LEARNING YEARS

LEARNING IN THE EARLY YEARS
A GUIDE FOR TEACHERS OF CHILDREN 3–7

Edited by
Jeni Riley

Paul Chapman Publishing

Paul Chapman Publishing
A SAGE Publications Company
1 Oliver's Yard, 55 City Road
London EC1Y 1SP

SAGE Publications Inc
2455 Teller Road
Thousand Oaks, California 91320

SAGE Publications India Pvt Ltd
B–42 Panchsheel Enclave
PO Box 4109
New Delhi 110 017

British Library Cataloguing in Publication data

A catalogue record for this book is available from the British Library

ISBN 0-7619-4105-3 (hbk)
ISBN 0-7619-4106-1 (pbk)

Library of Congress Control Number: 2002-110341

Typeset by Pantek Arts Ltd., Maidstone, Kent
Printed and bound in Great Britain by
Cromwell Press Limited, Trowbridge, Wiltshire

Contents

Contents

This book is dedicated to Imogen, who reminds me daily of the astonishing intellectual capability of very young children.

List of contributors

Carol Aubrey is Professor of Early Childhood Education in the Institute of Education at the University of Warwick. She trained first as a primary school teacher, as a researcher in applied psychology (dyslexia) and then as an educational psychologist. Later she spent a number of years in primary teacher education with a particular focus on the early years, first at University College, Cardiff, and then at the University of Durham, where she was Director of the Post-graduate Certificate of Primary Education (PGCE). She was Chair of Education (Early Years/Primary) at Canterbury Christ Church University College, where she led the Centre for International Studies in Early Childhood (CISEC). Her own research interests lie in the area of early learning and development, early mathematics and special educational needs. Her recent evaluation work has included the DfES telephone survey, *The Implementation of the Foundation Stage Curriculum in Reception Classes* (2002). She is chair of the editorial board of *Interplay* and UK editor of the new *Journal of Research on Early Childhood*.

Richard Bailey is Professor of Childhood Research at Canterbury Christ Church University College, where his main areas of work are physical education and philosophy of education. Before coming to Canterbury, he was Reader in Educational Studies at Leeds Metropolitan University and Head of the Centre for Physical Education and Sport Science at the University of Reading. Richard has worked as a secondary physical education teacher and as an infant school teacher. He has also worked substantially with children with special needs. His primary interest, both as a teacher and a researcher, is in infants, from 2 to 7 years of age. Richard currently directs an ESRC-funded project on the management of disaffected pupils in primary and secondary schools, a series of school-based projects on the identification of and provision for talented pupils, and a DfES Training and Development Fund project on the inclusion of pupils with special needs in physical education and sport. He is the author of numerous articles and conference presentations, and his recent books include *Supporting Physical Development and Physical Education in the Early Years* (Open University Press; with Jonathan Doherty), *Teaching Values and Citizenship across the Curriculum* (Kogan Page), *Teaching Physical Education 11–18* (Continuum) and *Education in the Open Society* (Ashgate).

Patti Barber is Lecturer in Primary Education at the University of London Institute of Education. Patti taught for many years in inner London primary schools where she was a deputy headteacher of an infants' school and a mathematics advisory teacher. Her particular interest is mathematics in the early years. She was a co-founder of the Early Childhood Mathematics Group, which is affiliated with the Association of Mathematics. Patti has been very involved with BEAM mathematics and has worked on many of their publications. She has co-written *Nursery Mathematics* and *Foundation Mathematics*, published by Heinemann. Most recently she has been involved in writing materials for the National Numeracy Strategy about the transition for children from reception to Key Stage 1. She has worked at the University of London, Institute of Education, since 1990 and has, in recent years, co-ordinated the mathematics component of the primary PGCE. She is also involved with the early years course and was deputy course leader of the part-time primary PGCE. Through her work at the Institute she has been involved with colleagues in research into trainee teachers' subject knowledge. This has lead to further ongoing research with Cambridge and York Universities.

Lynne Broadbent is Director of the British and Foreign Schools Society National Religious Education Centre at Brunel University. She has extensive experience of working with primary and secondary teachers and student teachers in the areas of religious, personal and social education.

Liz Brooker was an early years teacher for nearly 20 years but is now teaching students of early childhood at the Institute of Education University of London, and at University College Northampton. Her research has been mainly in the field of young children's home and school learning. This has included studies of parental involvement in their children's learning; of the reception class experiences of children from diverse backgrounds; and of nursery children's use of the computer. Her book, *Starting School: Young Children Learning Cultures*, was published in 2002 by the Open University Press.

John Cook is a part-time lecturer in primary education at the Institute of Education, University of London. He has been a primary headteacher in London and a humanities inspector and assistant chief inspector in the London Borough of Tower Hamlets. His long association with the development of the humanities curriculum includes involvement in the preparation of resource material for teachers to support 'distant locality' work with particular reference to Jamaica and the Netherlands.

Jonathan Doherty is Head of Early Childhood Education at Leeds Metropolitan University where he has responsibility for training intending teachers at undergraduate and postgraduate levels in the 3–8 age range. Prior to taking up his current post at Leeds, he was an early years teacher for a number of years. As a PE specialist, Jonathan lectures in the Carnegie Centre for PE and Sport at the university, mainly in psychology, skill acquisition and child development, and he has delivered many in-service training courses in PE to specialist and non-specialist teachers. A member of various working parties and committees relating to PE, he acts as a consultant to the Amateur Swimming Association National Education Committee and the QCA Physical Education and School Sport project. He has presented to national and international audiences and has written a number of papers and journal articles. Recent publications include *Supporting Physical Development and PE in the Early Years* (Open University Press; with Richard Bailey) and *Observing Children Moving* (PEAUK). His current research interests involve thinking skills in relation to movement in young children.

Esmé Glauert has worked with young children for many years in playgroups, nurseries and in primary schools. She has wide experience as a teacher educator in science contributing to initial teacher education, in-service training and masters programmes. Currently she is a lecturer in primary education at the Institute of Education, University of London, where she is course leader for the primary PGCE programme. Her research interests include pedagogy in initial teacher education and young children's learning in science. Her book, *Tracking Significant Achievement in Science* (Hodder & Stoughton) was published in both Japanese and English.

Caroline Heal is a lecturer in primary education at the Institute of Education, University of London, where she has gained experience as a teacher educator at both primary and secondary levels. Within the primary PGCE course she has the responsibility for the development of the history component. Her main research interest is in the development of teachers' thinking and practice through professional dialogue, especially in the context for 'mentoring'.

Russell Jago is a Post-doctoral Research Fellow within the Behavioral Nutrition and Physical Activity research group at the Children's Nutrition Research Center (CNRC), Baylor College of Medicine, Houston, Texas. Before his current appointment Russell was a research technician in the Department of Physical Education and Sport Science at the University of Reading. With his colleagues at the CNRC, Russell is currently a co-investigator on an American Cancer Society-funded project that is developing a new physical activity badge for the American Boy Scout Association. He is also a co-investigator on a National Institute of Diabetes, Digestive and Kidney Diseases project that is developing a middle school intervention programme to reduce the prevalence of obesity and diabetes among American youth. His primary research interest is school and community-based promotions of childhood physical activity and their effect on physiological risk factors for cardiovascular and metabolic disorders.

John Matthews is an artist and educator with experience as a teacher at nursery, primary and secondary level, as well as at university level, in Britain and Singapore. His research work is about the origin and development of art in early childhood. For many years he taught at Goldsmiths College, University of London, in the School of Arts and also early years education in the Faculty of Education. Presently he is Associate Professor in the Division of Visual and Performing Arts, National Institute of Education, Nanyang Technological University, Singapore. He has written many papers and addressed international conferences about the significance of the art of very young children. His books include *Children and Visual Representation: Helping Children to Draw and Paint in Early Childhood* (Hodder & Stoughton) and *The Art of Childhood and Adolescence: The Construction of Meaning* (Falmer Press).

Roy Prentice is Head of Art, Design and Museology at the Institute of Education, University of London. Over many years he has gained wide experience of art and design in different educational contexts, as a teacher, an LEA art adviser and a university academic. His long-standing commitment to the role of practical workshops in courses of primary teacher education and to the development of practice-based research in the field of art and design education is reflected in his teaching, writing and research. He is a practising painter.

David Reedy is currently the Head of Primary English for the London Borough of Barking and Dagenham and a Visiting Fellow at the Institute of Education, University of London. He has been responsible for the development and implementation of the Barking and Dagenham Primary English project which has substantially raised attainment in the borough's primary schools. David, when a practising teacher, has experience with children all through the primary age phase, including nursery children, and he continues to teach on a regular basis. His main research interests are the place of dialogic teaching in the primary classroom and the teaching of writing. His publications include *Guiding Reading – A Handbook for Teaching Guided Reading at KS2* (Institute of Education, with Angela Hobsbaum and Nikki Gamble) and *Developing Writing for Different Purposes – Teaching about Genre in the Early Years* (Paul Chapman Publishing, with Jeni Riley).

Jeni Riley is Head of Early Childhood and Primary Education at the Institute of Education, University of London. Before being appointed to the Institute of Education, Jeni's main teaching experience was in the early years and with the advisory service in Oxfordshire. Since her appointment at the Institute of Education in 1986, Jeni Riley has focused her research energies on the teaching and learning of language and literacy in the early years of education. Currently, she is directing a research project which is studying the ways of effectively enhancing the spoken language skills of reception children in two inner-city, multicultural schools. Jeni teaches on primary and early years PGCE courses, at MA level and also undertakes doctoral supervision. She co-ordinates in-service courses and also works as a consultant in the field of language and literacy. Her recent books are *The Teaching of Reading at KS1 and Before* (Stanley Thornes) and *Developing Writing for Different Purposes: Teaching about Genre in the Early Years* (Paul Chapman Publishing, with David Reedy).

Helen Taylor is a principal lecturer at Northumbria University in Newcastle where she leads initial teacher education as the Programme Area Director. She joined the university in 1993 as Head of Music Education. Having trained as a singer at the Royal Academy of Music in the late 1960s, she went on to train and teach in London before moving to the North East. Working in mainstream, special schools and as a freelance consultant, she has substantial experience in both music and early years education. In higher education she has worked with undergraduate, PGCE, MA and Phd students. She has recently developed a new Advanced Studies in the Early Years specialist ITT undergraduate course. The present focus of her research is into the impact that musicians have on children in the early years.

Introduction

Jeni Riley

> *A society can be judged by its attitude to its youngest children, not only in what is said about them but how this attitude is expressed in what is offered to them as they grow up.*
>> (Goldschmied and Jackson, 1994, cited in Abbott and Gillen, 1997)
>
> *All children should be given the opportunity to experience the very best possible start to their education.*
>> (Hodge, 2000: 2)

In this Introduction, I explain the purpose of this book, its rationale and its structure. Each of Chapters 2–7 focuses on the curriculum content and pedagogy within an area of learning as identified in *Curriculum Guidance for the Foundation Stage* (DfEE/QCA, 2000). This Introduction deals with the current political and operational context and it also addresses the key issues which affect young children's learning and which are evident in the discussion throughout this book. These issues are:

- the potential of play-based activities;
- the importance of the practitioners' subject knowledge; and
- information and communications technology and learning in the early years of education.

This book takes its structure from the curriculum guidance document and it aims to support practitioners with an overview of the six areas of learning along with a consideration of the relevant subject knowledge and 'developmentally appropriate' pedagogy. It will help students and practitioners to make useful connections between the Foundation Stage requirements and the National Curriculum for Key Stage 1, and also with the traditional body of knowledge which has informed learning in early childhood education. The book provides new insights from recent research that are relevant to teaching and learning within the 3–7 age range and, we believe, this book is highly relevant to early years practitioners in pre-school, reception and Years 1 and 2 classrooms.

Chapter 1 deals with the foundations of early learning and includes a discussion of the following:

- The responsibility we have to maximize each child's astonishing potential as demonstrated by recent scientific studies on the brain.
- The idea of a changing concept of childhood and different views on the child's place in society today.
- Issues about effective teaching and learning in the early years of education focused on the role of the adult in supporting the child's development and thinking.

Throughout the book we discuss the recommendations of the two documents from the DfES advising on the curriculum for 3–7-year-olds: *Curriculum Guidance for the Foundation Stage* (DfEE/QCA, 2000) (3–5 years) and the Key Stage 1 (5–7 years) section in the National Curriculum (DfEE, 1999) to explore their relationship with each other in terms of continuity of subject content and the associated 'developmentally appropriate' pedagogy.

The message of this book is essentially an optimistic one. Research findings emerging from the most recent studies are providing robust evidence which reaffirms many of the long-held beliefs of early childhood educators. But within this message is a clearer, more rigorous and harder-edged focus relevant to education today.

Why was it important to write this book?

The rationale for the book

The education children experience during the earliest years of their life lays the foundations for all that follows. The nature and quality of the care, the experiences and the learning opportunities that are offered to children, from their birth and then onwards through infancy and early childhood, affect their educational potential and their life chances in a profound and lasting way. The recognition by both wider public opinion and the government of the vital importance of the early years has resulted in a massively heightened interest in the quality of early childhood provision and education. Driven by this concern, substantial funding has been allocated to developing early childhood education and services. Considerable energy and effort have been directed into rationalizing, standardizing and improving the many and diverse services which at present cater for children before they reach full-time, mainstream primary education. Additional resources have been made available:

- for the integration of childcare and educational provision;
- for intervention projects with both the babies and their parents in UK's most economically deprived areas (e.g. the Sure Start initiative); and
- to improve the quality and to upgrade the professional training of the adults working within the pre-school sector.

The government's introduction of an official Foundation Stage (3–5 years, pre the statutory National Curriculum), along with its associated document, *Curriculum Guidance for the Foundation Stage*, further demonstrates a determination to improve the educational provision in England and Wales for all children in the 3–5-year age range. This book deals with the way, in practice, this guidance can complement the National Curriculum (DfEE, 1999) document at Key Stage 1 (5–7 years).

In a situation where there is increasingly tough competition for public funds, what has convinced a government that this immense commitment will be rewarded?

Evidence of the benefits of early childhood education

There have been many studies of interventions in early childhood education (see Ramey and Ramey, 1998) but one particular longitudinal study undertaken in the USA provides convincing evidence on the long-lasting value of pre-school education. The High/Scope Perry Pre-school evaluation (Schweinhart et al., 1993) is a robustly designed intervention programme and associated evaluation with a random sample of 123 participating individuals who at the time were living in deprived circumstances. The evaluation has provided extensive data over a wide variety of real-life measures covering a long timespan. Analyses of the data (which were collected annually from children 3–11, and then at 14, 15, 19 and 27) show the indisputable long-term benefits of an early educational intervention for children brought up in poverty and at high risk of school failure. The High/Scope study has also famously shown the impressive cost benefits to society of early intervention. The programme participants were more successful at school compared with those individuals who were living in the same circumstances but who had not received the educational programme. This was demonstrated by the participants:

- being less likely to be placed in programmes for mental impairment;
- having higher average school grades;
- graduating on time from high school more successfully; and
- having higher levels of literacy by the end of secondary education.

At 27 years of age, participants in the High Scope Programme:

- were earning a higher salary;
- were more likely to own their homes;
- were less likely to receive social service support; and
- had a lower rate of involvement with crime.

Although these findings have been very influential, more precise evidence is needed. For example, are the benefits so striking because this study was conducted on a very deprived group of people? Are all early education pro-grammes equally effective? If not, then what appear to be the key features of an effective pre-school programme?

Features of effective pre-school provision

Ramey and Ramey (1998) suggest that there are six 'developmental priming mechanisms' with a potential role to enhance learning:

1   encouragement to explore the environment;
2   mentoring basic intellectual and social skills;
3   celebrating new skills;
4   rehearsing and expanding new skills;
5   protection from inappropriate punishment or ridicule for developmental advances; and
6   stimulation in language and symbolic communication.

Evidence emerging from the Researching Effective Pedagogy in the Early Years (REPEY) project (Siraj-Blatchford et al., 2002) supports the dual emphasis described above and the value of encouraging equally both cognitive and social development. Findings from the REPEY study, derived from both quanti-tative and qualitative data, suggest that the greater than expected levels of development in children in the most effective settings were associated with:

● adult–child interactions that involve open-ended questioning to extend children's thinking and, very importantly, through what the researchers describe as 'sustained shared thinking';
● practitioners possessing high levels of subject knowledge of the curriculum as well as knowledge and understanding of child development;
● formative feedback to children during activities;
● shared educational aims with parents; and
● behaviour policies in which staff support children in being assertive, at the same time as rationalizing and talking through conflicts.

The findings of this important study and their implications for practice are discussed in more depth in Chapter 1.

Research evidence on the attainment and progress of children starting school

As every reception class teacher knows, there is a very wide range of develop-ment shown by each class of new school entrants. Extensive evidence of pupils' social, intellectual and behavioural attainment assessed in a variety of ways when they enter school confirms that this is so (Tymms, 2002). The wide range in the functioning of children is influenced by the type of home background, particularly their socioeconomic status, ethnic origin and gender, and is also affected by whether the child is a singleton or a twin.

The aim of the Performance Indicators of Primary Schools Project (PIPS) (Tymms, 1999) is to provide high-quality data on the attainments, attitudes and progress of children throughout their primary school careers. In addition, the findings offer reliable and up-to-date demographic information which is useful for teachers concerning the context within which they work.

Demographic information on pupils' start to school

The PIPS data indicate that, in English schools:

- it is common practice now for children to go to mainstream school when they are 4 years old. In 2000–1 only 13% started school at 5;
- 85% of these pupils start in the September of the academic year of school entry;
- 7% of school entrants do not have English as their first language;
- the vast majority will have attended pre-school with an average of two terms at a nursery and just over a term at a playgroup;
- approximately 0.7% have been identified already as having special educational needs; and
- 17% are eligible for free school meals.

The range of attainment shown at school entry

Details of the span of attainment at school entry across and within the different groups of children are discussed fully by Tymms (1999; 2002) and make compulsive reading. To take a few examples, in spoken language, some children starting school do not know or use basic and commonly used household words whilst others have in their vocabulary such words as saxophone, jewellery and cosmetics. Some children have a very limited understanding of how books and print work whilst one child in 500 is able to read a long passage fluently. In mathematics, one child in five cannot recognize the number 4 but one in a hundred knows the number 164.

The particular and long-lasting importance of the reception year

The design of the PIPS research project measured the reception pupils' progress and found that it is very rapid. Not only that, but the progress made in the first year of school is the greatest that pupils achieve over the entire seven years of primary school. In addition to this, some schools and their teachers have a greater effect on the progress made over and above what might be expected from the children's entry scores. In other words, in terms of a 'value added' effect (i.e. the influence of a school or a teacher which exceeds that which might be expected from a class of pupils' beginning-of-school-year scores) there is as much as a 40% variance in the relative progress made. This percentage is extremely high. In comparison with this figure of 40%, school effectiveness research at secondary level indicates that a positive school/teacher effect is approximately only 10–15% of the variance.

The important point to make is that the school and the teacher have the single and greatest influence on the progress made by classes of pupils. And the most progress occurs during the first year of school. Therefore reception teachers have an awesome responsibility: they need to build sensitively and knowledgeably upon the foundations that pre-school and home have laid whilst also taking into account the wide individual differences in young pupils. Two smaller studies (compared with the PIPS project) investigating the progress made during the reception year in literacy (Riley, 1996) and mathematics (Aubrey, 1994) provide detail on some of the factors and processes which appear to lead to positive learning outcomes for new school pupils. The quality of the training and experience of the teacher is key. Children arrive in school with a vast store of knowledge but it is highly idiosyncratic and individual. Capitalizing on that knowledge is the key for children to make sound progress. Teachers need strong subject knowledge across the curriculum and also to be aware of the appropriate pedagogy for teaching it. Early years teachers have to be skilled assessors of the children's levels of development so that they can offer a close match of teaching with children's levels of understanding. The findings of these studies described in this section support those from the REPEY study (Siraj-Blatchford et al., 2002). They also confirm the ideology and theories of early childhood education held for over a century.

Which type of curriculum is the most effective?

Debate exists about the type and content of an early years curriculum. What should be the main focus of education during the years 3–7? Clearly there will be a change of emphasis during this timespan. But in which direction should educators place most of their energy? Should adults working with young children be encouraging them to become autonomous learners, or should they be concerned mostly with developing socially competent young pupils to enable them to cope and integrate into the community of the setting? Or should greatest emphasis be put upon offering learning opportunities in the subjects of a curriculum? These aims are not mutually exclusive, naturally, but research evidence is providing answers here too.

'Play is the work of the child' (Froebel, 1876). Play based-activities as an effective vehicle for learning appear to meet all three of the above educational aims. Traditionally play has a place at the heart of early childhood education as the recognized way that young children learn most effectively. It is argued that play offers opportunities from which children will benefit hugely, both cognitively and socially. On the intellectual side, play-based learning – because of its highly motivating, self-directing qualities – encourages engagement, concentration, task completion and the development of problem-solving abilities. Social and communication skills of negotiation and collaboration with peers are also demanded in many play situations.

Play has its critics, however. Studies (e.g. Bennett et al., 1997) have shown that play activities can be low in intellectual challenge and often repetitive and time wasting for children, particularly in Key Stage 1. Researchers have found that infant teachers have an idealized, somewhat sentimental view of play, considering it to have educational validity at all times and in all circumstances but without a clear sense of how or why. It appears that some teachers underexploit its learning potential. Debate whether play is as educationally valuable as early years teachers would like to believe comes from a lack of clarity about what is and what is not play. This is despite many attempts at precise and comprehensive definitions! One way forward is a categorization of play-based activities developed in order to assess the educational value of play. How can activities which can be described as 'playful' be categorized?

Play-based activities

Widely used criteria for evaluating play events

Researchers have developed frameworks which take into account the nature of play and its complexity by categorizing the way in which it can cover a variety of dimensions. Brooker (2002) has summarized the research evidence on the learning outcomes of play. Parten (1932) described the developmental changes that occur in the social groupings that arise when children are playing and noted that, "as they grow older," children engage in more associative and co-operative play and play less on their own. Her categories are as follows:

- *Unoccupied* and *onlooker*, which describe a child who is observing but not participating in an activity.
- *Parallel*: in this category the child plays alongside others but not *with* other children.
- *Associative*: the child plays and shares the action with others.
- *Co-operative*: describes the child who displays a higher level of social behaviour and there is a defined division of labour and role.

Evidence from observational studies

Smilansky (1968; 1990) investigated the frequency and complexity of children's 'socio-dramatic' or 'fantasy' play and she suggests that socio-dramatic play in pre-school and school settings is a valuable stimulus for emotional, social and intellectual growth. Smilansky claims that 'it is the make-believe process . . . that is pivotal' (1990: 35). She developed the following criteria with the potential to develop children's intellectual capacity:

- functional play;
- constructive play;
- symbolic play; and
- games with rules.

Research evidence from the Oxford Preschool Research Project

Sylva et al. (1980) developed criteria which were used in the most informative research studies designed to undertake detailed 'target child' observations on 3–5-year-olds. The researchers coded the behaviour of each 'target child' on action codes, social codes and play bouts, using children in different forms of pre-school provision (120 children aged 3.6 and 5.6). They looked for the 'task settings' and 'social settings' associated with a high level ('yield') of cognitively challenging and complex play.

Their main findings lead them to recommend that:

- activities should have a clear goal structure;
- children should work in pairs; and
- adults should have a tutorial role.

The most beneficial situations in terms of the level of the cognitive demand on the child and which led to intellectual gains include construction materials of all kinds, structured tasks and art activities, as well as pretend play and small-world play; and settings in which a child interacts with a peer or adult.

The categories Sylva and colleagues developed aimed to take account of the complexity within both social and cognitive dimensions in the following way:

The context for observation – the social setting
- child alone
- child parallel
- child–child pair
- child in child group
- child in child group plus adult
- child–adult pair.

The context for observation – the task setting
- structured materials
- pretend
- small construction
- art
- large construction
- manipulation
- gross motor play
- informal games
- scale-version toys
- games with rules
- rough-and-tumble play.

Activities which meet the criteria potentially offer valuable learning opportunities for children to develop in a variety of ways and across a range of dimensions. However, progress depends upon the level of intellectual and social maturity of the children and the relationship between it and the activity in which they are engaged.

The importance of play

We return to the issue of the importance and nature of play throughout the 3–7 age phase in Chapter 1 of this book, with a particular focus on the research findings of the REPEY project (Siraj-Blatchford et al., 2002). This study shows that the children who made the most progress had been offered play-based learning opportunities which had both curriculum and social learning objectives and which were also intended to develop positive learning dispositions and communication skills. These children had developed best in effective learning environments and alongside adults who engaged with them in mutually enjoyable 'sustained shared thinking'.

The Qualifications and Curriculum Authority (QCA) is convinced that play is an appropriate way for valuable learning to occur in the Foundation Stage, so much so that play is in place within the official advice given to practitioners, which states that:

Through play children can:

- explore and represent learning experiences that help them make sense of the world;
- practise and build up ideas, concepts and skills;
- learn how to control impulses and understand the need for rules;
- be alone, be alongside others or co-operate as they talk or rehearse their feelings;
- take risks and make mistakes;
- think creatively and imaginatively;

- communicate with others as they investigate and solve problems;
- express fears or relive anxious experiences in controlled and safe situations.
  (DfEE/QCA, 2000: 25)

And this probably understates the case; no mention is made here of the many opportunities that play offers for children to acquire knowledge and understanding across the entire curriculum. Play has the potential to be the major, unifying pedagogical approach for the child's transition from the Foundation Stage to Key Stage 1. When playing, children are able to engage at a level which is best suited to them given the self-chosen, 'differentiated by outcome' and flexible nature of the activities. It is the practitioner's responsibility to be aware of the range and possibilities of the learning potential of a particular activity. Adults must also observe and monitor the play, with individual children's learning needs in mind, in order to ensure that sufficient cognitive and social challenge is present. The well-known saying of early years education 'observe, support and extend' holds true today. Let us take as an example children's 'sociodramatic', 'fantasy', 'pretence', 'make believe' or 'symbolic' play in both pre-school and school settings. Smilansky has showed that there are genuine gains for cognitive development in sociodramatic play. She claims that it '. . . activates resources that stimulate emotional, social and intellectual growth in the child, which in turn affects the child's success in school' (1990: 25). Role-play areas are an essential part of the learning environment in all pre-school settings and can and should be an effective and staple offering for Year 1 and 2 pupils. A travel agents' shop, for example, offers active, authentic, enjoyable learning experiences in communication, language, literacy, mathematics and knowledge and understanding about the world, to mention only some curriculum areas of learning.

The structure of this book

This book considers the curriculum and the associated 'developmentally appropriate pedagogy' in the age phase 3–7 from the perspective of the six areas of learning identified in *Curriculum Guidance for the Foundation Stage* (DfEE/QCA, 2000). It aims to support practitioners in their understanding of how guidelines for the Foundation Stage and the National Curriculum work together in practice. It shows how educators can use this framework of intellectual, social, aesthetic, spiritual and physical development for 3–7-year-olds as they meet the requirements of both documents. The issues particularly associated with the curriculum and 'developmentally appropriate' teaching approaches in both the Foundation Stage and Key Stage 1 are discussed in depth in Chapters 2–7. The book is organized in this way as an effective education for 3–7-year-olds demands an underpinning and unifying framework which spans the whole curriculum. A rigorous and comprehensive grasp of the curriculum is required of early years educators working in all pre-school settings, in reception and Year 1 and 2 classrooms, so that 'developmentally appropriate' learning experiences and teaching can be offered across all the curriculum subjects.

Issues of difficulty and confusion

There are two areas of potential difficulty with the *Curriculum Guidance* document, which has otherwise been widely welcomed. A high level of practitioner's subject knowledge has been assumed by the document and, in addition, it does not provide a useful support for planning. The 'Stepping Stones' of the 'Early Learning Goals' are not a curriculum framework but suggest rather an ideal place on a ladder of learning which needs to be reached by the end of the reception year on entry to Year 1. Research evidence suggests that 'the requirements for the Foundation Stage' presume levels of curriculum subject knowledge from early years practitioners that are overoptimistic (Siraj-Blatchford et al., 2002). Whilst at Key Stage 1 the issue appears to be reversed, through the recent initiatives in initial teacher education, primary teachers have stronger subject knowledge but they are less confident concerning child development and how to employ 'developmentally appropriate' teaching approaches, particularly through play-based activities.

In addition to this, advice early in the introduction of the National Literacy Strategy (in 1998 and 1999) was prescriptive: it was too whole-class-teaching focused and inappropriate for many children in reception and some Year 1 classrooms. This is not to deny that the curriculum content in the Framework for Teaching is relevant and broadly in line with current research evidence and thinking. The Framework for Teaching is helpful to the adults working with children at these ages, particularly in terms of planning for continuity and progression.

Recognition of the need for primary teachers to be well equipped with a sound understanding of the curriculum now requires no defence. An extensive subject knowledge enables a teacher to select content and to identify key points more appropriately. Such a practitioner is more accurate in assessing the level of the child's understanding. Research shows that this type of teacher is able, also, to interest the children more and to teach in a more engaging fashion. Teachers with strong subject knowledge ask more appropriate questions and are able to incorporate the pupils' contributions into the lesson. Aubrey (1994) made a strong case that educators supporting the earliest years of schooling need to be equally well informed. She suggests that:

> Those who teach children in the early years may, however regard other criteria such as the way young children learn and develop at a particular stage as more important. Clearly taking account of young children's interests, preferred activities and out of school experiences as these relate to teaching subject matter is vitally

important. Early years teachers may have different orientations to different subjects, as well as different knowledge bases, adopting a child centred approach to, for instance, children's literature and history and a fact-centred approach to mathematics and science. (Aubrey, 1994: 5)

Research evidence is highlighting further the vital importance for early years practitioners to be well qualified and with high levels of subject knowledge and expertise. This ensures that they are able to plan rich learning opportunities for children in the 3–7 age range and to engage and support the learners through discussion and skilful, open-ended questioning (Siraj-Blatchford et al., 2002). Children taught by adults of this quality make more progress than those who are not.

ICT and education in the early years

The debate regarding the effects of ICT (information and communication technology) on young children's development and learning is being resolved. Convincing evidence is emerging from studies being undertaken by DATEC (Developmentally Appropriate Technology in Early Childhood) regarding the nature and the role of ICT for nursery children. The studies are providing examples of exceptionally strong practice. One study (Brooker and Siraj-Blatchford, 2002) cites many instances where children are delighting in and benefiting across a variety of subject domains and dimensions of learning. The software packages, Henry's Party (Marshall Media, 1995) and Tizzy's Toybox (Sherston Software, 1997), appear to have been particularly valuable. The first program offers a series of locations to visit, in which clicking on items produces a huge range of effects and interactions, based on 'helping' characters (such as farm animals) to find and sort objects.

Brooker and Siraj-Blatchford give enchanting examples of groups of children (aged 3 and 4) interacting as they work with the computer. The interaction, in turn, supports language development, promotes pro-social behaviour and assists the performance of less experienced peers. Also, the researchers found that the interaction aids collaboration and stimulates play behaviours. Just two examples are included here (Learning Stories I.1 and I.2).

The principle which appears to underpin this valuable learning is the type of software package itself. Open-ended and interactive programs which encourage collaboration rather than those which are single-answer, drill-and-skill based, offer far more potential benefit with regard to the cognitive, social and linguistic gains listed above. The knowledge base of the practitioner and her sensitive balance between support at the appropriate point and non-intervention is another important factor. As we have discussed with traditional play-based opportunities, the nature of the adult's support is key to the child's sustained involvement and the progress made.

Learning Story I.1 Afternoon nursery interaction

It is 1.55 p.m. Three children are working with Tizzy's Toybox. Two not very skilled children (Khaleda and Sabena) are working with a more skilled child (Khanderley).

Khaleda doesn't know how to mouse-point at all; when I tell her to point to the game she wants to play, she puts her finger on the screen and is totally surprised to be told to move the mouse to point! But Sabena stands and instructs her ('Click'); she becomes frustrated by Khaleda's inability to point and to click, and makes her take her finger off the screen, points to her hand on the mouse, and insists (in Bengali) that she uses the mouse to point with (all this despite her own difficulty in pointing accurately). Khaleda makes steady progress. Sabena and Khanderley collaborate choosing letters with her, pointing to the screen to show her where to click. Khaleda has very little English but practises it whenever she recognises an object she knows: 'ball, ball', 'baby, baby' and repeats words after the computer has named the objects.

Learning Story I.2 Morning nursery interaction

It is 9.50 a.m. Amy, Annabelle, Tabitha, Ziaur and Jubed are working with Henry's Party.

Amy gets stuck on matching numbers to sets (cheeses with holes in) and Annabelle helps her to select the right match. All the girls continue to co-operate on finding the missing kittens, which requires skilful anticipation and well-judged timing as well as manual dexterity. The whole group enjoys the special effects obtained by clicking in the kitchen, which prompt group glee (singing and dancing). Amy returns to the number-matching to practise and perfect this task. She asks Annabelle for help once again, and she obliges. Alice arrives to watch.

The six areas of learning: Chapters 2–7

As stated earlier, this book has taken the areas of learning as described in the document *Curriculum Guidance for the Foundation Stage* (DfEE/QCA, 2000) as the organizing framework in order to give ideas coherence. All organizing structures are open to debate, and the areas of learning and their relationship with the subject areas of the National Curriculum at Key Stage 1 (DfEE, 1999) are not straightforward or tidy. Some curriculum subjects might have been placed in two or even three of the Foundation Stage areas of learning –

'dance' is one of these. Others are integral to the whole curriculum, such as communication and language. The authors of Chapter 7, when considering opportunities for creative development, acknowledge that creativity is not exclusively developed through the arts. The purpose of this book, therefore, is to address the particular and potential contribution which certain subjects offer to the overall development of children and their education. The view of learning which has been adopted is a consideration of the development of the whole child through the lenses of subject specialists with expertise in the early years of education.

Finally, what emerges from this book is the complex relationship between a practitioner's expertise across the curriculum and the quality of the learning experience that is offered to the children in the setting or class. We have aimed to inform, to delight and to inspire so that professionals can ensure that all children are given every opportunity to maximize their potential through access to the diverse ways of knowing and being intelligent.

References

Abbott, L. and Gillen, J. (1997) *Educare for the Under Threes – Identifying Need and Opportunity*. Report of the research study by the Manchester Metropolitan University jointly funded by the Esme Fairburn Charitable Trust.

Aubrey, C. (1994) *The Role of Subject Knowledge in the Early Years of Schooling*. London: Falmer Press.

Bennett, N., Wood, E. and Rogers, S. (1997) *Teaching through Play: Teachers, Theories and Classroom Practice*. Buckingham: Open University Press.

Brooker, E. (2002) 'The importance of play' (Institute of Education, London, ITT Resource File, Appendix B), in *The National Numeracy Strategy: Teaching Mathematics in Reception and Year 1*. London: DfES.

Brooker, E. and Siraj-Blatchford, J. (2002) 'Click on Miaow! How children aged 3 and 4 experience the nursery computer', *Contemporary Issues in Early Childhood*, 3(2): 251–72.

DfEE (1999) *The National Curriculum*. London: HMSO.

DfEE/QCA (2000) *Curriculum Guidance for the Foundation Stage*. London: QCA.

Goldschmied, E. and Jackson, S. (1994) *People under Three: Young Children in Daycare*. London: Routledge.

Hodge, M. (2000) 'Introduction', in *Curriculum Guidance for the Foundation Stage*. London: QCA.

Marshall Media (1995) Henry's Party.

Parten, M.B. (1932) 'Social participation among pre-school children', *Journal of Abnormal Psychology*, 27: 243–69.

Ramey, C. and Ramey, S.L. (1998) 'Early intervention and early experience', *American Psychologist*, 53(2): 109–20.

Riley, J.L. (1996) *The Teaching of Reading: The Development of Literacy*. London: Paul Chapman Publishing.

Rubin, K. (1977) 'Play behaviours of young children', *Young Children*, September: 16–23.

Schweinhart, L.J., Barnes, H.V. and Weikart, D.P. (1993) *Significant Benefits: The High/Scope Perry Preschool Study through Age 27*. Ypsilanti, MI: High/Scope Education Research Foundation.

Sherston Software (1997) Tizzy's Toybox.

Siraj-Blatchford, I., Sylva, K., Muttock, S., Gilden, R. and Bell, D. (2002) *Researching Effective Pedagogy in the Early Years. DfES Research Brief* 356. London: HMSO.

Smilansky, S. (1968) *The Effects of Sociodramatic Play on Disadvantaged Pre-school Children*. New York, NY: Wiley.

Smilansky, S. (1990) 'Socio-dramatic play: its relevance to behaviour and achievement in school', in E. Klugman and S. Smilansky (eds) *Children's Play and Learning: Perspectives and Policy Implications*. New York, NY: Teachers College Press.

Sylva, K., Roy, C. and Painter, M. (1980) *Childwatching at Playgroup and Nursery School*. London: Grant McIntyre.

Tymms, P. (1999) *Baseline Assessment and Monitoring in Primary Schools: Achievements, Attitudes and Value-added Indicators*. London: David Fulton.

Tymms, P. (2002) 'The attainments and progress of children starting school. Research review', *Interplay*, Spring: 35–8.

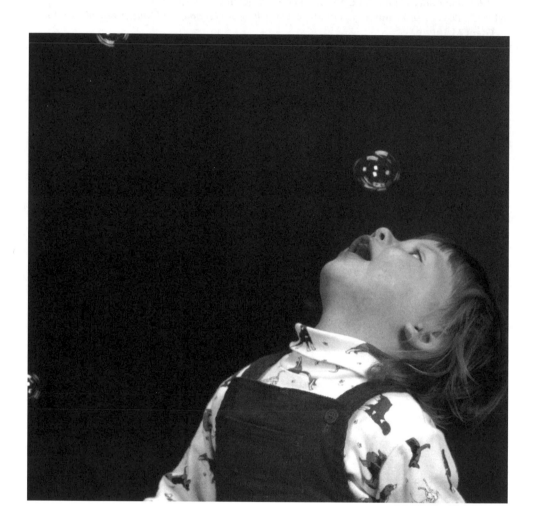

1

The child, the context and early childhood education

Jeni Riley

. . . . : the belief that children are highly active and efficient learners, competent inquirers, eager to understand . . . More and more evidence keeps coming to support this view that it is true of human beings from the earliest months of life. Children's minds are not at any stage – not ever – to be thought of as receptacles into which stuff called knowledge can be poured. Nor do children wait in a general way for us to prod them into learning. They wonder, they question, they try to make sense. And, not infrequently, when they direct their questions at us they push to the limit our ability to answer them, as every adult who has spoken much with children knows.

(Donaldson, 1993: 36)

The child

Our understanding of the child is at the heart of this book. It is the most obvious and appropriate place to start when considering education in the early years of schooling; the child, her capabilities, and how she learns are the focus of this first section. The wider social context within which the child lives will also be considered.

Nearly 30 years ago, the child development lectures that formed an essential part of my initial teacher training course focused heavily on the limitations of babies in their functioning. Born almost blind like kittens, the world appears to them, so we were told, as a 'buzzing, booming incomprehensible place'. Likewise, intellectual functioning was described mostly in negative terms that emphasized the young child's deficits and inabilities. This seemed strange to me as a teacher in training and as a young mother – the small children I knew well were not like this.

My 10-month-old daughter, hardly able to stand but clutching the coffee table for support, bent her knees and wriggled her bottom in time to the music played on the radio. The 1-year-old moves towards the controls of his father's music system the instant he is put down on the living-room floor, his accuracy of trajectory akin only to a missile. The 13-month-old, sitting at her father's feet whilst he is shaving, gently brushes his legs with a hairbrush. After a suspiciously long silence, the 18-month-old emerges from her mother's bedroom adorned with three necklaces and a bright smear of lipstick from ear to ear.

Are these the constrained, restricted thinkers referred to in the old child development textbooks? Are these the impoverished learners I was told about as a student, incapable of making connections and solving problems? I knew from my own observations that babies and very young children are able to think, observe and reason. Confirmation of this first came to me through Margaret Donaldson's book, *Children's Minds* (1978), in which she reported study after study revealing that children were capable of far more advanced intellectual operations than psychologists previously had believed. Young children consider evidence, draw conclusions, do experiments, solve problems and search for the truth. As Donaldson so succinctly puts it: ' . . . children are highly active and efficient learners, competent enquirers, eager to understand'(1993: 36).

How might this extraordinary competence demonstrated by babies and young children be explained? Why and how are they able to learn so effectively? It would appear that, first, a baby's brain closely resembles the most powerful computer imaginable, comprising millions and millions of neurons rather than silicon chips. Secondly, babies have innate, impressively effective learning mechanisms. And, thirdly, parents are genetically programmed to support and foster the development of their own children in a very potent and unique way.

Studies of the brain

Before recent advances in computer technology, most neurobiological research was conducted on mammals as the study of human brain tissue could be undertaken only at autopsy. Techniques now exist for brain imaging, such as functional magnetic resonance imaging (fMRI) and positive emission tomography (PET) which measure activity in the brain as tasks are performed. Research studies that involve these techniques suggest that the human brain is plastic and capable of continued development when used extensively. Babies' brains are especially active. The brain of a 2-year-old child has energy consumption at the full adult level; by 3 years old it is twice as active as an adult's brain, at which level it remains until 9 or 10 years of age when (amazingly) it starts to decline. Recent research in the field of neu-roscience has suggested that there are three important findings that have the potential to influence thinking about education in the early years.

1 *There is a very rapid increase in the development of the number of synapses (the wiring of nerve connections) between neurons (brain cells) in infancy and childhood.* This synaptic proliferation enables the frequently used nerve connections to be strengthened; and this period is followed by a phase of synaptic elimination or reduction when the less utilized connections become weakened and die. The reduction in synapses does not lead, neces-sarily, to diminished functioning but more towards a strengthening of the more utilized neurone pathways which in turn results in the specialized, mature performance of a skill (e.g. serving a tennis ball or tying a shoe-lace).

This is obvious in language development. At birth, brain-imaging studies indicate that babies respond equally enthusiastically to all the sounds it is possible for any human being to produce. After a few months, however, discrimination has occurred in favour of merely those sounds in the phonol-ogy of the particular mother tongue to which the child is exposed. By adulthood, the specialization is complete to the extent that we cannot hear the distinction between sounds that are not present in the sound system of our own language (e.g. Japanese people simply cannot discriminate between the sounds of *r* and *l* although they are tested many times).

The human brain has slightly fewer neurons at birth than in adulthood but the important factor that accounts for levels of intellectual functioning is not the number of neurons but the synaptic density. Immediately after birth, bombarded by stimulation of all the senses, the synapses begin to form prolifically and this continues up to sexual maturity; thereafter it decreases. The most important phase of experience-dependent synaptogenesis is thought to be from birth to 3 years. Different areas of the brain develop synapses differently and at a variety of rates. In the human brain, in the frontal cortex (which is responsible for planning, integrating information and decision-making), synaptogenesis occurs later than in the visual cortex and the reduction process takes longer. Pre-school children have brains which are more active, more connected and more flexible than an adult's brain. They undergo substantial, rapid change and development, and this continues throughout adolescence in some of the areas of the brain. The young child is 'literally an alien genius' (Gopnik et al., 1999).

2 *It has been suggested that there are 'critical periods' when sensory and motor systems in the brain require experience for maximum development. It is as if the brain can only develop optimally in this timespan.* For the last 30 years it has been known that animals require certain stimulation at very specific times during development if sensory and motor systems are to develop normally. The irreversible conse-quences for kittens of early visual deprivation (Wiesel and Hubel, 1965) are often

cited to support the argument for high-quality education for human children in their early years. However, there is debate about this, and now neuroscientists and psychologists believe that 'critical periods' are not as fixed or inflexible as was once thought. It is also debatable as to whether the brain has a biologically determined period of optimal learning for some specific skills or whether the neural pathways form to the advantage of some kinds of learning and are inhibitors for others. Perhaps a more apt term is 'sensitive periods', which allow the plastic, flexible and receptive brain to be shaped and moulded throughout childhood and adolescence for full capacity to be developed.

3 *In some mammals it has been shown that the more enriched and complex their environment, the greater the number of synapses will form.* Rats reared in stimulating laboratory conditions developed a thicker cortex in their brains and were able to solve maze problems more efficiently. Conversely, the observational studies of Romanian babies being reared in severely deprived conditions lacking sensory and social stimulation show that they are more likely to have delayed motor skills as well as impaired social, emotional and cognitive development (O'Connor et al., 1999). The brain continues to 'rewire' as it is greeted with successive forms of stimulation and each novel experience that requires a response. Experience changes the brain. Everything that a baby sees, smells, hears, tastes and touches alters the way the brain develops in an increasingly situation-appropriate way.

The findings of this neuroscientific research appear to provide sufficient evidence powerfully to reinforce an argument for an enriched environment and sensitive adult support very early in life: 'Children can take advantage of an innately determined foundation, powerful learning abilities and implicit tuition from other people' (Gopnik et al.,1999: 186). The far-reaching implications of this for early childhood education are explored later in this chapter.

From brains to minds

Human beings are marvellously equipped for, and are well supported in, their task of learning and making sense of their world. Now the technology of the video camera to record ingeniously designed experiments has enabled information to be gathered about exactly what babies know at birth and how very quickly they make use of that knowledge and build upon it. In the last 30 years we have come to realize the extent and competence of the baby's thinking skills.

Sensory development

In the womb, the foetus has begun to learn actively; sounds and sensations are noted and remembered. The music tracks played to pregnant women soothe their babies more quickly after birth than other music. The voice of a baby's mother is conducted to her, albeit imperfectly, via the spinal column whilst she is still *in utero*. My 1-day-old grandaughter, born nearly 3 months premature and weighing only 3 pounds, turned her head towards her mother's voice in delighted recognition when lifted from the incubator for the first time. Newborns prefer a human face to other visual stimuli and will gaze longer at the face of their own mother rather than at a picture of a stranger. They show that they crave novelty by learning to operate an audio or video tape-recorder through the strength of sucks on a teat; babies suck harder in order to alternate and play a variety of tapes.

Making sense of the world: people, emotions and beliefs

Immediately after birth the gradual understanding of what it is to be human appears to dawn, in a piecemeal way. Even the newly born, and certainly a month-old baby, will respond to overtures of communication by imitating any facial expressions made to her. Mouths will open and tongues protrude in perfect synchrony to a human partner. Slightly later than the physical gestures of interaction, the seemingly bizarre sounds adults are pre-programmed to make in order to engage an infant's attention (namely, 'coos', 'goos' and 'oohs') are responded to and imitated; next smiles are exchanged. The communication is deeply and mutually satisfying and is the forerunner to full-blown conversation. This work seems to indicate that babies are aware at birth that they are members of the human race and that a grasp of the art of social intercourse is an essential part of that membership.

Studies indicate that infants recognize other people's emotions and respond appropriately. A 1-year-old, when introduced to an intriguing new object, will intently scan her mother's face for reassurance or discouragement before approaching it. Babies express distress at disharmony such as a noisy household argument. A 2-year-old will attempt to comfort a distraught adult by giving her his own favourite toy. Other people's likes and dislikes in food, even when it differs from their own preferences, will be recognized and respected by toddlers of 18 months. Two-year-olds will undertake deliberately timed experiments on the precise limit of an adult's patience when trampolining on a forbidden cream-coloured sofa. This crucial survival mechanism, the ability to 'read' other people and thus to be able to establish relationships with them, begins at birth. It is fostered through the opportunities offered by most family situations; emotional intelligence is developed within the cut and thrust of our home lives.

Another set of fascinating studies indicates that very young children develop the ability to recognize that other people think differently from themselves. This is a capacity which psychologists describe as 'theory of mind' – the sheer brilliance of a 4-year-old who is aware not only of her own intellectual functioning but also that someone else cannot be expected to think the same as herself if not in possession of the appropriate information. Experiments conducted with sweet boxes containing pencils show that, at 3 years old, although a child will agree that a box holds pencils rather than the sweets illustrated on the lid (because he has seen them exchanged), cannot appreciate that the friend who did not observe the swap has no reason to think the same. The 4-year-old realizes that the act of knowing the true situation depends upon seeing the exchange.

Scientists undertaking neurobiological studies on the brain usually attempt no explicit connections between their findings and the implications for early education. Educationalists, however, are doing so. Blair (2002) offers a suggestion that the research findings on the relationship between emotional stability and cognition in turn facilitate adjustment to school. The use of neuroscientific measurement techniques demonstrates the optimum conditions for infants to develop the emotional maturity which provides resilience, enhances the ability to regulate behaviour and to concentrate – all aptitudes which school demands of the young pupil.

Malaguzzi, the inspiring founder of the nurseries in Emilio Reggio in northern Italy, uses the term 'the rich child'. This concept is not new to psychologists. For several decades the extraordinary capacity, the amazing intellectual competence of the young child have astonished researchers.

The world which the child will inhabit

The declared aim of this book is to consider an educational provision of the highest possible quality for the youngest of the pre-school and school population. In so doing we cannot ignore the changing context in which the children live. Education does not and cannot exist in a vacuum. Those responsible for educational provision need to consider the kind of world for which we are preparing these already amazingly capable young children. For what sort of society must we equip the next generation? We can only guess at what the social, economic and cultural landscape will look like in 20 years' time. It is self-evident, however, that fuelled by the rapid advances in technology, particularly global communication systems, life is becoming ever more complex and multi-layered. It is constantly changing. This restlessness makes many sectors of our society uneasy and insecure. Age and experience (if they ever were) are no longer synonymous with wisdom. Five-year-old children are more comfortable surfing the Internet or programming the family video than their 55-year-old grandmother. This is both endearing and frightening. Older generations are no longer automatically revered for their maturity and wisdom; the young have inherited and, some would argue, commodified the earth. The idea that our society is no longer moving forward in a linear, logical progression towards an ultimate nirvana with a well-educated, affluent population makes fundamental shifts of perspective occur. The nature of life, its cultural patterns, a sense of community and even the reason for human existence are brought sharply into question. We struggle to make sense of the transformation we see daily.

Modernism and postmodernism

In the eighteenth century, a pre-industrial society developed the concept of modernity. This philosophy suggested that the knowledge accumulated by individuals working freely and creatively would, eventually, liberate the human race from the irrationality of superstition and religion and the arbitrary use of power in order to build an enlightened world. These ambitious goals encompassed concepts of progression, linearity and continuity; the knowable world revealed through a constant, universal 'truth'; and the emancipation of the individual, socially, culturally and politically (Habermas, 1983, cited in Dahlberg et al., 1999; Harvey, 1989). Central to this view of modernity is the view of a predictable, preordained world that is ordered and controlled by stable, autonomous individuals. This philosophy for education implies that there is a stable, agreed, preconstituted body of knowledge which can be transmitted by one generation to the next generation of children.

The seismic technological changes that took place in the latter half of the twentieth century shattered the certainty and optimism of modernity; the lofty ideals of modernity, it is claimed, have been revealed to be unworkable. Harvey (1989) and Bauman (1991, cited in Dahlberg et al., 1999) suggest that modernity set itself unachievable tasks with its pursuit of absolute truth and the pure art of liberating humanity; of humankind operating within an ordered, certain, harmonious world progressing towards the end of history. The major emphasis of the philosophy of modernity sees order as the key to all that society is able to achieve. Any notion of complete certainty and perfect order, Dahlberg et al., suggest, has now imploded.

Postmodernity is a philosophy which embraces, even encourages, uncertainty, complexity, non-linearity, muliple perspectives and diversity. From a postmodern perspective, there is no position of absolute certainty, no universal understanding that exists for all time and in all cultures. There is no defined canon of knowledge to be acquired by every educated individual which will enable her to cope with all circumstances and all eventualities. If order and its pursuit are the key to modernity, the world and knowledge of it, in postmodern thinking are seen to be socially constructed with each individual having an active part to play in the process of construction. Difference and plurality are celebrated by those who subscribe to such a viewpoint. Great store is placed on meaning-making in collaboration with other social beings rather than the seeking and finding of the ultimate truth:

> Social construction is a social process, and in no way existent apart from our own involvement in the world – the world is always our world, understood or constructed by ourselves, not in isolation but as part of a community of human agents, and through our active interaction and participation with other people

in that community. For these reasons, knowledge and its construction is always context-specific and value-laden, challenging the modernist belief in universal truths and scientific neutrality.

(Lather, 1991: 99, cited in Dahlberg et al., 1999)

In essence, the postmodern view of the world is, first, that it is provisional and unstable and, secondly, that it is made up of many alternatively constructed perspectives which, by their nature, are culturally embedded and value-laden. This position challenges the idea that there is a shared social reality but suggests, instead, that there are only multiple, individual realities; each personal reality is equally valid and, in essence, diverse and distinct. The relevance of these ideas and influences of postmodernity is very great for the field of early childhood education. This philosophical explanation of the world makes it necessary for educators to re-examine the conceptual framework within which they work. The notion of a postmodern world demands that we think anew our practice in education. Are there ideological beliefs of enduring value, and what might constrain our vision for the education of the child?

We need not, necessarily, discard and reject all the goals of modernity; the very concept of postmodernity allows us to accept multiple perspectives and plurality. But it is essential we reconsider the theoretical position which underpins early childhood educational practice in order to empower learners.

The concept of childhood

The concept of childhood is a social construction. The idea that there is a stage of life that is a preparation for fully functioning maturity is a relatively recent idea which stems from the philosophies discussed in the previous section. The suggestion was that there is a 'state of adulthood', which is clear cut and the individual is fully formed. In pre-industrial society children were regarded merely as small adults useful only for the continuation of the human race. Investment in them was in direct relationship to their survival rate to adulthood and, in consequence, was low. The Industrial Revolution brought with it a necessity for more complex life skills, and the period of infancy and childhood began to be viewed as a buffer zone during which preparation took place for the adult life ahead. Economics played its role, undoubtedly: a stable, well-prepared, self-supporting workforce creates wealth for society but, whilst this is the over-riding rationale for this view, it is far too simplistic to leave the discussion there. Just as with the philosophical explanations of the world and the complex influences that mould our thinking, tensions also exist between the various perspectives of the child and the purpose of childhood: 'Children's lives are lived through childhoods constructed for them by adults' understandings of childhood and what children are and should be' (Mayall, 1996: 1).

Views of the child

The blank tablet

In the seventeenth century, Locke presented his idea of the child born as a blank sheet, a *tabula rasa*, or an empty vessel waiting passively to be filled with a predetermined body of knowledge, receptive to having transmitted to her a defined range of skills and existing cultural values. This is a child whose period of childhood must be used to equip and train her for the demands of later education and adulthood by preparing her for the accomplishment of the successive stages of life. The young individual is viewed as valuable physical capital. Childhood is seen therefore as a period of time which provides an opportunity to educate a population effectively in order to promote a nation's well-being. The well-chosen metaphor used for early childhood education as the first rung of a ladder that requires successful negotiation aptly describes this way of thinking.

The innocent

Competing with the view of the child as a potential asset of society is the image of the child as a primitive being, an innocent inhabiting the golden age of childhood. This is Rousseau's child who is seen as intrinsically good and in need of adult protection from the evils of life. This sentimental perspective has had an enduring influence on early years education which is felt centuries later. Adults shelter children from a world in which they are very much a participant. The resulting tensions arising today from the hangover of these views are discussed later in this chapter.

The product of science

A third view is of the child with fixed biological stages, a child born with inherent characteristics and who moves successively through a predetermined path of development in an isolated way towards complete realization. Developmental theorists have contributed greatly to this view of childhood, particularly Piaget.

Piaget

Major theorists have viewed cognitive development and its sources of influence very differently. Piaget (1896–1980), a brilliant Swiss biologist and naturalist, has had a profound impact on the way in which learning is viewed by early childhood educators. He and his wife meticulously recorded the development of their three children. These scientific records showed that their babies were extremely competent learners and that their view of the world was complex and structured but, Piaget suggested, it was qualitatively different from an adult's view. He concluded that thinking is an essentially biological mechanism. Cognitive development occurs as a result of the dynamic interaction of two processes within the individual. These are assimilation, in which new information is taken into the pre-exising concepts, and accommodation, in which these concepts change to fit new information.

This notion of the interaction between the child and her environment is critical and has greatly influenced the views of developmental psychologists and early years teachers. Piaget's best known contribution is that cognitive development occurs in stages, during the succession of which the child's thinking changes qualitatively. The main point here is that a stage theory is linear, sequential and hierarchical, moving from concrete to abstract thinking – essentially a modernist perspective.

Vygotsky

Vygotsky (1896–1934), the Russian psychologist, brought a dimension largely ignored by Piaget to the field of education – the view of the adult as fundamental to the child's development. Educators in the west see his work as hugely important for early years practice. Vygotsky, like Piaget and Donaldson, views cognitive development as a series of stages, during which the individual's thinking becomes increasingly flexible and powerful. However, he suggests that the greatest influence on this development is the support offered to the learner by an experienced practitioner. The social situation of the developing child is considered by Vygotsky to be the key influence on the thinking of the maturing individual. Vygotsky suggests that children's thinking develops through their social interactions with a 'significant adult', particularly interactions conducted through the medium of spoken and written language which, in turn, enable the child to form her own understandings or, in Vygotsky's words, to 'internalize the concepts'. This view of intellectual development places great value on the role of an adult (the teacher) in supporting a child's thinking and learning. This notion is immortalized by his proposal that the knowledgeable adult (or experienced practitioner) can support the novice into functioning at a level of her 'zone of proximal development' (ZPD): 'What the child does in co-operation with others, he will learn to do alone' (Vygotsky, 1978). Piaget saw the child as being innately programmed to learn. Vygotsky saw culture transmitted through language as the most natural and effective teaching tool. *Independent learner*

Bruner

Bruner (1966), whose ideas over the past four decades have inspired educational thinking, also suggests a stage theory and sees the child as increasingly able to represent her world in more and more complex ways through the three stages of:

1 *enactive representation*, during which the individual can only think in a way that is based on actions;
2 *iconic representation*, during which the child can employ the use of images to think without the objects having to be present; and
3 *symbolic representation*, during which stage the child is able to think in terms of symbols to represent the world (an example of this is the essential ability to use spoken and written language).

Unlike Piaget, Bruner developed a theory of instruction to accompany his stages of cognitive development and harnessed the Vygotskian notion that thinking can be facilitated. Through a collaboration between experienced and less experienced practitioners, Bruner proposes that a fruitful, learning relationship can exist, and that it is one in which the the novice is 'scaffolded' to attain higher levels of intellectual competence (or ZPD) than otherwise would be achieved.

Donaldson

Donaldson also suggests that children's thinking moves through qualitatively different stages, developing from what she describes as 'point mode', through 'line mode' and 'construct mode' to finally, 'transcendent mode'. In 'point mode' the infant is limited to thinking in the here and now, but in 'line mode' the child can operate in the past and in the future in terms of time. By the 'construct mode' the child is able to generalize from events, albeit still in the concrete mode and, later still, with the 'transcendent mode' the child, with even more advanced thinking, can distance herself in time and space (Donaldson, 1992).

In addition, Donaldson proposes that a child's thinking can be enhanced through both the nature and the way in which problems are presented to her. The essential feature of the tasks that appear to facilitate intellectual performance occurs when the problems make 'human sense' to the child. The tasks that the young child finds most difficult are those that require a type of thought that Donaldson calls 'disembedded' thinking.

It is beyond the scope of this short introductory chapter to do justice to the ideas of many important theorists who have made significant contributions to our understanding of the nature of cognitive development and to the ways in which it can be supported. Piaget, Bruner and Donaldson share the view that the thinking of the individual becomes increasingly complex, flexible and subtle as intellectual functioning advances through the various stages of development. This is shown by intellectual feats – such as the ability to operate with thoughts in the absence of the concrete object, having a concept of past and future, being able to account for a different perspective from one's own and understanding that something can stand in place of an object. These literally mind-changing levels in the capacity of thought are acknowledged in a child's assertion that 'If we didn't think there wouldn't be a us' (Fisher, 1990).

Vygotsky, Bruner and Donaldson give us the starting point for thinking about the ways through which adults can promote intellectual development, but still we are left to deal with the question: 'Are there indeed stages or universal patterns of cognitive development, through which all must pass?' On this Meadows says:

> The degree to which Piaget's stages can be seen in children's cognitive
> behaviour has been the matter of fierce debate and considerable uncertainty,
> such that John Flavell, one of the most informed people in the field, published
> two incompatible decisions in the same year and called himself 'undecided to
> the point of public self-contradiction'. (1993: 348)

The discussion continues about the extent to which stage theories are either valuable or restricting. But the contributions of the four theorists to which reference has been made already reveal a shared belief that the child's thinking develops with maturity enhanced with the appropriate experience and, crucially, with the relevant adult support. Thinking moves from a preoccupation, in infancy and early childhood, with the physical, the sensory and the immediate, towards being able to operate at a greater distance from the concrete presence of the context of thought.

This achievement in mental operations, during the years of middle childhood has, as its ultimate goal, the ability to think in the abstract. Not that all mature thinking is abstract; nor is abstract thinking necessary for all the intellectual functions required of an adult but, without the ability to shift gear into abstract thought, an individual is relegated to the bottom rungs of the educational ladder. The capacity to use a personal and flexible repertoire is essential in order to be able to move fluidly between operating either in abstract or concrete thinking, as required.

The qualitative shifts in intellectual functioning are demonstrated, for example, by the ability to conduct mathematical and scientific mental operations of reversibility; to be able to divide numbers accurately; and, most importantly, to know when to use division as a means to solve a problem. Another crucial cognitive leap is the ability to operate within a symbolic system, the obvious demonstration of which is the ability to use the alphabetic code to represent spoken language and to be able to employ a mathematical language and its conventions in order to conduct numerical operations.

Donaldson (1993) says that the ability to read and write offers the opportunity to use a symbolic system and that, through operating within it, thought is made more systematic and ordered. The interactive nature of learning in and through the different curriculum subjects requires a range of cognitive functioning, but it is through being able to operate in the symbolic communication systems of advanced societies that the individual has, in turn, the level of her thinking enhanced. Donaldson says:

> . . . the thinking itself draws great strength from literacy whenever it is more than a scrap of an idea, whenever there are complex possibilities to consider. It is even more obvious that the sustained, orderly communication of this kind of thinking requires considerable mastery of the written word. (1993: 50)

In addition, thinking is enhanced by being able to read texts in which the meaning is, of necessity, 'disembedded'. Donaldson goes on to say:

> But the kind of written language we are now concerned with is also more impersonal in the details of its form. It entails the use of phrases like; 'It is possible that . . .' or 'The causes of this seem to lie . . .' or 'One reason is . . .' or 'What this means is . . .'. (1993: 51)

The constraint resulting from the dominant influence of developmental psychology in early childhood education, Dahlberg (1985) suggests, is that this is a scientific child based on a model of natural growth. Aspects of functioning are separated out for ease of description and analysis into distinct, measurable categories – namely, social development, intellectual development and motor development. The reality and the complexity of the inter-related parts and how they operate together in a holistic educational experience is neither explained nor wholly accounted for (ibid.).

Perhaps, for the present purpose, the most useful aspect of this discussion is that throughout infancy and childhood the individual demonstrates marked changes in intellectual behaviour and, during the years 3–7, children's thinking advances substantially. It is useful, therefore, for early years educators to be aware, first, of the qualitative shifts in thinking that occur; secondly, how they might be developed through the different curriculum subjects; and, thirdly and most crucially, in what ways thinking can be promoted in order to maximize the level of intellectual functioning of children.

The generator of labour

There is a fourth view which competes with the previously described views, and this is that of the child as a labour market producer. The contribution of women to the economic well-being of both western and developing worlds is established and accepted, in addition to which many studies have challenged prevalent thinking that very young children (between 0 and 3 years at least) need their mothers as the prime caregivers. Governments are encouraging an economically driven argument that the provision of high-quality childcare (now termed educare) is a cost-effective approach to maintaining a stable, skilled and female workforce.

The four constructions of the child discussed here have their roots in a modernist philosophy, and they are relevant today and still dominate early years practice. Their influence reflects an ideological stance on behalf of the educator regarding issues such as the 'innocence' of children and the necessity to protect them from evil (e.g. the way films are certificated in attempt to preserve childhood ignorance). The purpose of this chapter is not to offer value judgements, solutions or answers but to offer an alternative perspective in order to develop and deepen understanding of the context in which early childhood education operates and also to offer newer ideas from other disciplines for consideration.

The power

From a postmodernist perspective, the practices of early childhood education need to be questioned. Constructions of the child and childhood in line with current social and economic change have to be rethought. Children, it can be argued from this viewpoint, have an independent place in society; they have recognized rights and are seen also to be functioning members of society in their own right. Complementary to this view is the image of the powerful child. Culturally this is self-evident. In contrast to the eighteenth century, children are now hugely demanding of their parents' resources in terms of their time, energy and expense. First, pregnancy and childbirth offer commercial opportunities and then, later, the babies and infants are even bigger business. Childhood is a highly profitable industry. Babies grow into pre-school and primary school children, and all are multi-billion pound consumers of technology, clothes and toys. The term 'edutainment' has been coined to describe the books, TV programmes, videos, computer games and educational toys which are designed to teach, inform and entertain the young learners. Television promotion of these items is deliberately and cynically intensified before Christmas: and not only does commerce sell to children via their parents in this way but it also sells to the parents direct through their children. Ever more sophisticated and relentless marketing capitalizes on the seductive, appealing image of the beautiful young child in order to sell commodities to adults such as transport, holidays, clothes and perfumes – take, for example, the advertisement which links an expensive, fast car with an image of the 30-year-old 'new' man holding his baby.

The active co-constructor of knowledge

The final perspective we will deal with here is the one in which the child is seen operating within an actively negotiated set of social relations and conditions. Childhood, whilst a biological phase, is socially determined by the time, place and culture. The construction placed upon childhood varies within each and every society and is affected by class, gender and socioeconomic level. The concept of childhood, therefore, means different things to different communities. There is no worldwide, universal concept of childhood. Diversity is celebrated.

However, there are tensions within and between community perspectives and contextually constructed patterns of childcare. In western society children are given earlier and earlier access to designer clothes, cosmetics and adult entertainment such as videos and the Internet but the same children are condemned for becoming sexually active and for experimenting with drugs.

The postmodern perspective also sees the child actively participating in the construction of her own childhood in order to determine her own life in a powerful, positive way. This is demonstrated through an analysis of adult/child relationships – the somewhat surprising recognition that the child also has power in the negotiation of her relationships with adults. Adults have power certainly, but children also have the ability to resist that power. The distinction between this view of the child and the previous one is in recognizing that the child has rights for her own sake and with these rights comes power. There needs to be a genuine, respectful recognition of the child's power and enormous capacity rather than a manipulation of it for commercial gain.

■ The implications for early childhood education

The implications of this perception of childhood and the child are far reaching, challenging and exciting. If, through the lenses of postmodernism, you see the child as an active negotiator in her own learning and as a co-constructor of knowledge, nursery settings and schools become different places from many of those currently operating. We have discussed the impressive intellectual competence of the young child, and we suggest that layered on to this there is the disturbing notion that there is no agreed, predetermined body of knowledge in today's world to transmit to the child. Rather, we have only shifting perspectives of what society requires as its needs constantly change. The postmodern perspective sees it as no longer possible to fall back on knowledge as something as universally accepted, absolute and predetermined. All learners must take responsibility for their own meaning-making. What is our task? It is a high-risk one but necessary. We must educate the child by capitalizing on and maximizing her competence in a collaborative venture in order to co-construct knowledge for today and the uncertainties of tomorrow.

In Reggio Emilio, thinkers such as Malaguzzi have been reconceptualizing early childhood education in these terms for over 20 years. Their worked-through philosophy translated into early years practice is the concept of the 'rich child' – Malaguzzi says that children are 'rich in potential, strong, powerful and competent'. Learning is not seen as an individual act taking place in the head of one child, but a co-operative activity in which children and adults construct knowledge together in order to make meaning. Children are active, valued partners in the co-construction. Psychologists have described to us these learners engaging actively with the world, who are born well equipped to interrogate the world. Malaguzzi suggests that children lose part of their full capacity in a formal school system where pupils are regulated, made to conform, restrained and constrained by adults thinking that they know what there is to be learnt. He writes strikingly about 'the hundred languages of children' which are lost one by one in many educational systems.

In this book, by developing the ideas promoted by the Reggio Emilio pedagogues, we can conceive, implement and sustain practice that enables young children to develop into the flexible, skilled thinkers that society will need, who will achieve personal fulfilment in the world they inherit but who are motivated also to reshape it.

Research evidence on what makes early education more or less effective

The findings of the 'Competent Children' study in New Zealand (Wylie, 1998) suggest that, by 6 years of age, the intellectual functioning of children is affected by the following factors:

- The age at which children started in early childhood education (before 3, the greater the impact).
- The quality of staff interactions with children.
- The extent to which children are allowed to finish activities.

Important questions also arise concerning the nature and quality of the curriculum as well as types of pedagogy and their effectiveness when considering the benefit of early education programmes. Such issues are particularly relevant in a book of this nature. These essential questions are beginning to be answered by the extensive and hugely comprehensive DfEE-funded 'Effective Provision of Pre-school Education' (EPPE) study (Sylva et al., 1999), which shows that a significant boost to children's progress beyond the pre-school years can be attributed to attendance at particular early years settings. The gains can be accounted for by the quality of particular settings rather than explained by the children's personal characteristics, their home circumstances or parental education. More detail and explanation for the gains are still emerging as the vast amount of diverse data from the study are being analysed, considered and the findings published.

The curriculum experienced by the 3,000 plus children in most of the huge variety of settings investigated by the EPPE project (1997–2003) became more explicit and subject focused as the study progressed: it spanned the impact of the introduction of, first, the Desirable Learning Outcomes (1996) which was followed by the Early Learning Goals (2001). The extent and nature of this curriculum guidance from the DfES will be discussed fully in the later chapters of the book.

Curriculum and pedagogy

What precisely do these two complementary terms mean? Over time different 'models of learning' have generated a variety of metaphors to encapsulate what occurs as education in an array of schooling establishments. The term 'kindergarten' offers a developmental image of a rich environment in which children are encouraged to grow. Thus the terms curriculum and pedagogy, both semantically and practically, are entwined in early childhood educational settings. They are influenced, Murphy (1996: 11) suggests, by '. . . the belief that a child's development towards scientific rationality emerges spontaneously as she explores and "plays" with the environment'. How the child learns is seen as equally important as what she learns. Both contribute substantially overall to the type of learner she becomes; a learner who is able to operationalize intellectual capacity in order to maximize on whichever learning situation she finds herself in later in life. Katz (1992) argues that the inculcation of positive learning dispositions should be foremost in the early childhood educator's mind. It is knowing how to learn, to be able to engage, to concentrate and to persevere which empower an individual to succeed in education.

Learning dispositions

Five domains of learning disposition might be described by:

1 taking an interest;
2 being involved;
3 persisting with difficulty;
4 communicating with others; and
5 taking responsibility (Carr, 2001).

These prerequisite skills and abilities without which no individual can develop into a proactive, autonomous learner underpin all that is conducted in the name of education in early years settings, and the opportunity to develop these learning dispositions makes up a large part of what is conceptualized as a curriculum. In New Zealand, this is even more explicit. The metaphor 'Te Whariki' (Maori for 'woven mat') is used to promote a curriculum with these learning dispositions as the basis. A community and context-appropriate curriculum is woven by New Zealand early years educators for their specific setting. The EPPE study has, for the purposes of the conceptual framework of the research project, separated curriculum from pedagogy.

The curriculum

The 'curriculum' in this context is described as broadly meaning the knowledge, skills and values an educational establishment aims to impart to its pupils. Curriculum theorists have written at length on the idea that there are, in truth, two curricula, one that is explicit and acknowledged and one that is 'hidden' and which influences the learning of pupils in many subtle and unintentional ways. Children learn, for instance, what pleases an adult, they try to guess the 'right' answer to a question through her facial expression and body language. They learn also what attitudes are appropriate and what kind of behaviour is expected in order to fit the 'ethos' of the particular setting of which they are part.

Pedagogy

Pedagogy is often referred to as the activity of teaching and whether teaching can be considered, in its practice, an art or a science. In the early years of education, pedagogy does not necessarily refer to a direct and didactic transmission of knowledge but, rather, it will include the considered provision of an effective learning environment with planned opportunities for play and exploration. Pedagogy in a pre-school setting embraces talking to children, discussing things with children and drawing facets of a shared situation to their attention. If pedagogy is the pursuit of an educational goal and if learning can occur through a variety of approaches, the term implies that it is instructive in some way. The researchers on the EPPE project have defined pedagogy to describe the set of instructional techniques and strategies which enable learning to take place and also the organization of the setting in which the learning occurs. This learning includes opportunities for the acquisition of knowledge, skills, attitudes and dispositions within a particular context. The EPPE study aimed to identify more fully the range of techniques used by the most effective pedagogues practising in those early childhood settings (in the project) in which the children made the most progress.

Developmentally appropriate practice

Different settings regard valuable learning experiences from a variety of perspectives and offer different criteria for making judgements about them. Enabling young children to learn is a highly skilled endeavour. The impressive intellectual capacity of the young child has been discussed earlier, and the moral obligation to develop that capacity to its maximum potential is not in question. Children acquire knowledge and understanding from an (at present) undefined period before birth and continuously from then on. In addition, that store of knowledge is idiosyncratic and different for each and every individual. So there is considerable consensus that, if a learning experience is to facilitate learning, it has to meet the learning needs of the child; in this way such an experience can be termed 'developmentally appropriate'. The notion of appropriateness can be described as the extent to which a learning activity:

- exercises and challenges the capacities of the learner;
- encourages and helps the learner to develop unique patterns of interests, talents and reach goals; and
- presents experiences in which the learner is able to master, generalize and retain concepts, skills and knowledge which relate to previous experiences, whilst linking to future learning expectations (adapted from Hohmann and Weikart, 1995: 15).

Play and pedagogy

It has been long recognized that most high-quality, well-planned and developmentally appropriate experiences in a pre-school setting will have play as the means to promote learning. Through the motivating nature of play-based activities the child has the opportunity to experiment, to explore and to engage for long periods of time. It is an 'active' form of learning of extraordinary potential.

Piaget and Vygotsky have proposed that there are strong links between symbolic play and the development of the child's intellectual ability to be able to represent and to transform what she knows about the world using language, literacy and mark-making. Much is also learnt socially in play situations through negotiating, interacting and constructing understandings. Adult support is also an important factor in the quality of the learning that occurs.

In providing these type of opportunities for children, *Curriculum Guidance for the Foundation Stage* (DfEE/QCA, 2000) upholds this theoretical position on the educational value of play when it states that the early years practitioner should '. . .establish relationships with children and their parents, plan for the learning environment and curriculum, support and extend children's play, learning and development' (p. 1) and '. . . Practitioners need to plan learning experiences of the highest quality . . . Well-planned play is the key way in which children learn with enjoyment and challenge during the foundation stage' (p. 7).

Scaffolding learning

The idea of the adult scaffolding children's learning has been touched upon earlier and is an important aspect of pedagogy in the earliest years of schooling. Scaffolding is related to Vygotsky's notion of a 'zone of proximal development' which is a level of functioning, and one that, without assistance from a more experienced individual, the child is not likely to reach.

·tioning vary within and between cultures, societies and experi-
...eveloped in joint activity, within a meaningful, social context
...ild and supported by interaction and in collaboration with a more
...ienced person.

Embedded in a concept of effective support for an individual are certain pre-requisite conditions that have to be met by the learner herself, the very least of which is engagement. Therefore, for learning to take place the child has to be motivated in order to engage with a cognitive challenge. Encouraging and enabling the child to participate at this high level are perhaps the most important feature of scaffolded learning in the early years. Pascal and Bertram (1997) suggest that effective learning demands an almost symbiotic relationship between child and adult. These writers describe an 'involvement' of the child which flows from and is influenced by the 'engaged' teacher. The characteristics of an involved child are those which enable her to be focused and persistent in an activity. Mutual collaboration in the learning act is described by Pascal and Bertram in the following way: '. . .not only does the adult's style of engagement directly effect the children's level of involvement, but the children's involvement effects the adult's style of engagement' (1997: 135). The centrality of which is the notion of reciprocity.

Co-construction and scaffolding learning

Other theorists have drawn to the attention of early years educators the importance of this co-construction, where both parties, adult and child, engage with each other's understandings (or constructions) in order for learning to occur. Wells (1985), in his language study, found incidences of this nature in the homes of those children who acquired language rapidly. Other studies have shown how mothers intuitively adapt their language to the limits of their child's linguistic competence and comprehension in facilitating ways. Wood (1986) and Bruner (1966) have both developed this concept with positive implications for the consideration of effective pedagogy in the early years. These writers suggest that the adult, in order to enhance learning, needs to know very precisely what the child already knows and can do when scaffolding during a learning experience. The role of the learner within the activity can be enhanced positively by an adult who:

- highlights the critical features of the activity;
- buffers the child's attention through distractions;
- channels the child's activities to ensure success;
- uses errors to encourage learning;
- enables procedures to be commented upon and explained; and
- allows responsibility for the activity to be gradually transferred to the learner contingent upon her success (adapted from Meadows, 1993).

Substantial and convincing evidence from empirical research is now adding to the validity of these ideas.

Findings of the Researching Effective Pedagogy in the Early Years (REPEY) project

Before looking at the findings of the REPEY project, it is necessary to look first at the Effective Provision for Pre-school Education (EPPE) project (1997–2003), which followed the developmental progress of over 3,000 children in 140 pre-school settings across England. The EPPE study assessed the children's developmental progress on a range of intellectual, social and behavioural measures in order to determine which settings fostered higher levels of development over and above what might have been expected from the results of assessment of the child on entry to pre-school. Family background factors and the child's gender and health were also taken into account. EPPE is the study which identifies the 'value added' boost to children's progress afforded by the pre-school provision they have experienced.

The REPEY study, on the other hand, is based on case studies of 14 selected Foundation Stage settings from the much larger sample of the EPPE study itself. These settings had shown that they provided 'good or excellent practice' on the basis of the social/behavioural and cognitive outcome measures of the children from the EPPE study. In investigating the pedagogy of a setting, as has been suggested earlier, a clear distinction was made between 'pedagogical interventions', which can be described as face-to-face encounters with children, and 'pedagogical framing'. This covers all that occurs in an early years setting in order to offer positive learning opportunities, such as the arrangement of the space, the establishment of routines and provision in terms of the materials and resources used. The analyses of the REPEY study have been most insightful in explaining the quantitative data from the parent project in the most effective settings and in suggesting how it was that the pupils had made more progress than their peers in the indisputably less effective settings. Four areas of impact were investigated closely:

1 Adult–child interactions.
2 Differentiation and formative assessment.
3 Parental partnership and the home education environment.
4 Discipline and support in talking through conflicts.

Adult–child verbal interactions and 'sustained shared thinking'

The quality of the adult–child interactions is the most compelling feature of the settings with the highest ratings and these settings were where the children had made the greatest progress. It can be assumed from the theory that these interactions will occur most frequently where children are offered direct and immediate experiences within which to operate. The level of stimulation will be high, and the child will have the opportunity to be active and to construct her own understandings. As Hohmann and Weikart (1995: 15) say about this type of learning, it is 'active learning' and '. . . learning in which the child, by acting with people, ideas and events constructs new understandings'.

In the most effective settings, the REPEY team observed examples of what Bruner describes as 'joint involvement episodes' in which it was observed that both the child and the adult were highly motivated to engage with the understanding of the other participant. The learning is achieved through a process of reflexive 'co-construction' which means that both parties are involved in the learning episode and that also the content is instructive. From the analyses of the data, the researchers have added to the literature on the concept of 'scaffolded learning' in suggesting that, for learning to be most effective, there has to be an element of 'sustained shared thinking' in the dyad. It is this phenomenon that supports the most effective learning.

The project report supplies several examples of the staff enjoying being with the children and sharing a joint activity. The level of engagement of both participants was high. The following example demonstrates this well, with an adult entering into and extending the child's imagination through play:

[A nursery nurse (NNEB) and a group of children are seated at a table working with play dough.]

BOY 1 (3.11) hands her a ball of playdough.

NNEB 1 'I wonder what is inside? I'll unwrap it.'

NNEB 1 quickly makes the ball into a thumb pot and holds it out to BOY 1. 'Its empty!'

BOY 1 takes a pinch of playdough and drops it into a thumb pot. 'It's an egg.'

NNEB 1 picking it out gingerly, 'It's a strange shape.'

Another child tries to take the 'egg'.

'Be very very careful. It's an egg.'

To BOY 1 'What is it going to hatch into?'

BOY 1 'A lion.'

NNEB 1 'A lion? . . . Oh I can see why it might hatch into a lion, it's got little hairy bits on it.'

NNEB 1 sends BOY 1 to put the egg somewhere safe to hatch. He takes the egg and goes into the bathroom. (After a few minutes BOY 1 returns to the group.)

NNEB 1 'Has the egg hatched?'

BOY 1 'Yes.'

NNEB1 'What was it?'

BOY 1 'A bird.'

NNEB 1 'A bird? We'll have to take it outside at playtime and put it in a tree so
it can fly away.' (Siraj-Blatchford et al., 2002: Document 421, Vignette 8)

This type of sensitive interaction encourages children to engage with their
play, to fantasize and to learn in an active, participatory way. Research has
suggested that a wide range of techniques and strategies are appropriate
to enable pupils to acquire different types of knowledge. On occasions
simple 'procedural knowledge' can be acquired through direct teaching.
Procedural knowledge covers issues such as 'knowing about the things
in the world and how to act on them'. The support for the development of
'conceptual knowledge', which includes ideas and the understanding
of principles and their relationship to each other, requires a different
approach – a constructive process. The most valuable is when the co-
constructivist process occurs and the knowledge is developed jointly by an
experienced and less experienced learner.

The type of knowledge of the highest level which an individual needs to
acquire in order to develop the ability to think in an advanced and flexible
way is 'metacognitive knowledge'. This is an understanding about one's
own thinking. Knowledge of this type is developed through learners being
offered opportunities which require them to reflect upon and to regulate
their own thinking. It is this type of intellectual development which is
powerfully facilitated by what the REPEY research team have termed 'sustained shared thinking' and which occurs between children and adults or
more advanced peers. The following is an example from the REPEY project
of this type of scaffolded learning:

BOY 8 (4.1) who has been watching the various items floating on water, 'Look
at the fir cone. There's bubbles of air coming out.'

NURSERY OFFICER 1 'It's spinning round.'

(Modelling curiosity and desire to investigate further.)

BOY 8 'That's 'cos it's got air in it.'

NURSERY OFFICER 1 picked up the fir cone and shows the children how the
scales go round the fir cone in a spiral, turning the fir cone round with a
winding action, 'When the air comes out in bubbles it makes the fir cone
spin around.'

GIRL 2E (4.9) uses a plastic tube to blow into the water. 'Look bubbles.'

NURSERY OFFICER 1 'What are you putting into the water to make bubbles? . . . What is coming out of the tube?'

GIRL 2E 'Air.' (Siraj-Blatchford et al., 2002: Document 421)

This type of activity – *sustained shared thinking* – is, the REPEY team argue, a necessary prerequisite for the most effective pedagogy. They define it as:

1 the teacher having an awareness of, and responding to, the child's understanding or capability vis-à-vis the particular subject/activity in question;
2 the child's awareness of what is to be learnt (i.e. what is in the teacher's mind or the 'curriculum'); and
3 the active co-construction of an idea or skill.

Both participants contribute to the learning process, although not necessarily equally. The child might be, and often was, the initiator of the episode, but it was crucial that the adult responded positively, sensitively and empathetically. The research team observed occasions where 'sustained shared thinking' occurred and, mainly, these take place in the centres defined as 'excellent' in the REPPE project – they declare it to be a powerful way of extending children's thinking. They admit, however, that the episodes of 'sustained shared thinking' are not common even in the most effective settings.

The features of high-quality adult–child interaction

Types of questions The types of questions used by practitioners are proving to be significant. Research indicates that the questions which are most facilitative in supporting learning are those which are more open-ended and provide a framework for conversation with the child (Tizard and Hughes, 1984; Wells, 1985). The data from the case studies suggest that open-ended questioning is associated with higher levels of cognitive achievement but, again, this does not occur frequently and only made up 5.1% of all the interactions compared with 34.1% of closed questions.

Subject knowledge of practitioners The data from the case study observations are indicating very clearly that, in order for high-quality 'sustained shared thinking' to take place, the practitioners need sufficient subject knowledge of the various curriculum areas in which children are engaged in order to support and extend the child's understanding. The REPEY team found occasions when the subject knowledge of adults was inadequate, and this led to missed opportunities or what the team term as 'uncertain outcomes'. An additional facet to the learning outcome for the children is the level of the practitioner's 'pedagogical subject knowledge' (Shulman, 1986). This term describes the way in which we are able to make our own knowledge accessible to others. This is heavily dependent, in turn, on the level of the subject knowledge itself: the deeper the understanding an individual has of the subject, the better usually is her ability to engage others with the content area. The report continues: 'However, even in these more effective EPPE case study centres we found enough evidence to suggest that early years staff in the Foundation Stage require more support in developing their subject knowledge and their knowledge of how to scaffold children's learning' (Siraj-Blatchford et al., 2002: 76). The implications for the training of early years teachers and their initial teacher education are clear, as has been suggested in the Introduction to this book.

In conclusion

The evidence cited here from the EPPE project is the most substantial, longitudinal evidence to date on the type of effective settings that support competent young learners. The study provides the empirical quantitative data on the proven benefit of specific forms of provision and pedagogy. The findings are confirmatory of much of the theory of early childhood education and they uphold the ideology of some of the greatest thinkers in the field, both past and present. The EPPE and REPEY projects uphold and endorse the views of Pascal and Bertram, and of Malaguzzi in the Reggio Emilio nurseries, on the most effective ways of supporting children's learning through rich first-hand experiences and working alongside pedagogues and professionals involved with their own practice (artists and designers). We have here Malaguzzi's active co-constructor of knowledge as she participates in Siraj-Blatchford et al.'s episodes of 'sustained shared thinking'. The EPPE project also points to the way forward on how to improve further on what is offered. The findings are both illuminating and affirmatory but also challenging. There is no room for complacency as there is much to be done. The place of this book on the shelves of early years practitioners is assured.

▮ Suggested further reading

Dahlberg, G., Moss, P. and Pence, A. (1999) *Beyond Quality in Early Childhood Education and Care*. London: FalmerRoutledge.

Gopnik, A., Meltzoff, A. and Kuhl, P. (1999) *How Babies Think*. London: Weidenfeld & Nicholson.

Siraj-Blatchford, I., Sylva, K., Muttock, S., Gilden, R. and Bell, D. (2002) *Researching Effective Pedagogy in the Early Years. Research Report* 356. London: DfES.

References

Bauman, Z. (1991) *Modernity and Ambivalence*. Cambridge: Polity Press.

Blair, C. (2002) 'School readiness', *American Psychologist*, 57(2): 111–27.

Bruner, M. (1966) *Toward a Theory of Instruction*. Cambridge, MA: Harvard University Press.

Carr, M. (2001) *Assessment in Early Childhood Settings: Learning Stories*. London: Paul Chapman Publishing.

Dahlberg, G. (1985) *Context and the Child's Orientation to Meaning: A Study of the Child's Way of Organizing the Surrounding World in Relation to Public Institutionalized Socialization*. Stockholm: Almqvist & Wiksell.

Dahlberg, G., Moss, P. and Pence, A. (1999) *Beyond Quality in Early Childhood Education and Care*. London: Routledge Falmer.

DfEE/QCA (2000) *Curriculum Guidance for the Foundation Stage*. London: QCA.

Donaldson, M. (1978) *Children's Minds*. London: Fontana/Collins.

Donaldson, M. (1989 [1993]) *Sense and Sensibility: Some Thoughts on the Teaching of Literacy*. *Occasional Paper* 3. Reading: Reading and Language Information Centre, University of Reading. Reprinted in Beard, R. (ed.) (1993) *Teaching Literacy: Balancing Perspectives*. London: Hodder & Stoughton.

Donaldson, M. (1992) *Human Minds: An Exploration*. Harmondsworth: Penguin Books.

Fisher, R. (1990) *Teaching Children to Think*. Oxford: Blackwell.

Gopnik, A., Meltzoff, A. and Kuhl, P. (1999) *How Babies Think*. London: Weidenfeld & Nicholson.

Habermas, J. (1983) 'Modernity: an incomplete project', in H. Foster (ed.) *The Anti-aesthetic: Essays on Postmodern Culture*. Port Townsend: Washington.

Harvey, D. (1989) *The Condition of Postmodernity*. Oxford: Blackwell.

Hohmann, M. and Weikart, D.P. (1995) *Educating Young Children*. Ypsilanti, MI: High/Scope Educational Research Foundation.

Katz, L.G. (1992) *What Should Young Children be Doing?* Urbana, IL: ERIC Clearinghouse on Elementary and Early Childhood Education, University of Illinois.

Lather, P. (1991) *Getting Smart: Feminist Research and Pedagogy with/in the Postmodern*. London: Routledge.

Mayall, B. (1996) *Children, Health and Social Order*. Buckingham: Open University Press.

Meadows, S. (1993) *The Child as Thinker*. London: Routledge.

Murphy, P. (1996) 'Defining pedagogy', in P. Murphy and C. Gipps, (eds) *Equity in the Classroom: Towards Effective Pedagogy for Girls and Boys*. London: Falmer Press and UNESCO.

O'Connor, T.G., Bredenkamp, D. and Rutter, M. (1999) 'Attachment disturbances and disorders in children exposed to early severe deprivation', *Infant Mental Health Journal*, 20 (10): 10–29.

Pascal, C. and Bertram, T. (1997) 'A conceptual framework for evaluating effectiveness in early childhood settings', in *Researching Early Childhood 3: Settings in Interaction*. Goteborg: Goteborg University, Early Childhood and Research Centre.

Schweinhart, L.J., Barnes, H.V. and Weikart, D.P. (1993) *Significant Benefits: The High/Scope Perry Preschool Study through Age 27*. Ypsilanti, MI: High/Scope Educational Research Foundation.

Shulman, L.S. (1986) 'Those who understand: knowledge growth in teaching', *Educational Researcher*, February: 4–14.

Siraj-Blatchford, I., Sylva, K., Muttock, S., Gilden, R. and Bell, D. (2002) *Researching Effective Pedagogy in the Early Years*. DfES Research Brief 356. London: DfES.

Sylva, K., Sammons, P., Melhuish, E., Siraj-Blatchford, I. and Taggart, B. (1999) *Technical Paper 1. An Introduction to the EPPE Project: A Longitudinal Study Funded by the DfEE, 1997–2003*. London: University of London, Institute of Education.

Tizard, B. and Hughes, M. (1984) *Young Children Learning.* London: Fontana.

Vygotsky, L. (1978) *Mind in Society: The Development of Higher Psychological Processes* (M. Cole et al. eds). Cambridge, MA: Harvard University Press.

Wells, G. (1985) *Language Development in the Preschool Years.* Cambridge: Cambridge University Press.

Wiesel, T.N. and Hubel, D.H. (1965) 'Extent of recovery from the effects of visual deprivation in kittens', *Journal of Neurophysiology*, 28: 1060–72.

Wood, D. (1986) 'Aspects of teaching and learning', in M. Richards and P. Light (eds) *Children of Social Worlds.* Cambridge: Polity Press.

Wylie, C. (1998) *Six Years Old and Competent: The Second Stage of the Competent Children Project – A Summary of the Main Findings.* Wellington: New Zealand Council for Educational Research.

2

Personal, social and emotional development: the child makes meaning in a social world

Liz Brooker and Lynne Broadbent

It is now very clear that unless a child achieves at least a minimal level of social competence by about the age of six, he or she is at risk for the rest of his or her life. The risks are not only in subsequent social functioning – many aspects of mental health, the ability to form stable relationships, to maintain employment, and to function well in marital and parental roles; the current evidence indicates that insufficient social competence leads to premature dropping out of school.

(Lilian Katz, in Dowling 2000: vii)

Introduction: what do we mean by PSE?

This chapter, like all the others in this book, is about the child as a *learner*. But perhaps even more than other chapters it is conscious of the child as a learner from *birth*, in every moment of his or her experiences – learning in infancy whilst being bathed and dressed, soothed and rocked; learning as a toddler from walking to the shops, watching children in the park, waving goodbye to friends. Personal, social and emotional development (PSE) is a lifelong process. In focusing here on children's learning in this area from 3 to 7, and in educational settings, we are always aware that this is a small, though significant, part of a complex process which takes place in many settings.

In stressing learning, too, we are emphasizing that personal, social and emotional development in children occurs *through* learning and is not something that 'just happens' in the early years. Although we know that babies are endowed with some personality traits and tendencies from birth, we know too that a very large part of the person they become results from learning through social interaction in an ever-widening set of contexts. A small child's first move out of the family and community into an institutional setting such as a school or pre-school brings with it huge new opportunities for learning.

Personal, social and emotional development is the first area of learning in the Foundation Stage curriculum (DfEE/QCA, 2000) and we can understand its position in two ways: first, that PSE learning is the most essential aspect of the curriculum for 3–5-year-olds; and second, that this aspect is the necessary context for all other curriculum learning to take place. Most early childhood practitioners and researchers would agree with both these views. When children move into Key stage 1, the curriculum requirements (DfEE/QCA, 1999) change rather abruptly. Personal, social and emotional matters become more implicit, located in the 'aims' and values of the curriculum and in the non-statutory guidance. Practitioners working with this age group know, however, that children do not suddenly complete their personal, social and emotional development at the age of 5, and that support in this area is still needed in Year 1.

In this chapter we show how the important themes from a child's earliest home experiences and his or her pre-school learning can be carried through into the National Curriculum years. At the same time, we explore the links between these areas and the moral and spiritual development of children, showing how closely the ideas from each perspective interweave and overlap in children's daily lives at home and school. Through examples from our own experience we try to show that opportunities for promoting children's personal, social and emotional development can occur spontaneously, as well as through planned activities, and that the role of the skilled practitioner is to be alert to the multiple meanings of children's everyday experiences in and out of the classroom.

By the age of 3 a child has taken many giant strides: towards constructing a personal identity, or sense of self; towards learning about relationships with others; and towards discovering the intrinsic pleasure of learning itself. Most 3-year-olds can tell you who they are and who they belong to, their preferences (what they like and dislike) and their accomplishments (what they are good at and not so good at). Most of them, once they have settled into a new setting, are 'ready, willing and able' to go on learning. Planning for the PSE curriculum should ensure that *all* children not only reach this point of readiness but also maintain it, with sufficient reserves and resilience to see them through the later school years when learning cannot be guaranteed to be fun or self-initiated.

How this chapter is organized

We have divided this chapter into parts, corresponding to three major strands of learning in the area from 3 to 7: learning about myself, learning about relationships and learning dispositions. As every practitioner will know, the three strands are interwoven and indivisible in reality, but we have tried to discuss each separately, with some examples (or 'learning stories') from children across the age range. Three aspects of the learning process are also exemplified throughout:

- Learning through the child's own exploration of the environment.
- Learning through interaction with peers and siblings.
- Learning with adult support and guidance.

We begin by looking at the documents which guide this area of learning.

Starting points in planning for PSE

The Foundation Stage curriculum

The current *Curriculum Guidance* for 3–5-year-olds (DfEE/QCA, 2000) describes six strands of development and learning in PSE, which lead towards 'goals' related to:

- dispositions and attitudes;
- self-confidence and self-esteem;
- making relationships;
- behaviour and self-control;
- self-care; and
- sense of community.

All these too are obviously inter-related – the child who can 'select and use activities and resources independently' (a goal for self-care) is probably also 'confident to try new activities' (a goal for dispositions and attitudes); the stepping-stones towards self-confidence and self-esteem include the ability to 'show care and concern for self' – but we can recognize some as having a very direct bearing on particular aspects of development. These strands will be woven through the sections that follow and taken on into the Key Stage 1 curriculum.

The Key Stage 1 curriculum

The revised National Curriculum (DfEE/QCA, 1999) is framed by statements of value and purpose and non-statutory guidance, which indicate a powerful underlying concern for the development of the whole child – personal and social, moral and spiritual. Its statement of aims includes:

The school curriculum should contribute to the development of pupils' sense of identity . . .

The school curriculum should promote pupils' self-esteem and emotional well-being and help them to form and maintain worthwhile and satisfying relationships, based on respect for themselves and for others . . .

The non-statutory guidance for Key Stage 1 includes goals related to developing:

- confidence and responsibility and making the most of their abilities; and
- good relationships and respecting the differences between people.

Although teachers are not required to plan specifically for these goals, it is clear that they are intended to underpin the ethos and organization of the school and classroom and the ways that teaching and learning take place in the setting.

Spiritual and moral development

In many respects, features of personal, social and emotional development reflect those features often referred to as spiritual development. The idea that learning environments can contribute to children's spiritual development is certainly not new, and recent documents have tried to foster teachers' understanding of the 'spiritual'. *Spiritual and Moral Development – A Discussion Paper* (NCC, 1993) argued that spiritual development applied to 'something fundamental in the human condition', that it was to do with 'the universal search for individual identity' and the 'search for meaning and purpose in life and for values by which to live' (p. 6). It described the term 'spiritual' as having many inter-related aspects, including:

- the development of personal beliefs;
- a sense of awe, wonder and mystery;
- the experience of feelings of transcendence;
- the search for meaning and purpose and for self-knowledge;
- thoughts, feelings and emotions;
- relationships and a sense of community; and
- creativity and imagination.

The links between these aspects and the first of the Early Learning Goals are self-evident, whilst the claims that 'spiritual development is fundamental to other areas of learning' and that 'without the exercise of imagination, insight and intuition, young people would lack the motivation to learn' are implicit in both the Foundation Stage and the Key Stage 1 planning documents.

We turn now to how different aspects of children's learning develop across the years from 3 to 7. We begin with 'the self'.

Learning about myself

Where are we at 3?

> Developing a sense of self is often seen in Western cultures as the long process
> of becoming a self-aware individual – becoming aware, for example, of what
> you look like, your gender, what makes you happy and sad, what roles you play
> . . . All the things which delineate you as an individual. (Miell, 1995: 190)

How does this process come about? Research shows us that it begins very early, and proceeds very rapidly, in an infant's life. Babies soon learn about themselves from seeing themselves mirrored in the attentions of others, especially their 'significant others' such as early caregivers. Early interactions with caregivers are bi-directional – babies socialize adults as much as adults socialize babies. Their spontaneous sounds and movements are mimicked by loving adults and become a part of the infant's unique and expanding repertoire. Their accidental effects on their environment (knocking a mobile with a flailing arm, dislodging a soft toy with an energetic leg movement) teach them that they have agency of their own and encourage them to repeat each movement over and over to confirm that they themselves are the cause. From 15 months babies begin to demonstrate awareness of their own appearance and, by 24 months, they can identify themselves by name and by gender – most babies' early experience of adult talk, after all, consists of being told they are a 'good boy' or a 'clever girl'.

At the same time another important aspect of the child's identity is emerging, of great concern to early educators: the child's self-esteem. Self-esteem has been described as the *value* a child assigns him or herself: attempts to 'measure' or describe it have focused on the disparity between what a child would *like* to be like and that child's view of how he or she actually is. But in early childhood it principally reflects the value the child perceives he or she has in the eyes of others, particularly those 'significant others' whose opinions count the most for the child. And although children in the later pre-school years can separate and evaluate different aspects of themselves (being good at football, drawing or making up stories), young children have a simpler, 'global' self-concept. For this reason, 'Self-esteem is only likely to be fostered in situations where all aspects of all children are esteemed' (Dowling, 2000: 9) and is very vulnerable to the views of important people in children's lives.

Learning about myself from 3 to 5

For all children, even the most confident, entering a pre-school setting is more than a step into a new world, full of promise; it is a step away from the familiar world of home and carries with it innumerable anxieties which may revive memories of the child's earliest experiences. Literally from birth, children have undergone the pain of separation and loss. Most will have come to terms with temporary absences and feelings of grief and learnt that their important people do, usually, come back to them. Nevertheless, the dawning understanding that this new stage in their lives means something different – means saying goodbye, regularly and for long periods, to their familiar caregivers and acquiring new caregivers to take their place – is something that many children understandably resist. The 'self' which for many children has developed gradually, separating itself in tiny steps from the others who surround and enfold it, now has to take on an independent identity, mirrored in the eyes and actions of a whole new company of 'significant others'.

Transitions

Dealing with separation may dominate the child's early pre-school sessions, but most parents and practitioners have strategies for supporting children at this time. Close links between home and 'school' adults are usually established through home visits to the child and parental presence in the setting; children's own important objects – teddies, books or special blankets – are usually accommodated until the child no longer needs them; daily feedback from key workers to parents, as well as news from the home, is especially important during a child's settling-in period, however long that may be.

Dowling, however, reminds us that we are wrong to attempt to 'jolly' children out of their unhappiness at times of transition. 'Children have the right both to witness and to experience difficult feelings', and learning about sadness is a stage in their emotional development. Rather than distracting children to try to make them forget their feelings, she suggests 'A simple acknowledgment of sympathy will at least show the child that she is being taken seriously' (2000: 62).

Every change of setting is momentous for young children and, even within the Foundation Stage, the strange routines involved in the move to a new classroom can cause anxiety, as Barry's story shows (see Learning Story 2.1).

Learning Story 2.1 Barry: the first week at school

Barry started school aged 4 years 5 months, in the same classroom that his sister Linzi had just left to move into her Year 1 room. For the first few days he was very quiet but not obviously unhappy: he was familiar with the room and the teacher from bringing Linzi every day. His mother felt he was 'just taking it all in' but was quite happy to come to school.

All this changed at the beginning of the second week: Barry's mother came in, very embarrassed, to report that she could not get Barry to come in to school and had left him in the playground, howling and struggling, with her friend. After lunch that day she brought him in briefly, clinging tightly to her hand. He hid behind her and refused to stay in the classroom. This pattern was repeated the following day but on the third day when she brought the unwilling Barry through the door, it was with the information that 'He says he's frightened of doing *Gladiators*'. Since this did nothing to resolve the mystery, at group time the teacher decided to invite the views of the other new children: 'Barry's mummy says he is frightened to come to school because he doesn't want to do *Gladiators*. But we don't do *Gladiators* [an adult TV contest, watched by children] in our class.' The children quickly explained: the previous Friday, the teacher, in the course of informing them about the things they had to look forward to in their second week of school, had mentioned 'Apparatus' [the large indoor climbing equipment used in school PE]. None of them had known for sure what was meant by this term and several were aware of Barry's alarm. A phone call to Barry's mother enabled the difficulty to be resolved the following day.

The skills of children (like Barry's classmates) in understanding, empathizing and supporting each other are one of the practitioner's biggest assets.

Self-concept

Separation brings with it a very positive step in any child's learning: acquiring a sense of themselves as 'being a person' in more than one setting. As life at school, playgroup or the childminder's becomes an integral part of the child's experience, it contributes to the expansion of identity: the child can now see herself as someone who drinks from the family's mugs at home, but from a plastic beaker at nursery or a Disneyland mug at the minder's; who throws her cardigan over a chair at home but hangs it on her peg at pre-school; who tips her toys into a toybox at home but tidies things into separate crates in daycare; who *belongs* in more than one place. This awareness of one's different roles enables the child to reflect more consciously on her own identity: on occasion she may have to introduce herself to new adults in the setting – 'I'm Katie but I'm in Patti's group' – and explain about her life outside the setting – 'I get picked up by Kelly's mum because my mum has to get my big brother first'. Through these experiences the child's own self-concept and self-awareness expand dramatically.

Belonging

It follows from this that the sense of belonging – in different settings, with different people and possibly among different sets of cultural values – is one of the most important aspects of identity development. In the early years curriculum in New Zealand (*Te Whariki*), 'belonging' is one of five key strands in children's experience. The Foundation Stage guidance, which has drawn on these earlier models, indicates that, as they grow in their early childhood setting, children should:

> Have a sense of belonging . . .

> Have a sense of self as a member of different communities . . .

Many features of the traditional nursery environment contribute to this sense – the name on the coat peg, the picture on the mug, the photo above the snack table, the key worker group and the 'home base'. It is reinforced when practitioners draw children's attention to the different aspects of their lives, talking with them about their homes and families, their journey to and from the setting and their activities in the community. As the guidance says, children should 'talk freely' about these other parts of their lives, and this is particularly vital when practitioners do not share the background of children in their setting. Knowing that you 'belong' to your own group in pre-school *and* to your own family and community helps the child to become aware of the many sides to his or her identity.

Self-esteem

Early childhood settings rightly emphasize the importance of self-esteem. As we have seen, 'Children's self-esteem is a key factor not only for their well-being but also for learning outcomes' (Roberts, 1998: 161), and it is very vulnerable in this period.

One unfortunate outcome of practitioners' traditional advocacy of self-esteem, however, has been an equally traditional tendency to over-praise. Starting from children's earliest days in a setting, they have sought to encourage and reassure them by constant approval and admiration – *Well done! Good girl! Lovely! You're a star!* Such enthusiasm is well-meant and may make all the difference while a child is feeling especially vulnerable. But when it becomes a habit it ceases to hold meaning or value for the child. It may even do harm, in two ways: first, because it makes the child dependent on adult approval, showing him or her that the adult's judgement of his or her efforts are necessary to give them value – so that the adult actually controls the assessment process and, in consequence, the learning process. Secondly, because it gives the child no information on which to base his or her *own* independent assessments of his or her efforts and discourages him or her from making the kinds of assessments which can inform the child's learning. As Roberts argues: 'the use of strategies such as habitual empty praise, gold stars, smiley stickers and meaningless statements, are more likely to feed children's self-preoccupation and narcissism than to help them form a genuine sense of their own worth' (2002: 106). In the end, real self-esteem comes from a realistic assessment of one's efforts and outcomes. In the end, too, when children are praised for efforts of which they are not particularly proud, they may come to question the trustworthiness of the adults (Gura, 1996).

The honest alternative to praising is to give the child both *attention* and *information*. Although it takes more time, a long look at a painting, a question ('Did you do the blue bit first? Is this anybody I know?') and a comment ('This red bit's all dribbly, we must have made the paint too runny') will reward a child far more than an enthusiastic cry of *Lovely!*

Responsibility

Closely linked with small children's sense of their worth – and contributing to this – is their acquisition of a sense of responsibility. Too often, when children are much older, both parents and teachers lament their *lack* of such a sense. Do they ever think back to when those children were small and anxious to be involved in everything their caregivers and older siblings did?

Early years settings often attempt to inculcate this sense with their routines, involving children in 'helping' with taking the toys outside or washing the paint tables, handing out the snack or fetching the Sellotape. All too often, however, these tasks are quite limited and undemanding: the truth is that they are conceived by adults as childish routines, as training in being sociable rather than as real learning. When children volunteer to help with a real task, such as lifting equipment, switching on a plug at a socket or fetching a sharp knife, they are frequently shooed away and told that only grown-ups do that. Yet these same children – some of them – will be used to taking responsibility at home: caring for a younger sibling or handling tools alongside responsible adults. Researchers in cross-cultural settings have shown just how widespread this 'apprenticeship' to adult life is, outside the English-speaking world. Even within the UK, many of our children, including those from Traveller families and from the Asian community, experience such 'guided participation' in adult life and in social as well as cognitive learning in their homes and communities.

Roberts points out that 'learning to be responsible happens as a result of being given responsibility . . . Children can not become responsible beings on their own, they need adults to hand over to them real responsibilities through which they can learn' (1998: 157). In settings as in homes, children's physical safety must never be compromised. But there are many ways in which they can learn about responsibility and come to view themselves as competent, without putting themselves at risk. Talking about responsibility is one valuable means to achieving this particular 'goal', as Darren's story shows (Learning Story 2.2).

Learning Story 2.2 Darren: thinking about responsibility

Darren had a new baby brother. He had announced the news as soon as he had entered the reception class that morning. Sitting on the carpet the teacher encouraged other children to talk about their siblings. She introduced language such as 'a new brother or sister becoming part of your family'. The conversation continued with discussion about what babies did, the clothes they wore and the care they needed and, at this point, the teacher asked Darren what he could do for his new brother. Through question and answer it was established that Darren would be able to tell mum when the baby was crying; he would be able to distract the baby's tears at times by talking to him, touching his hand or playing with his soft toys; he would be able to assist at nappy-changing time and could help mum gain greater access to the supermarket shelves whilst pushing the baby by fetching shopping items for her. Some of the children then moved to the home corner and practised bath and nappy-changing time and experienced pushing a baby around in a buggy. By the end of the morning, and through the teacher's skilful questioning and improvised plans, Darren and the other children had developed an understanding of what it meant to belong to the social group of the family and a sense of joint responsibility for different members of that group and, most importantly, a whole repertoire of skills which they could put to immediate use in the care of a brother and thus be able to experience being an accepted and responsible member of a social group.

Learning about myself from 5 to 7

Getting started in Year 1 is not seen as one of life's major landmarks; by now many children have already made two big transitions – from home to pre-school and from pre-school to the 'real school' in which their reception class is housed. Ideally, their reception year should have acclimatized them, from within the secure framework of the Foundation Stage curriculum to the world of statutory schooling. Ideally too they should be ready for the next step: a more formal learning environment in which large chunks of the day's activities are predetermined – not by the teacher but by the statutory requirement to introduce the National Literacy and Numeracy Strategies by the end of reception.

The Early Learning Goals suggest what children may have achieved by now in constructing a self-concept and identity. The framework for PSE at Key Stage 1 is intended to build on these goals so that pupils 'learn to recognise their own worth, work well with others and become increasingly responsible for their own learning'. If we look again at the aspects of a sense of self which dominated the pre-school years, we can identify some of the opportunities (and difficulties) of securing their continued development in Year 1.

Transitions

Separation from familiar caregivers and settings is given little consideration at this stage but may well prove significant for children. Earlier transitions in their lives were managed with supportive strategies and thoughtful planning: continuity between homes and schools, parents and professionals, is highlighted throughout the Foundation Stage; routines such as group times are carefully designed to make room for children's emotional needs; informal instructional sessions allow for continuous social talk between children and adults; and the play-based curriculum enables children, ideally, to learn in their own way and at their own pace, as well as by following their own interests. Few of these conditions are found in Key Stage 1. Too often, the drive to complete statutory requirements by lunchtime forces teachers to ignore parents who are waiting to chat, and to rush through the morning group time without offering children opportunities to express their concerns and needs. A child who is distressed or a parent with a problem to communicate may be seen as obstacles in the path of teachers with a crowded timetable to manage.

Although most children adapt quite quickly, practitioners need to be alert to their feelings and remember that home influences on the child's learning are still extremely important, and that links between families and schools are vital. Parents' interest and involvement in their children's school learning may *appear* to dwindle once the children leave the Foundation Stage but, research tells us, this is not the case (Hughes, 1996). The increasing separateness of the settings in which the children pass their lives, as Bronfenbrenner (1979) has shown, is not beneficial for their social, emotional or cognitive learning.

Self-concept

Self-concept, which for many children may have been comfortably achieved in their early settings, again becomes vulnerable and subject to rapid transformations as the child enters a more formal regime. The process of 'becoming a pupil', which begins in the Foundation Stage, now assumes major significance (Boyle and Woods, 1998; Brooker, 2002). Pupils are socialized into the discourse of the school and adapt their behaviour to its ethos and expectations. Some pupils are less successful than others in making this adjustment: as Schaffer reminds us, self-concept 'is affected by experience, especially of success and failure and the feelings of competence or incompetence derived therefrom' (1996: 159). The child who discovers that he or she is viewed as less competent by a new teacher or new classmates risks becoming less competent in his or her own self-evaluation.

Two aspects of children's identity are particularly vulnerable in this process. Recent studies (Connolly, 1998) have demonstrated the strongly sexualized and racialized discourse used by children aged 5–7 in construct-ing their own and other children's identities in the classroom and playground. Although name-calling and other stereotyping exists among the under-5s (Siraj-Blatchford, 1994), early years educators have more time and space to observe and deal with it. In Key stage 1, and particularly during unsupervised playground games, very damaging attacks on chil-dren's identity and sense of self may occur. Many practitioners will recognize the importance of using a brief group time at the start of every session to discuss and defuse fears, anxieties and hostilities that have arisen in the playground. Despite the pressures of the timetable, we should try to preserve this important routine.

Belonging

On the positive side are the new opportunities for belonging afforded by the new role of pupil. Classroom rituals and routines, so long as they are fair and inclusive, can bind children together into a supportive subculture: most prac-titioners spend important sessions with their new class deciding on the 'golden rules' for their group – rules which should acknowledge the impor-tance of the learning process as well as the rights of the individual child and the fostering of social relationships. Another perspective on the self is now available to the child as he or she reflects on him or herself, not only as a member of his or her continuing family and new class but as someone with a history in different settings – someone who *used* to attend a particular pre-school or reception class and is now a member of a new social group. Both the continuity of self and the changing nature of self become part of the child's reality as he or she formulates this new view of him or herself as a person with many guises.

Self-esteem

Parents are well aware of the effects on children's self-esteem of new, more formal methods of instruction and, possibly, more explicit and critical forms of assessment – they too may feel somewhat helpless and excluded by the new regime (Hughes et al., 1994). Both the ethos of the school and the ethos of the individual classroom are crucial in providing a framework in which children and parents can feel secure and supported as they nervously embark on a new stage in their educational career.

Responsibility

We conclude this section with another example of the way that responsibil-ity in the classroom can contribute to a child's sense of self – see Learning Story 2.3.

Learning Story 2.3 Omar: taking responsibility in Year 1

Omar had learning difficulties: a physical speech impediment combined with language delay in his first language and limited proficiency in English made communication in class a great struggle for him. Although his teacher had established ground rules for supporting Omar with the class, she was not able to ensure that he was always included in children's self-directed activities.

The class operated a 'helper' system whereby a new child each day – the next child in an alphabetical list of first names – took responsibility for collecting the register, bringing children to the carpet for group times, instigating clearing up, leading the children to lunch and so on. The first time the list reached 'O', Omar was absent, somewhat to his teacher's relief but, as his turn approached again, Omar was visibly excited, waving his arms at the list and stammering desperately in his efforts to communicate his awareness of his impending role. When the day arrived, Omar pulled his mother into the classroom, marched over to the name chart and moved the marker to his name, then set about arranging the small chairs and cushions for group time, blurted his intention of fetching the register and sat quietly waiting to hand it to his teacher with the appropriate pens. The children responded patiently and respectfully all day to his instructions and management: Omar signalled tidy-up time by walking around the room banging a drum, and the children quickly reminded each other to pack away; Omar tried to tell them to wash their hands before lunch and they went more quickly than usual; Omar chose a picture book for story-time and several children said 'Oh, thanks, Omar, I like that one'. Not only was this, in his teacher's view, the happiest day in school ever for Omar, but its effects persisted in improved confidence for Omar and improved relationships with his classmates.

Learning about relationships

Early relationships

All personal and social learning, as we have seen, begins in interactions so that 'learning about myself', the child's first concern, is achieved *through* relationships. Between the ages of 3 and 7, however, relationships with others, both adults and children, become increasingly important in their own right as the child's focus of attention moves outwards. Children's play behaviour provides clear evidence of this shift. Studies of children's self-directed play (Sylva et al., 1980) confirm what most practitioners know from their own experience: from around the age of 3, children who have previously been observed in 'solitary' or 'parallel' play gradually spend more time playing sociably with others, and by 5 peer friendships assume great importance in the lives of some children. At the same time, adults continue to play a vital role in supporting and extending children's learning. Early years settings are built around this seemingly 'natural' development in children's lives, but relationships with peers and teachers are central to the learning environment throughout childhood. As Dowling (2000: 24) points out: 'We all need other people to help us learn and young children need adults and other children. Thus, a child's ability to form good relationships not only enhances her personal development but helps her progress intellectually.'

Learning about relationships from 3 to 5

The curriculum guidance for the Foundation Stage, which includes as a goal 'Form good relationships with adults and peers', frames these specific objectives within some overarching principles, including a commitment to play as 'a key way in which young children learn with enjoyment and challenge'. Learning about relationships through play begins with the earliest peek-a-boo games played by infants and their caregivers and continues throughout their early years. We identify here some important aspects of this learning.

Social competence

> A three-year-old is a socially aware person who is capable of making and keeping friends and of negotiating interesting cooperations and tests of understandings with a wide range of acquaintances. (Trevarthen, 1998: 97)

In order to make and sustain relationships, we need to acquire a range of related social 'skills'. These include learning about turn-taking, sharing, negotiating, co-operating and empathizing. All these skills may be learnt from the modelling behaviour of adults towards children, but all spring too from an important underlying ability which is achieved during the early years – the ability to take the perspective of others, to understand and appreciate their point of view. If we identify and foster this ability in children, we will recognize them as agents in their own social development and learning; as individuals who will develop appropriate social strategies because they are able to construct an authentic reason for them, based in part on their recognition of the needs of others.

Despite evidence to the contrary, there is still a 'folk belief' that children are self-centred and egocentric throughout the pre-school years and into the start of formal schooling. Early childhood practitioners can do a great deal to counter this belief. We know, for instance, that children who hear feelings discussed are able to empathize and take on the perspectives of others from an early age – possibly as young as 2 – and that in most families girls are far more likely to be offered this opportunity than boys.

Part of the challenge for practitioners concerned to reduce gender stereo-typing is to create an environment in which everyone's feelings count and the discussion of feelings is for everyone to share. Stories are an excellent starting point for such discussions

Realistically, we can expect young children to be motivated (as we all are) by a mixture of self-interest and altruism. Adults supporting children in their play disputes intuitively offer both perspectives to children, pointing out that sharing a toy enables both children to enjoy it, that taking turns allows more children to participate, that relinquishing a desired object to a play-mate leaves the child free to take up another offered activity. When these cause-and-effect relationships are made explicit to children, they can include them in their own repertoire of strategies for resolving conflicts *and* in their own social-justice vocabulary of what is 'fair' and 'not fair'.

Social play

Almost every aspect of play in a social group involves negotiation and con-versation: over the ownership of bikes and blocks or the right to be the princess or the daddy in the home corner. Good relationships with peers and adults can both ease the pain of the small sacrifices made and demonstrate the rewards: the emotional satisfaction of developing friendships and the pleasure of prolonged and successful play bouts in which the negotiated 'rules' enable exciting improvisations, as well as familiar repetitions to occur.

Play theorists have focused on socio-dramatic, or 'pretend', play as the pre-eminent vehicle for such learning. The theories of Piaget, who saw *symbolic play* as the characteristic activity for 3–6-year-olds, and Vygotsky, who taught us to look at the value of peer interactions for learning language and culture, are cited in support of this view, and research has shown strong associations between children's engagement in pretend play and their learning in several dimensions (Smilansky, 1990). There can be no doubt that perspective-taking is a prerequisite for successful pretend play: most children will concede that if someone else is the mummy, she must be allowed to get on with the cook-ing, however much the child with the role of baby or dog would like a turn with the pots and pans.

Faulkner (1995) argues that all forms of play and games can contribute to children's development of social competence. Vygotsky, she points out, 'saw play between children as creating a zone in which their performance is in advance of their actual developmental level'. This zone (the ZPD) can be seen as 'a sort of inter-psychological, social space in which children can explore new knowledge and ideas through conversation and other forms of interac-tion' (Faulkner, 1995: 241). Not only pretend play but social play of all kinds – with sand and water, with blocks and bricks, with small-world toys and malleable materials – lends itself to such explorations.

Many of these activities can be shared and supported by adults as well as peers. And although socio-dramatic play invites children to explore feelings, early years settings are full of such opportunities. Experienced practitioners know what happens when they quietly sit alongside children who are playing with dough or Plasticine or making patterns with pegs and cubes. These are often the occasions when children, in a relaxed and unhurried manner, confide their stories about happy and unhappy events and their worries about changes in their lives. They may also be occasions when adults should suppress the impulses of their professional training (to verbalize, elaborate and extend children's thoughts and words) and simply listen!

Friendship

Children's friendships develop, in the Foundation Stage years, from associations based on convenience and contingency (mixing with the children of neighbours; playing with the other children in the child's key worker group or home room) to relationships based on shared identities and individual preferences. By the time they are 4 it is commonly observed that many boys play almost entirely with boys, and that minority ethnic children in a setting are usually found together. Since children are working hard at their gender and ethnic identities during these years, the choice of same-sex same-race playmates provides both a scaffold and a safety net in avoiding risky mistakes about appropriate attitudes and behaviour.

When children meet new challenges, such as transition to a new class or a new school, these friendships support and sustain them, providing 'the emotional and cognitive resources necessary for successful adaptation to their social world' (Faulkner and Miell, 1993: 25). The Foundation Stage curriculum includes countless contexts for making friends – including, to some people's surprise, learning at the computer (see Learning Story 2.4).

Learning Story 2.4
Georgia: playing together at the computer

The nursery class at Barrack Road Primary is a microcosm of the local neighbourhood: its intake includes children whose parents are from Bangladesh and Pakistan, Somalia, Sierra Leone, Turkey and Kosovo. Despite the staff's efforts to encourage children from different linguistic backgrounds to mix, most interact almost exclusively with others from their own group.

Georgia (age 4, white UK), who is quite a skilful computer user, joins a small group of less experienced children who are attempting to find their way though an open-ended software program called *Henry's Party*. These four – Kol, a boy from Kosovo; Hafsa, a girl of Bangladeshi background; Alican, a boy from Turkey; and

Ali, a boy from Somalia – crowd round her enthusiastically as she starts to play. She clicks on a 'birthday party' where farmyard animals are singing 'Happy Birthday' and all five children sway and sing along with the music. But when she starts to select other options, by clicking on different parts of the picture, Georgia rapidly becomes annoyed: all three boys are standing with their hands or fingers on the screen to request an item, and she is unable to see to make her own choice. She complains loudly and brushes their hands aside whilst they protest verbally in the limited English they can command ('it my turn', 'no, him one').

When Georgia selects a sorting game she demonstrates both her physical skill and control (dragging and dropping items on screen) and her lack of cognitive sophistication (she sorts almost every item incorrectly). The other children seem to believe that she is making deliberate mistakes: they all happily join in saying 'uh-oh' with the computer, as each incorrect choice is made. Ali roars with laughter and Kol turns to the nearby researcher to make sure she has understood the joke. All five children are engrossed in their shared experience of the activity, although they are otherwise unable to communicate with each other at all.

Not all children find it easy to make friends, and practitioners may need to do some 'social engineering' to protect children who – for individual reasons or because of ethnic or social differences – are not accepted within the group culture of the setting. Fortunately most practitioners are very alert to such exclusions and have strategies for protecting the self-esteem of 'outsiders'.

Learning values: the moral and spiritual curriculum

The Foundation Stage guidance suggests that values are learnt by children through their daily activities and relationships in the setting. Children are expected to 'work as part of a group or class' and to understand the need for 'agreed values and codes of behaviour for groups of people'. They should also 'understand what is right, what is wrong, and why'.

Relationships with adults and peers are fundamental to children's moral development and their acquisition of values. The values in any setting are modelled for children by the adults, as well as demonstrated to them: 'Concepts of individual worth, honesty, right and wrong, justice, entitlement and collective endeavour are within the scope of young children's understanding, provided they experience these things in a concrete way' (Roberts, 1998: 160). Concrete learning of abstract concepts occurs when adults take time to discuss with children the fairness of decisions (about sharing toys and taking turns), the consequences of speech and actions (intentional and unintentional harm to others) and the kinds of behaviour which have positive outcomes for the 'common good' of the whole group, rather than benefiting one child.

Psychologists have distinguished *moral behaviour* (doing the right thing) from *moral understanding* (knowing why it is the right thing to do). Most practitioners would agree that the latter – rather than obedience or compliance – is the real goal for children's acquisition of values. Moral understanding, it is clear, involves perspective-taking, and some children will need to experience many concrete examples before they are persuaded that it is a good idea to sacrifice their own self-interest. Supportive adults in the setting help them to reach such decisions.

When they are 4 or 5, many children begin to take an interest in the 'big' questions of belief: the purpose of life, the existence of God and the meaning of death. Adults working with children often feel ill-equipped to discuss such issues, but both picture books and spontaneous events in children's lives can provide a starting point. Often there is no need for the adult to present her own point of view, and she certainly isn't required to 'teach' children about these issues: listening to children, accepting their feelings and supporting their efforts to share them is often the most important contribution a practitioner can make. The children in Learning Story 2.5 are responding, without prompting, to a story they have just heard.

Learning Story 2.5
Talking about feelings: the Grasshopper and the Butterfly

The reception class had shared a story about a Grasshopper and a Butterfly. In circle time, the children began to talk:

Amy   I'm playing sad music for the grasshopper (strumming the sole of her shoe) 'cos he's died.

Ashley   I think God will make the Grasshopper alive again. Once there was a snail outside getting near the water, by the pond. I moved it in case it fell in and it can't swim.

Rachel   If you see a little bird and it can't fly, put a plaster on it and put some flowers if it's died. And water. That's to say we loved the thing that died, and the water's for the bird and the flowers . . .

Navdeep When my grandma died I put lots of flowers on my grandma, on the body, I've got a picture of her in my house and, in my garden in India, I did hold a bird. (Bennett, 1997: 10–11)

Circle time provided these children with a space and a time to reflect on the story, to make links with their own experiences and to share these within the social context of the group. In terms of the 'spiritual' curriculum, they were enabled to explore their experiences of awe and wonder at the natural world, their feelings of sadness and love and their attempts to make sense of patterns of life and death, whilst the process of sharing, listening and being listened to fostered their feelings of self-confidence and their sense of community relationship.

Learning about relationships from 5 to 7

'Becoming a pupil' in Key stage 1, as we suggested earlier, may mean adopting a quite different persona and entering into quite new relationships in which there may be little scope for considering personal feelings and emotions. The non-statutory guidance, however, recommends that pupils should be *taught* how to develop good relationships which are respectful of the differences between people. This teaching, which may not necessarily be explicit, builds on the Foundation Stage goals. The outcomes are that children should:

- recognize how their behaviour affects other people;
- listen to other people, and play and work co-operatively;
- identify and respect differences;
- care for friends and family; and
- understand teasing and bullying.

These aspects of learning not only extend children's personal, social and moral development but they also provide the foundations for ideas of citizenship.

Social competence

In the Key stage 1 classroom, the social competencies children have acquired through informal interactions and play experiences become essential prerequisites for interactions around 'work' of an increasingly formal kind. In a large group (in which whole-class tasks often replace group activities), sharing resources and taking turns, and respecting the space and needs of others are priorities for harmonious working. Some children will still have difficulty in adopting such other-orientated behaviour but the group culture should support them in their efforts. Most classrooms display lists of negotiated class rules: the discussion of these rules is part of the essential settling-in period in a new class, and skilful practitioners work with children to construct rules which are positive rather than prohibitive. Children generally find it easy to generate a long list of 'don'ts' – don't fight, don't poke, don't shout, don't throw rubbers – and the activity of transforming these into positive statements is an important piece of modelling for children of this age. Positive rules almost always involve *thinking about the effect on others* of one's own wayward, or simply thoughtless, behaviour: if children are encouraged to include this practice naturally and instinctively in their daily decision-making, they will learn not only to be an effective pupil but to be an effective member of society.

Playing games

Practitioners as well as parents observe with pleasure children's growing ability in these years to participate in 'games with rules', described by Piaget as the characteristic form of play as children approach middle childhood. The need for rules such as turn-taking and fairness is evident to children once they are old enough to organize their own game-playing, and many are fanatical about seeing fair play!

Children's enthusiasm for games, and genuine involvement in them, is a context for both social and cognitive learning. Games, such as board and card games, quizzes and puzzles, and computer games, are an appropriate vehicle for much of the teaching and learning in the Key Stage 1 curriculum. Although many other play opportunities – role play and dressing up, large blocks and sand and water – are disappearing from Year 1 and Year 2 classrooms, games and puzzles, as well as smaller construction toys, allow children to continue to construct their own learning through interactions in an environment where direct instruction can threaten to dominate. Even the teacher-controlled, highly prescriptive Literacy and Numeracy Hours provide opportunities for learning through small-group games, including computer programs. The view of play as a zone of proximal development, a social space in which peer interactions among a group with different levels of knowledge and skill provide support for less experienced participants, is as appropriate when the game is Snakes and Ladders or Scrabble as when it is Mummies and Daddies.

Playtimes

Whilst games are seen as the staple ingredient of life in playgrounds, research has shown that playtime is not always a time for innocent fun and amusement and that some children have experiences which are very damaging to their self-esteem in this child-ordered environment. One study (Sluckin, 1987) demonstrates that hierarchies constructed by children to include and exclude particular individuals and groups mirror those of the adult world and may be rooted in forms of gendered and racial prejudice and discrimination. Sluckin argues that children's social interactions in the playground, though conceivably a 'preparation for life', are a negative experience for many.

Few practitioners would argue for banning playtime or policing it more strictly, and most will recognize the valuable space it offers for privacy and friendships as children grow into middle childhood. But our awareness of playground cultures should tell us that the curriculum guidance on relationships (including the knowledge that 'there are different types of teasing and bullying, that bullying is wrong, and how to get help to deal with bullying') must be taken seriously and included in explicit teaching from the start of primary school.

Friendship

By the time they enter Key Stage 1, children have learnt that there are cultural rules both for initiating new friendships and repairing damaged ones. As children's experience of school learning and classroom organization becomes more formal, their friendship groups become part of the group dynamic of the setting, a force to be reckoned with by a teacher in her planning for social learning and in her everyday management of the class. Friendship groups support children in their continuing identity formation and in their negotiations with school adults: any particular group will identify itself against other groups (starting with girls' and boys' frequent rejection of each other's tastes and preferences) and in relation to perceived authority, such as the teacher in the classroom. Wise practitioners will build on their knowledge of children's friendship groups when planning for group work and active learning, and will be prepared to undertake 'social engineering' on behalf of isolated children.

Citizenship

As the children's social world widens, their understanding of 'relationships' can slowly grow to embrace ideas of 'citizenship' – sharing experiences and responsibilities with those in the wider community. The non-statutory guidelines indicate that pupils should 'learn that they belong to various groups and communities' and 'identify and respect the differences and similarities between people'. Learning Story 2.6 shows how closely these goals link to the moral and spiritual curriculum as well as to the RE syllabus.

Learning Story 2.6 Celebrating diversity in Year 1

The classroom assistant was getting married and had invited the Year 1 children to attend the wedding service! The class teacher decided that the RE programme for that term should focus on weddings, which would include learning about the ceremony, the symbols used to show that the couple were joined together and the promises made to each other. The children learnt about and constructed replicas of the church building, they focused on the symbolism of the wedding ring and discussed why promises are made and what those promises should be. As the school was in a multi-faith area, the class then visited the local *gurdwara* to learn about Sikh weddings and, on their return to school, role played a Sikh wedding with the couple walking around the holy book and symbolizing their union through the scarf, or *chunni*, wrapped around them.

This planned learning experience fostered the children's social development both through the visits to religious buildings in the local community and through the role-play experience; it developed their knowledge of different communities and practices and challenged their thinking about personal values and relationships in relation to the making of promises.

Learning values

Theories of moral development generally emphasize the active participation of the child in constructing beliefs about right and wrong, but our knowledge of bullying and discrimination reminds us that children's moral development cannot be left to occur unsupported. Adults working with children must take responsibility for ensuring that every child has the opportunity to reflect on values and is supported in reflecting on the outcomes of his or her actions. As in the Foundation Stage, adults play a crucial role, not only in modelling 'moral' behaviour but in modelling the process of thinking about cause and effect. This includes thinking through the consequences of actions for other people (both altruistic acts such as making a card for a classroom assistant who is unwell, and selfish ones such as using equipment that another class planned to use), and making time to unravel the rights and wrongs of playground disputes. Taking bullying, name-calling and racism seriously may be the most important lesson in values a practitioner can offer. Once again, the skill of perspective-taking is essential to this process, as Vincent's story shows (Learning Story 2.7). Over the year, Vincent's class learnt to discuss issues of prejudice knowledgeably and openly, and when the local mosque was despoiled many of the children spontaneously sympathized with, and supported, the Muslim children in the school.

Learning Story 2.7
Vincent: thinking about right and wrong

In Year 2, the curriculum required children to develop understanding and empathy for those remote from them in time and space – historical people and those in the 'distant places' of the geography curriculum. One class worked on these skills through the practice of 'talking to the child in the picture', which their teacher had introduced. A large photograph – of small children in a public playground in Delhi, for instance – would be discussed by the class, and individual children would then role play the children in the picture by answering questions put to them by their classmates: 'Is it hot where you are?' 'Um, yeah, it's really really hot, I need a drink!'

The same practice lent itself to discussions of *difference* (of age or appearance, gender or ethnicity) and to discussion of feelings. One such discussion revolved around a close-up photograph of a black child sobbing miserably. The children questioned 'the child in the photo' sympathetically: 'Did your mum say you can't play out?' 'Did your mate say he won't play?' and debated the appropriateness of such questions ('He wouldn't be *that* upset'). They gave lengthier consideration to a suggestion that the child's mother had gone to work without saying goodbye but were still unconvinced. The matter was apparently resolved for them by Vincent, a white child from a family rumoured to be both 'rough' and racist, who asked: 'Did they call you black bastard?' Some children gasped and many looked at their teacher for her reaction, but no one spoke; it seemed as if everyone thought Vincent had found the most likely answer.

Learning dispositions

Recent research on learning dispositions has confirmed something that experienced practitioners have known intuitively – that children's academic progress and their ultimate achievements depend in large part on their attitude to learning: their initial enthusiasm and openness and their longer-term persistence in problem-solving. Practitioners, like parents, have sighed over children who 'could do it if they wanted to', could 'get there if they tried a bit harder' or who 'have the ability, if only they didn't give up so easily'. Research has given us some insights into the reasons for children's different levels of motivation and persistence and, in doing so, gives some clues as to how we can foster these important dispositions in the early years.

Although babies are born with some innate *predispositions* – personality traits which are genetically acquired – these are not the most important influences on the *dispositions* they display in their pre-school and school settings. Dispositions, like the young child's other personal and social behaviours, are *learnt*, through early experience, and can be un-learnt through subsequent experiences. This may be one of the most important challenges for practitioners but it is one that pays off handsomely. The effort put into fostering positive dispositions is rewarded by children who are more purposeful and successful and less likely to become disaffected. As Anning and Edwards claim:

> Those of us who are involved in the education of young children . . . need to
> focus on helping children to become learners, to enjoy learning and to feel that
> they are people who are able to learn. This is no small challenge but it is a safe bet
> that investment in children's dispositions to learn will pay dividends. (1999: 59)

Developmental psychologists have demonstrated that children's own theories about learning produce specific and predictable patterns of behaviour when they are confronted with new learning tasks. These patterns were given the shorthand tags of 'helpless' and 'mastery' orientations towards learning and were seen in children who, respectively, gave up easily and relied on others to coach them through tasks, or took on new tasks with an enthusiasm and determination to succeed with them. The underlying theories children held (about intelligence and achievement) interacted with their experiences in educational settings so that their theories were, on the whole, confirmed by their real-life successes and failures (Dweck and Leggett, 1988).

Over the last decade, early years educators have translated this research evidence into recommendations for practice. Before turning to their suggestions, let us look at 4-year-old Kelly's dispositions in her second week at school (Learning Story 2.8). Kelly's teacher, clearly, needs to foster her fearless disposition and help Kelly to use it in a wide range of activities.

Learning Story 2.8 Kelly: creating challenges

Kelly, along with her classmates, was being assessed on a baseline measure of completing simple jigsaw puzzles. She was experienced with puzzles after spending a year in nursery and progressed rapidly through the array of increasingly difficult puzzles the staff had set out, seizing a new puzzle with one hand as she fitted the last piece to the previous one and pushed it away from her. Having exhausted them she quickly improvised her own challenge, turning a 12-piece puzzle upside down (so that the picture was hidden) and announcing 'Now I'm going to do it the hard way'. She completed the puzzle by trial and error, with considerable effort and concentration, and instructed the researcher, 'Now you mix some of them up for me while I shut my eyes, to make it harder this time'. Eventually she tried putting some puzzles together, by feel with her eyes still closed; after several failed attempts, when she remarked 'I've done it wrong, I'll have to have another go', she gave up and pranced away without further concern. At no time did she seem interested in the adult's view of her performance.

Theory into practice

The *Curriculum Guidance for the Foundation Stage* (DfEE/QCA, 2000) knows where it stands on learning dispositions for the very first set of 'goals' in the document is directed towards them: the early learning goals for dispositions and attitudes require that children should 'Continue to be interested, excited and motivated to learn' (p. 32). The stepping stones towards this goal specify that children should, during the Foundation Stage, 'Have a positive attitude to new experiences . . . Show confidence . . . Persist for extended periods of time . . . Take risks and explore . . .' All these attributes are associated with the 'mastery' dispositions which enable children to carry on learning when the going gets tough later in their school career. To this extent, the Foundation Stage really does lay the foundations for *all* subsequent learning.

Dispositions have been defined by Katz as 'relatively enduring habits of mind or characteristic ways of responding to experience across types of situations' (1995: 62). She goes on to stress that 'not all dispositions are desirable, and curriculum and teaching practices must address not only how to strengthen desirable dispositions but how to address undesirable one' (p. 63). Katz outlines some reasons why this should be a goal of early childhood education:

● Without appropriate dispositions, children in educational settings will acquire knowledge and skills which they do not then use: all children, for instance, know how to listen, but some children are not inclined to do so! Katz argues that, since skills improve with use, it is important to strengthen the disposition to use them.

● The process of acquiring knowledge and skills may actually decrease children's motivation to use them. Katz's example here is early formal instruction in reading, which may not only teach children to read but also teach them there is no fun in reading. In such a case it can be argued that the disposition to have a go at reading is more important than the skill of reading.

● Some dispositions to learn (such as exploration) are inborn – wired into the child's brain – but these dispositions can be damaged or extinguished for good by inappropriate learning experiences.

● Close observation of children at this age can show what kind of feedback from adults works for each child: some children for instance will be motivated by praise for their performance, whilst others will become dependent and unable to self-motivate if praised too highly. Striking the balance for each child is of paramount importance.

● Dispositions are most likely to be acquired through adult modelling of behaviours rather than through direct teaching. Early educators can model exploratory and curious behaviour and demonstrate that feeling uncertain and making mistakes are part of the learning process.

High-quality early education has consistently demonstrated the importance of efforts to strengthen learning dispositions. Systematic reviews of the long-term outcomes of well-planned programmes such as High/Scope (Schweinhart et al., 1993) show that a change in children's attitudes towards themselves and their learning, rather than a change in their measurable IQ, is the most important factor in transforming the life chances of children from disadvantaged communities. Reviewing the effectiveness of early education, Sylva (1994: 94) concludes that 'The most important learning in pre-school concerns aspiration, task commitment, social skills and feelings of efficacy'. This is the mechanism which enables early education to 'make a difference' in children's lives which stays with them into adulthood, so it is important to get it right.

Writing about the New Zealand *Te Whariki* curriculum, Carr (2001) lists the five domains which contribute to children's positive dispositions to learn:

- taking an interest;
- being involved;
- persisting with difficulty or uncertainty;
- communicating with others; and
- taking responsibility.

Carr further demonstrates the dynamic way that these domains can be put into practice when planning for children's learning and assessing the learning behaviours of individuals. She collapses the five domains into a deceptively simple formula of being *ready, willing and able* to learn within the setting. For any individual child, these conditions can only be fulfilled when he or she has a sense of his or her own efficacy (good self-esteem, based on realistic evaluations) *and* is presented with interesting and relevant opportunities, *and* feels safe and secure in his or her settings and his or her relationships. If these conditions are met, most children will be in a position to 'take an interest, get involved, persist with difficulties, communicate with others, and take responsibility' for their own learning.

Much of the responsibility for children's learning dispositions, as Roberts (2002) points out, lies with adults, who themselves need to be *ready, willing and able* to perform a supportive role as children acquire the learning dispositions that will see them through the lifelong learning ahead of them. Tyler's story (see Learning Story 2.9) shows how a skilled practitioner can transform a child's 'feelings of efficacy'.

Learning Story 2.9 Tyler: fear of failure in reception

Tyler started school with great promise. He had attended an excellent nursery and his mother had bought him as she said 'hundreds of books' as well as educational tapes and videos for early literacy learning. Tyler was a cheerful, sociable and articulate boy who enjoyed conversations with adults and quickly established good relationships. So it was surprising to discover that he wanted *nothing* at all to do with reading or writing: if an adult approached whilst he was drawing he would put his pencil down, push his paper away and say: 'I can't write, you know – I'm not gonna write.' If an adult sat close by whilst he was looking in a book, he would sometimes shut the book and say: 'I'm not reading, I can't read!'

Tyler's teacher realized that he had probably absorbed a certain amount of anxiety and unconscious pressure from his mother, who was desperately keen for him to learn to read. She adopted an entirely carefree and casual tone in her reading sessions with Tyler, sharing small jokes with him, drawing his attention to humorous illustrations, chatting about nonsense rhymes, but never focusing his attention on decoding the actual text in the early reading books. In her written messages to the family, in Tyler's home reading bag, she recommended the same practices, suggesting that his parents read to him, or invite him to 'read' the pictures rather than the words or make up nonsense rhymes. After a few months, to his great relief (and his mother's), Tyler began to notice that he *could* read – that he *knew what the words said*! Armed with this confidence he was able to get involved in all the learning activities of his literacy-rich classroom.

How does this supportive work continue into Key Stage 1? The National Curriculum guidance (DfEE/QCA, 1999) is not very specific, although its first aim clearly refers to learning dispositions: 'The school curriculum should develop enjoyment of, and commitment to, learning . . . It should build on pupils' strengths, interests and experiences and develop their confidence in their capacity to learn and work independently and collaboratively.' Transition and continuity are again of the utmost importance: a sudden jump from the informality and play-based learning of the Foundation Stage to the formal curriculum of Year 1 may undermine children's confidence in themselves as learners and undo many of the important lessons they have learnt. Practitioners need to allow for a period of adjustment and help children to become proud of their new, more grown-up ways of learning. The progress and behaviour of individuals must be carefully monitored in the early weeks of the new Key stage: children who are feeling insecure about their competence and status may find different ways of showing it, and both the shy withdrawn child and the boastful bullying one need sensitive support.

Strategies for fostering children's personal and social identity, discussed earlier in this chapter, are an essential foundation for the maintenance of good learning dispositions. Children who are secure in their relationships with adults and peers will be more willing to take risks, ask questions and admit difficulties. Circle times may be held less frequently because of timetable pressures, but once a week at least the class should have the chance to review what has been new, what has been difficult, what has been fun and what has been surprising for them, collectively and individually. Teachers play a crucial role in creating the ethos that informs these sessions so that children's contributions are both positive and realistic. As in the Foundation Stage, adults' modelling of dispositions and behaviours – of feeling curious, feeling fed up, deciding to have another try, admiring the success of others – helps children to identify these feelings in themselves and to recognize that they are all part of the learning process.

Assessment and self-assessment

Realistic evaluation and self-evaluation become even more important as children encounter the more difficult tasks, and more challenging curriculum, of Key Stage 1. The traditional types of teacher 'marking' of work can rapidly undo all the progress children have made in forming an appropriate sense of their own achievements, even for pupils who do well. If you hand your 'work' to a teacher and it comes back covered in ticks and stars, you may come to depend on the teacher's view of your work to validate your efforts: in future, your motivation may be satisfying the teacher rather than satisfying yourself. If it comes back covered in crosses and underlinings it is hard to feel motivated at all.

Children's disaffection begins at an early age and is hard to overcome (Barrett, 1989). One way to prevent is it to introduce self-assessment by children – a continuation of the kind of 'reviewing' of one's own activities that has been emphasized in the High/Scope curriculum in particular. Discussions with individual children about the activities they have completed are time-consuming but can be recognized as an integral part of the child's learning and an invaluable aspect of the teacher's teaching. Once children become skilled at evaluating their own and others' work, they slip into a routine where it is second nature and becomes an ongoing aspect of their work rather than an add-on at the end. Roisin's story (see Learning Story 2.10) describes the value of the practice.

Learning Story 2.10 Roisin: learning about self-assessment

Roisin was an expert on school: she had been instructed in the rules and routines of the classroom by an older sister and already knew about school practices before she began. In consequence she found it hard to assimilate messages which conflicted with these expectations. When her Year 1 teacher gradually introduced the practice of self-assessment, withholding her own comments on children's processes and products and inviting children to give *their* opinion of any project they had undertaken, Roisin was uncomfortable. Outwardly she appeared to accept the new routine but, in practice, she continued with her existing habits under a new guise: when invited to comment on a drawing, model or piece of writing she would instruct her teacher to write 'Lovely', 'Good girl' or 'Well done', and would add her own large ticks or a star before returning her book to her tray or her drawing to its pile. After a time her teacher noticed that Roisin was simply side-stepping the whole process of evaluation by adding the ticks and stars herself, at the same time as putting in a final full stop and disposing of her work without showing it to anyone. Once alerted, she made a point of spending time with Roisin as she completed tasks, discussing 'what you would like me to write about how you have worked' and gently probing the evaluative judgements ('Lovely work!'), encouraging her to replace them with informative ones ('I didn't know how to do "daddy" but Catriona showed me and now I know', 'I remembered about the spaces between the words but not all of them'). Roisin was helped in this process by peer modelling as she observed less self-conscious children discussing what 'comment' they would ask for, and comparing their writing and drawing with earlier examples and with each other's work.

▌ Summary

Children's personal, social and emotional development – and their moral and spiritual development – is, as our examples have shown, intertwined with every aspect of their experience in early childhood settings: with their play, their friendships and their conversations, as well as with the curriculum and the culture of the school. Careful planning is essential for these aspects of learning as it is for their academic learning. But just as essential is the practitioner's own sensitivity – her own ability to tune in to the ways that children's experiences, at home and at school, are shaping their emerging identity.

We might summarize by suggesting that practitioners should be:

- *ready* – to take children's emotional lives seriously and to prioritize these aspects of children's learning in their planning;
- *willing* – to listen and learn, from children, parents and colleagues, about their own concerns and priorities and the ways they think about them; and
- *able* – to exercise their skills confidently and flexibly, responding to children's personal, social and emotional needs as they present themselves.

▌ Suggested further reading

Brooker, L. (2002) *Starting School: Young Children Learning Cultures*. Buckingham: Open University Press.

Carr, M. (2001) *Assessment in Early Childhod Settings: Learning Stories*. London: Paul Chapman Publishing.

Dowling, M. (2000) *Young Children's Personal, Social and Emotional Development*. London: Paul Chapman Publishing.

Roberts, R. (2002) *Self-Esteem and Early Learning*. London: Paul Chapman Publishing.

References

Anning, A. and Edwards, A. (1999) *Promoting Children's Learning from Birth to Five: Developing the New Early Years Professional*. Buckingham: Open University Press.

Barrett, G. (ed.) (1989) *Disaffection from School? The Early Years*. London: Falmer.

Bennett, J. (1997) 'Can I tell that story something in a circle?' *Resource* 19(3): 10–11.

Boyle, M. and Woods, P. (1998) 'Becoming a proper pupil: bilingual children's experience of staring school', *Studies in Educational Ethnography*, 1: 93–113.

Bronfenbrenner, U. (1979) *The Ecology of Human Development*. Cambridge, MA: Harvard University Press.

Brooker, L. (2002) *Starting School: Young Children Learning Cultures*. Buckingham: Open University Press.

Carr, M. (2001) *Assessment in Early Childhood Settings: Learning Stories*. London: Paul Chapman Publishing.

Connolly, P. (1998) *Racism, Gender Identities and Young Children: Social Relations in a Multi-Ethnic Inner-City Primary School*. London: Routledge.

DfEE/QCA (1999) *The National Curriculum. Handbook for Primary Teachers in England*. London: DfEE.

DfEE/QCA (2000) *Curriculum Guidance for the Foundation Stage*. London: QCA.

Dowling, M. (2000) *Young Children's Personal, Social and Emotional Development*. London: Paul Chapman Publishing.

Dweck, C. and Leggett, E. (1988) 'A social-cognitive approach to motivation and personality', *Psychological Review*, 95(2): 256–73.

Faulkner, D. (1995) 'Play, self and the social world', in P. Barnes (ed.) *Personal, Social and Emotional Development of Children*. Oxford: Blackwell/Open University.

Faulkner, D. and Miell, D. (1993) 'Settling into school: the importance of early friendships for the development of children's social understanding and communicative competence', *International Journal of Early Years Education*, 1(1): 23–45.

Gura, P. (1996) 'What I want for Cinderella: self-esteem and self-assessment', *Early Education*, 19: 3–5.

Hughes, M. (1996) 'Parents, teachers and schools', in B. Bernstein and J. Brannen (eds) *Children, Research and Policy*. London: Taylor & Francis.

Hughes, M., Wikely, F. and Nash, T. (1994) *Parents and their Children's Schools*. Oxford: Blackwell.

Katz, L. (1995) *Talks with Teachers of Young Children*. Norwood, NJ: Ablex.

Miell, D. (1995) 'Developing a sense of self', in P. Barnes (ed.) *Personal, Social and Emotional Development of Children*. Oxford: Blackwell/Open University.

National Curriculum Council (1993) *Spiritual and Moral Development: A Discussion Paper*. York: National Curriculum Council.

Roberts, R. (1998) 'Thinking about me and them', in I. Siraj-Blatchford (ed.) *A Curriculum Development Handbook for Early Childhood Educators*. Stoke-on-Trent: Trentham Books.

Roberts, R. (2002) *Self-esteem and Early Learning*. London: Paul Chapman Publishing.

Schaffer, H.R. (1996) *Social Development*. Oxford: Blackwell.

Schweinhart, L.J., Barnes, H.V. and Weikart, D.P. (1993) *Significant Benefits: The High/Scope Perry Preschool Study through Age 27*. Ypsilanti, MI: High/Scope Education Research Foundation.

Siraj-Blatchford, I. (1994) *The Early Years: Laying the Foundations for Racial Equality*. Stoke-on-Trent: Trentham Books.

Sluckin, A. (1987) 'The culture of the primary school playground', in A. Pollard (ed.) *Children and their Primary Schools*. Lewes: Falmer.

Smilansky, S. (1990) 'Socio-dramatic play: its relevance to behaviour and achievement in school', in E. Klugman and S. Smilansky (eds) *Children's Play and Learning: Perspectives and Policy Implications*. New York, NY: Teachers College Press.

Sylva, K. (1994) 'The impact of early learning on children's later development', in C. Ball (ed.) *Start Right: The Importance of Early Learning*. London: Royal Society of Arts.

Sylva, K., Roy, C. and Painter, M. (1980) *Childwatching at Playgroup and Nursery School*. London: Grant McIntyre.

Trevarthen, C. (1998) 'A child's need to learn a culture', in M. Woodhead et al. (eds) *Cultural Worlds of Early Childhood*. London: Routledge.

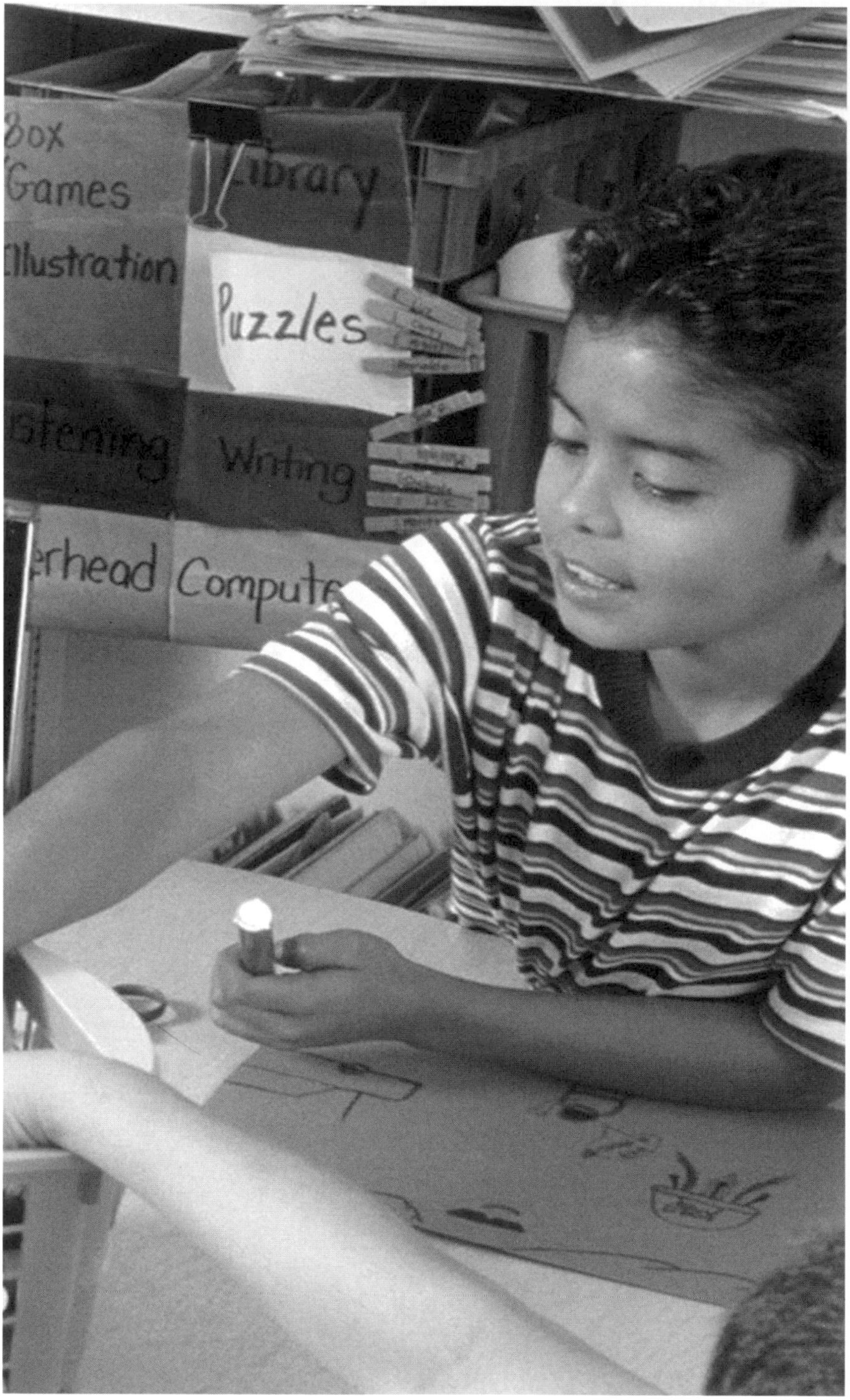
Box
Games
Library
Illustration
Puzzles
Writing
Computer

Communication, language and literacy: learning through speaking and listening, reading and writing

Jeni Riley and David Reedy

> *Language is a gateway to new concepts, a means for sorting out confusions, a way to interact with people, or to get help, a way to test out what one knows. It is the source of much pleasure for the child and the adult. It is a pervasive, persuasive, perpetual fountain of learning – and there is no equipment that will give children the interactive experiences that will power their progress.*
>
> (Clay 1998: 11)

The ability to communicate effectively is fundamental to all aspects of human development: the capacity to think and to learn and, ultimately, to be successful in life depends upon it. The *Curriculum Guidance for the Foundation Stage* (DfEE/QCA, 2000) recognizes the importance of developing spoken language as a key starting point for learning in pre-school settings. The Early Learning Goals emphasize that children should either have the opportunity or be able to:

- Interact with others, negotiating plans and activities and taking turns in conversations.
- Enjoy listening to and using spoken and written language. . .
- Sustain attentive listening, responding to what they have heard by relevant comments, questions or actions.
- Listen with enjoyment, and respond to stories, songs and other music, rhymes and poems and make up their own stories, songs, rhymes and poems.
- Extend their vocabulary, exploring the meaning and sounds of new words.
- Speak clearly and audibly with confidence and control and show awareness of the listener, for example by their use of conventions such as greetings, 'please' and 'thank you'.
- Use language to imagine and recreate roles and experiences.
- Use talk to organise, sequence and clarify thinking, ideas, feelings and events. (DfEE/QCA, 2000: 48–59)

Making relationships: in the beginning . . .

[Language] is something to do with the complex business of getting two minds in contact, because the exchange of meanings and language is at the centre of human communication. (Whitehead, 1997: 4)

Human beings are born with a predisposition to communicate and to form relationships. In the weeks before birth babies become aware of their mothers' voices, through transmission down the spinal column. Each newborn recognizes and reacts to it when held in her arms for the first time. The two individuals are now connected. Researchers agree that babies and their carers engage in mutually satisfying and conversational-type activities, by cooing and establishing eye contact soon after birth and, certainly, by the time the infant is 5 or 6 weeks old. The infant's drive to communicate is matched by the adult's desire to enable the child to enter into a world of shared meanings.

Speech develops through richly varied language experiences. Throughout the preschool years merely living in a family provides many opportunities to learn and practise language through watching, listening and playing with more experienced language users. Daily routines of washing, dressing and feeding are accompanied with commentary, with one-to-one conversations, stories, songs and rhymes. Spoken language develops through a range of experiences such as these. However, the ability to speak is not a single capacity but is composed of an array of skills which develop in order to fulfil different purposes and needs.

Development in spoken language

Classification of language functions

The development of spoken language, as we have discussed, is dependent upon both the opportunity and the need to communicate for particular purposes, and also through conversations that are, first and foremost, intensely satisfying. Gradually the use of language broadens through greater linguistic expertise and developing conceptual and social maturity. Halliday (1975) developed a classification system of the different functions of language. The following, using only three examples from his system, shows well how children use language in increasingly complex ways. To:

- speak in order 'to get things done';
- control of the behaviour of others;
- interact, which is concerned with the establishment and then the maintenance of relationships with others.

These stages of development reflect the growing complexity of the individual's social interactions through childhood (Halliday, 1975). Pre-school and primary teachers need to be aware of the different dimensions of function and use of oral language so that they are able to assess the level of a child's growing control over it. Wilkinson (1982) suggests another classification of language which compares interestingly with that of Halliday. This is based on questions surrounding three basic activities: 'Who am I?', 'Who are you?' and 'Who or what is it, was it, will it be?'

Children gradually learn to express their needs, thoughts and feelings more fluently and, in turn, so their ideas develop with the ability to talk. Using language more precisely enables pupils to generalize, to categorize, to manipulate ideas and to explore ideas of cause and effect. Language has a supportive role in clarifying and organizing the thought processes. In this way, thinking is developed through the child's growing control of spoken language. In addition, concepts are developed through the awareness of specific and precise vocabulary – for example, the particular features of a rectangle are learnt by knowing the mathematical term.

Looking for research evidence which might inform practice leads us to turn to a study, although over 20 years old, that has much to offer. Factors which encourage the development of spoken language were shown clearly by the much celebrated 'Bristol Study'. This research project (Wells, 1987) studied the language development of 128 children from the age of 13 months through to school age. It offers a rich source of information on a range of domestic situations and the variety and type of adult support of the children involved, it compares this information with the differing levels of the children's emerging competence in oracy. Wells and his colleagues provide information on the relationship between the progress of the children and their living circumstances and experiences.

'Motherese' and modelling and extending talk

As they analysed the huge mass of data from the audio-tape transcripts, the Bristol research team found that there was a great variation in the rate at which children acquire spoken language. The researchers suggest the reason for this is that adults are very good at enabling infants to speak. Mothers speak to their children in a manner described by psychologists as 'motherese', which is highly supportive in developing language. This is a form of speech that is raised in pitch and is simple and repetitive. The child's utterance is frequently expanded upon for the purpose of clarification and this also provides intuitive tutoring. The child says, for example, 'Ben sock!' and the adult responds, typically, 'Yes, that *is* Ben's sock. He must have his red socks on this morning'.

A real and interesting issue to discuss

All the evidence from the Bristol Study suggests that children learn language best not through drills and instruction but when adults attend to, and are interested in, what children are saying and enter with them in real conversations. Children's language skills need personal interaction in order to develop. If one believes that children learn through being taught to speak, rather as one would teach a parrot, this has important implications for the way in which the adults should interact with the child. Wells is clear from the evidence of his study that this is *not* the case. In fact, he cites examples where it is plainly counterproductive and discouraging when a mother, as in one of the examples he gives, deliberately sets out to teach and ignores the child's obvious lack of interest in the topic!

The extent and type of conversation

What, then, does appear to be valuable? If we take the view that children are largely constructors of their own personal version of spoken language, perhaps it can be argued that adults have little to contribute to the process. This is again patently not true. In order to make progress, children need feedback on the effectiveness of their efforts: to talk to people and, through conversation, to test hypotheses about the way language works and to have their hypotheses confirmed. The extent to which children have this opportunity is important. Wells identified a clear relationship between those children who were exposed to a large number of conversations and the rate at which they developed.

So the amount of experience of talk is important, but it is even more complex than that. Wells says:

> What seems to be important is that, to be most helpful, the child's experience
> of conversation should be in a one-to-one situation in which the adult is talking
> about matters that are of interest and concern to the child, such as what he or
> she is doing, has done or plans to do, or about activities in which the child and
> adult engage together. (1987; 44)

The explanation of the value of the shared experience is that it maximizes the possibility of the meaning being interpreted appropriately by both participants and built upon further. The less experienced language user is supported through interest and the context and, in this way, is motivated into sustaining the dialogue. The role of the more experienced speaker is crucial. Wells continues: 'This therefore places a very great responsibility on the adult to compensate for the child's limitations and to behave in ways that make it as easy as possible for the child to play his or her part as effectively as possible' (1987: 45).

Parents or carers are able to do this best at this stage of spoken language development as they have insight into the child's model of the world and her capability. This enables them to be skilful and co-operative listeners and to make a rich interpretation of the child's utterances.

'Shared sustained thinking'

In the Introduction and Chapter 1, we discussed the REPEY project's idea of 'shared sustained thinking' that was observed in the most effective early years centres. This concept echoes and builds on Wells' suggestions that mutual and pleasurable engagement with a topic is the most fruitful context for effective language development. As Wells says, it is a collaborative enterprise in which both are involved. Adults do not need to be over-analytical concerning the linguistic complexity of how exactly they are operating but they do need to know that the value lies in the *way* they respond:

> All that is required is that they be responsive to the cues that children provide as to what they are able to understand. Rather than adults teaching children, therefore, it is children who teach adults how to talk in such a way as to make it easy for them to learn (Wells, 1987: 48)

Children, therefore, play the major role in constructing their knowledge of language although they are greatly aided in this by adults. Children who made less progress were not as frequently enagaged in one-to-one conversations or with adults who worked hard at trying to make mutual sense of a situation.

The teaching points that emerge for early years educators from the findings of the Bristol Study are as follows:

> When the child appears to be trying to communicate, assume he or she has something important to say and treat the attempt accordingly.

> Because the child's utterances are often unclear or ambiguous, be sure you have understood the intended meaning before responding.

> When you reply, take the child's meaning as the basis of what you say next – confirming the intention and extending the topic or inviting the child to do so for him or herself.

> Select and phrase your contributions so that they are at or just beyond the child's ability to comprehend. (Wells, 1987: 50)

The development of spoken language in the Foundation Stage

By the age of 4 most children have acquired at least 1,600 words and can understand many more (Crystal,1987). The physiological mechanisms which produce speech are now well developed and speech becomes more intelligible and clear. The intellectual capacity to exploit the rules of language that have been acquired is shown by the child's overgeneralization of past tenses (as in 'goed' and 'see-ed'), the regularization of plurals with 'mouses' and 'foots' and the transformation of nouns into verbs (such as 'boxing' an object). These inventions illustrate that language acquisition is not a matter of simple imitation. The child uses language in order to be able to communicate, to get things done, to learn and to comment on the world and, most important of all, to make meaning.

Once in an early years setting or reception class, the child becomes involved with a wider social community which requires communication with many different people for a variety of purposes. Literacy has greater and greater impact on spoken language development. Speech structures become more complex and literary influences are evident in the child's oral language patterns and vocabulary. The presence of more elaborate connectives becomes evident, as does the awareness of cause and effect when the child experiments with constructions such as 'What I think is . . .' followed by 'because . . .', and 'When I get round to it I will . . .'. Uncertainty is expressed with 'maybe', 'perhaps' and 'probably' and the passive voice is understood but probably not used. Vocabulary expands with the acquisition of technical and subject-specific terminology through the need to meet the demands of school-based learning as the pupil now has the opportunity to experience specialist areas of the curriculum.

The situations in which children find themselves require language to be used in a variety of ways which, in turn, make different levels of demand on their developing oracy.

Supporting spoken language in the Foundation Stage

The dimensions of language use: contextualized uses of language

As we have seen, one of the main purposes of language is to establish and maintain interpersonal relationships. This is achieved through face-to-face conversation and the meaning is negotiated through gesture and mutual speaker and listener feedback; in addition, these exchanges are highly contextualized. The home is a very supportive place for the contextualized use of language to be developed. At home, talk usually fulfils the following criteria:

- It is mutually enjoyable.
- It provides a familiar audience.
- It uses known patterns of discourse.
- It achieves an immediate purpose.
- It supports successful communication.
- There is an appropriate length of exchange, depending upon purpose, situation and pleasure.
- Talk is usually between a child and a more experienced language user.

Decontextualized uses of language

Some homes prepare children to use language in a different way by encouraging a sharing of events that have not been experienced by everyone present. Such a decontextualized use of language presents challenges to many speakers as it requires an ability to present information to audiences who are at a distance to the speaker and who may share different levels of background knowledge. Snow (1991) suggests that language skills of this type are fostered through engaging in explanations and personal narratives, and through using language to create fantasy worlds and to convey information to relative strangers. The skills of decontextualized spoken-language use are the ones related most closely to higher levels of competence in written language acquired later in primary school, such as reading comprehension and reading ability.

At the centre of spoken language learning is the quality of the interaction between the speaker and listeners. As we have seen, listeners provide positive encouragement for the speaker to continue through what are called contingent responses. Non-contingent responses are ones that have little or no relationship to what the speaker has said or means. The exchange then becomes unsatisfying for both parties and finally breaks down.

Contingent responses:

- keep conversations flowing;
- indicate active listening;
- provide positive feedback;
- are emotionally satisfying;
- extend meaning; and
- achieve a clear purpose (Raban, 2000).

Speaking and listening are complementary: they reinforce each other as the conversation is jointly constructed. Good listeners anticipate what will be said – they check their own understanding of the meaning which then becomes shared. Speaking and listening are dynamic and interactive processes.

The role of books and stories in developing oracy

Purposeful conversations are embedded in the ebb and flow of daily life. Books also offer access to a wider and fascinating world. Narrative has its own important role in the intellectual and emotional development of young children but, in relation to this section on oracy, stories provide a basis for stimulation, for discussion, for debate and for fantasy. Children will talk extensively about the stories told and read to them. Imaginations are sparked by the colour, humour and intrigue held within the covers of a picture book. Meaningful interactions occur with books naturally, through sharing stories, predicting the possible outcomes and discussing the characters and their actions, and through 'reading' and interrogating the enticing illustrations. Experiences with other types of texts (such as receiving birthday and postcards and seeing notes, shopping lists and letters) will fuel genuine conversations.

Sharing books in the Foundation Stage

In early years settings, practitioners use colourful, illustrated picture books to stimulate interaction and to bring meaning to a text with a small group of children. This recreates the child/parent experience of sharing a book through conversations which extend all aspects of spoken language and demonstrate, at the same time, what readers do in order to make meaning.

An example of a well-loved picture book that is literally transporting is *We're Going on a Bear Hunt*, written by Michael Rosen and illustrated by Helen Oxenbury. It is published in both standard and enlarged text form for use in early years settings. This text invites participation and discussion as the children collaboratively make the meaning. The inclusive pronoun 'we' in the title refers not just to the characters but includes the group looking at the book.

Talking about the text

Before opening the book, young children will talk spontaneously about the story and speculate about what will happen. To some it will be familiar and they will say so. The adult, supporting and maintaining the dialogue around the text, will wait, enjoying hearing the children's contributions and responding to their comments: 'Yes, I've read it before too . . . you join in with the words when I read it!'

As the book is read, children engage with it on several levels. They comment on the immediate action in the text: 'I don't like mud', 'We've got a dog like that.' And they join in with phrases, supported by the repetition and the simple but strong rhythm. They savour the alliteration and onomatopoeia (*deep*, *dark forest*, *swishy swashy*, *swishy swashy*) and so they learn important lessons about the phonic system and the relationship between sound and symbol.

As the action heightens and the massive bear disturbed, the characters scamper home to the safety of a big bed. So the pace quickens, excitement builds and, finally, the book ends with the touching image of the bear walking hunched and alone along the beach. Commentary comes thick and fast:

- 'I wouldn't be frightened.'
- 'The bear looks lonely.'
- 'Is he sad?'
- 'Can we have it again?'

The narrative teaches the children about how books and language function. This experience with a story of such quality and power offers children a safe place where they can work through their own thoughts and feelings. With a picture book they can enter and leave when they wish.

This teaching approach ensures that there is an authentic conversation between the members of an early years setting. The adult is involved and responsive when pupils have a suggestion – she injects 'cognitive challenge' into the conversation and, in this way, develops the children's thinking. Thinking can also be taken forward by incorporating new vocabulary into the pupils' linguistic repertoire and so extending their language competence. Questions such as 'The bear looks so sad at the end – I wonder whether he was lonely and just wanted to play? What do you think?' give rise to real debate between children encouraging the use of complex language constructions such as:

- 'I think he's sad because . . .'
- 'I don't think so because . . .'

The genuine exchange of ideas helps pupils to see the importance of listening to and building on the ideas of others. Open-ended but focused questions are a key strategy on the part of the teacher to encourage not only the development of speaking and listening but also an understanding of the text itself. The interaction between illustrations and text builds rich and varied interpretation and establishes the basis for a deep personal response to written texts.

Speaking and listening can be developed through using the text as a focus for drama and role play. Drama offers further opportunity to articulate feelings and actions in role and to develop the action in new and interesting ways, extending their spoken language as they do so. Pupils explore the text actively, repeating words as they move through the poem or story.

Supporting language development in Key Stage 1

We need to look now at the types of talk that are the most valuable for developing language in schools. The research evidence demonstrates considerable variation between the home and the school setting. At home children are very much more likely to initiate a conversation (in some of Wells' analyses the percentage is as high as 70%) than at school. He cites several depressing incidences in which the teacher and the child appear to be talking completely at cross-purposes, with the result that both speakers became frustrated and disinclined to repeat the experience. Mutual enjoyment is far from the experience of the participants, and little learning is likely to have occurred. Worse still is the impression that Rosie (the most striking of the examples cited) has given to her reception teacher: one of linguistic incompetence which contrasts poorly with the transcripts taped at her home.

The barriers to effective language use and development in classrooms

The obvious issue in schools is the unrealistic expectation that one teacher can communicate effectively with 30 or more young pupils. But this is not the only factor that runs counter to a supportive linguistic learning environment in the Key Stage 1 classroom. It is a fact of life that teachers have pressures and a variety of different agendas with which to cope. This situation ensures that the interactions that occur in classrooms usually have a predetermined goal, concept or skill to be acquired. In Wells' opinion, this is counterproductive to any kind of valuable learning and leads to the 'Guess what is in my mind?' phenomenon. This is also a far cry from the 'sustained shared thinking' of the REPEY project discussed in Chapter 1 of this book.

Young children can be observed in their desperate search for clues (from the adult's facial expression and body language) that might lead to the 'correct' response before offering a reply. Some will rarely volunteer a suggestion, so intimidated are they by this school 'game'. Wells makes a plea for teachers to adopt a more genuinely conversational approach in their interactions with children so that, if one of several answers is appropriate, several suggestions are accepted and developed. Doing this encourages pupils to continue to offer responses and so to participate in the joint act of meaning-making that is the nature of communication and an exchange of ideas.

Similarly, Clay (1998) believes that talking to children one to one as often as possible is the most effective way to develop their spoken language. She suggests that adults should:

- talk to the ones least able to talk to you;
- talk when the going is hard;
- listen when the child wants to talk to you;
- reply and extend the conversation;
- note how many turns go back and forth;
- note that good talkers will talk most – adults need to identify those children; and
- identify those who need to have the most time spent with them.

Children for whom English is an additional language

The *Curriculum Guidance in the Foundation Stage* (DfEE/QCA, 2000: 19) recommends that bilingual children with English as an additional language should be offered activities and experiences which:

- build on children's experiences of language at home and in the wider community by providing a range of opportunities to use their home language(s), so that their developing use of English and other language support one another;
- provide a range of opportunities for children to engage in speaking and listening activities in English with peers and adults;
- ensure all children have opportunities to recognise and show respect for each child's home language;
- provide bilingual support, in particular to extend vocabulary and support children's developing understanding;
- provide a variety of writing in the children's home languages as well as in English, including books, notices and labels;
- provide opportunities for children to hear home languages as well as English, for example, through the use of audio and video materials.

The principles and examples of good practice suggested in the first part of this chapter should form the basis of working with all 3–7 year-olds. However, there may be a need for specific consideration for children for whom English is as an additional language (EAL) and who are at various stages of developing their competence in language in the early years setting or classroom. These children may be bilingual, trilingual or multilingual and, as such, will bring to the pre-school or classroom a wide variety of experience and use in their first and additional languages. Some settings may have substantial numbers of bilingual learners with one dominant first language; others may have small groups or individual learners who have a range of home languages. The children attending early years settings and schools in Britain represent several different categories of bilingual learner – they represent various stages of competence of English, some having arrived recently in Britain whilst many others (95%) are British-born ethnic minority children.

Supporting the development of an additional language

There is research evidence to reinforce the most supportive conditions that enable the effective learning of a second language to occur: first, if it is developed from the basis of a flourishing, maintained and supported first language (Cummins, 1978); and, secondly, if this language is respected and encouraged (ILEA, 1990), progress in the additional language is enhanced. Developing the children's spoken and written English provides access to the whole curriculum, to social interaction and to opportunity and power. The attitudes of the adults with whom the child comes in contact are vital in promoting these principles, particularly as early years educators are seen, by both children and their parents, as representatives of the whole educational system. A positive attitude will be demonstrated through both general policies and good classroom practice. The section that follows focuses on the latter.

A positive, enabling ethos

The education of bilingual children is underpinned by the same ideology as that of the education for all in the early years – namely, the adage 'observe, support and extend' learning. Adults will first establish what the child can do and understand through observation and assessment and the planning which needs to take place for the next stage of learning, using the motivating force of the child's interests and strengths as a starting point. The most effective way of working in a setting with bilingual pupils is one where the language support is fully integrated into practice which has a meaningful, active context. Acquiring or developing an additional language demands high levels of risk on the part of the learner. The ethos of the classroom, therefore, must be an enabling one so that the children feel secure and that their home or community language is valued and respected. This is achieved through the positive promotion of the first language so that the pupils are encouraged to use it, perhaps with other children or parents invited to act as interpreters for key events and for activities needing specific explanation. Favourite and class-made books can be translated into dual texts along with songs, rhymes and stories, which should also be enjoyed in the first languages as well as in English. The use of story boards, role play, drama and finger puppets makes the spoken language more accessible, visual and memorable by embedding learning in a concrete context.

The earliest stages of additional language learning

Children who are in the very early stages of learning English as a second or additional language are aware of the communicative purpose and function of a language but will go through similar, but accelerated, stages of English acquisition as the young infant. These are as follows:

1　A period of silence during which the children have an increasing receptive language capability indicated by what they can understand but they appear to have little or no productive ability. Communication will occur through gesture, mood and non-verbal utterance. This stage is followed by single words, such as 'Yes', 'Me', 'No', 'See', etc.
2　Children gradually begin to put together two and three words in order to express themselves in increasingly more complex ways (for example, 'Me too', 'Me go too?', 'Come see', 'Go away!') with the use of gesture and intonation appropriately emphasizing the intention.
3　It may take up to two years for children to achieve fluency in face-to-face contextually supportive situations, and much longer to use oral language accurately in abstract situations (Cummins, 1984).

During the period of second or additional language acquisition, the adults with whom the bilingual pupils are in daily contact have considerable opportunity to support their progress. The child's understanding of what is being said is important, and this is enhanced if visual and contextual support is used to accompany instructions or explanations with a practical demonstration and lively gestures, intonations, eye contact and frequent repetitions are also used. Sensitive grouping of children at different stages of competence can be used in order to provide the appropriate linguistic support in imaginative play and other activities – perhaps with a child more advanced in English on some occasions or with an adult on others.

Specific suggestions to develop oracy might include speaking and listening activities in a small group (with adult support), such as the ones shown in Figure 3.1. The emphasis at this stage will be on engaging children in practical, activity-based learning such as cooking, science and technology where the vocabulary used is embedded in the context of the activity and the understanding is supported by the 'doing'.

- Discussion and feedback sessions and nursery rhyme 'reading' with a large text.
- Games with repetition, imitation and action, such as 'Simon Says', and games involving naming and counting, such as pelmanism, Kim's game and animal dominoes.
- Sorting and matching activities.
- Listening and re-telling stories with the use of story boards, 'fuzzy-felts' or puppets.
- Adult-made books with repetitive structures, such as 'Faziah likes drawing but Ahmed likes painting'.
- The positive inclusion of all the pupils in class routines, in taking messages and in undertaking 'jobs'.

Figure 3.1 *Suggestions to develop oracy*

Developing language through ICT

The use of information and communication technology (ICT) is becoming increasingly valuable in supporting learning across the curriculum and for developing spoken language in particular. An example drawn from an element of the requirements for ICT in the Foundation Stage (based on the use of ICT in everyday life – making toast/using a toaster) is given in Figure 3.2.

This practical activity provides a supportive context for learning a second or additional language. Using a toaster enables some simple vocabulary, such as *on, off, switch on, switch off, bread, plug in,* to be embedded in the activity.

The adult/teacher might begin by asking such questions as:

- What do we have to do first?

- Why isn't it working? Oh, we haven't plugged it in! Now we need to switch it on.

- What does this knob do? Let's turn it around a bit and see what happens to the toast.

Speaking and listening can be further extended by getting the children to tell others the sequence they went through to make the piece of toast, what they needed to do and so on. Again, simple sequencing vocabulary, particularly temporal connectives such as *first, then, next, after, last,* can be demonstrated and then used by the pupils themselves.

Figure 3.2 *Making toast*

Another example is given in the DATEC (Developmentally Appropriate Technology in Early Childhood) project, which is reported by Brooker and Siraj-Blatchford (2002). Two bilingual boys, Mahib and Jubed, aged 3 and 4, are working with a computer using a software program which clearly scaffolds the children's attempts through a structured but accessible format and through suitable vocabulary (Learning Story 3.1).

Learning Story 3.1 Mahib and Jubed

Mahib has changed to 'Pencils': he knows how to answer this correctly and tells me 'That is tall pencil' then repeats after the computer voice, 'That is the tall pencil'. He points to a red balloon ('No') and says 'That is no'.

Jubed very deliberately repeats each message from the computer: 'That is the tall pencil . . . Yes. That is the short pencil.' Mahib informs me of the colours of the pencils in Bengali.

Two further examples, also reported by Brooker and Siraj-Blatchford, are given in Learning Stories 3.2 and 3.3.

Learning Story 3.2 Jahez and Ziaur

Jahez knew some of the items in the kitchen but also received lots of advice, in Bengali, from Ziaur, who told him all his favourites. Jahez obliged him by clicking on them repeatedly. He began by talking aloud to himself and me in English: 'Where . . . cat . . . milk?' (he had difficulty locating the kittens but then managed it): 'I did it . . . I did it' (with enormous effort and concentration, caught all three kittens). He discovers how to 'break a window' and shouts 'I did it – glass'. He experiences a lot of frustration trying to drag and drop birthday candles (expressed as 'Oh! My hand!' – pointing to it in despair).

Learning Story 3.3 Jahez and Amy

Jahez goes to favourites and verbalizes as he goes: 'Look, in the house go!', 'Look it man clock!', 'Look, I break window' and as always after completing any activity an exultant 'I did it! I did it!' He discovers a new favourite (matching pairs of cards) and delivers a running commentary concluding with 'I did it, I did it!' and does it again. When Amy arrives there is a discussion about him giving the computer up to her:

Jahez: 'She doesn't want to.'
Amy: 'Yes, I do want to.'
Jahez: 'She wants to go in there [barn]?'
Amy: 'Yes I do want to go in there, I do.'
Jahez: 'OK.' He gets up and leaves.

Learning to read and write

The relationship between oracy and literacy

Learning to read and write is dependent upon learning to speak. Through learning to read children come to understand the way in which symbols represent speech. In addition, through literacy children gain an explicit knowledge to add to their considerable implicit knowledge about language. This explicit knowledge about language is expressed as language about language (called metalanguage – Clark, 1976) and includes the use of terms like 'word', 'sentence' and 'phrase' and, with respect to writing, 'letter', 'capital letter' and 'full stop'.

Linguistic awareness develops at both a surface and at a deep structure level. When learning spoken language with its focus on meaning, awareness of structure is nevertheless acquired as well as an understanding of the sound system and how it is represented by symbols, letters and groups of letters also needs to be developed before any real progress can be made in literacy.

Developing literacy: the Early Learning Goals

The *Curriculum Guidance for the Foundation Stage* (DfEE/QCA, 2000), in the Early Learning Goals, addresses the understandings, concepts and skills needed in order to be able to read and write. The order these are presented in the document is misleading and illogical for adults working in the Foundation Stage and they also assume considerable levels of subject knowledge. The document suggests that, by the time of entry to Year 1, children should be able to:

- Hear and say initial and final sounds in words, and short vowels in words.
- Link sounds to letters, naming and sounding the letters of the alphabet.
- Use their phonic knowledge to write simple regular words and make phonetically plausible attempts at more complex words.
- Explore and experiment with sounds, words and texts.
- Re-tell narratives in the correct sequence, drawing on language patterns of stories.
- Read a range of familiar and common words and simple sentences independently.
- Know that print carries meaning and, in English, is read from left to right and top to bottom.
- Show an understanding of the elements of stories, such as main character, sequence of events, and openings, and how information can be found in non-fiction texts to answer questions about where, who, why and how.
- Use their phonic knowledge to write simple regular words and make phonetically plausible attempts and more complex words.
- Attempt writing for different purposes, using features of different forms such as lists, stories and instructions.
- Write their own names and other things such as labels and captions, and begin to form simple sentences, sometimes using punctuation.
- Use a pencil and hold it effectively to form recognisable letters, most of which are correctly formed. (DfEE/QCA, 2000: 60, 62, 64, 66)

Continuity between *Curriculum Guidance*, the National Literacy Strategy and the National Curriculum for English at Key Stage 1

The *Curriculum Guidance for the Foundation Stage* (DfEE/QCA, 2000), the National Literacy Strategy and the National Curriculum offer guidance, continuity and progression on the teaching of literacy. They also acknowledge the interactive and complex nature of the literacy process. The curriculum content is consistent and coherent across all three documents, but there are different emphases regarding the concepts, understandings and skills to be acquired for pupils to become literate. The pedagogical approaches are at odds, however. Early years practitioners and teachers in nursery and reception classes will offer both literacy learning experiences and one-to-one or small-group teaching. In a reception class this approach will form the majority of the 'instructive experiences' (Siraj-Blatchford et al., 2002) although the whole class will be drawn together for short periods of shared reading and writing, for listening to stories and for discussion – but only then, most probably, towards the end of the first year in school. By Years 1 and 2 the pedagogy will consist mainly of group and class teaching. All through the Foundation Stage and Key Stage 1, practitioners will include in their planning the following:

- The provision of a literacy-rich environment.
- Literacy opportunities offered through play, particularly in a role-play area.
- The opportunities that books offer for developing spoken and written language and the links between the two.
- Further ways of making the links between oracy and literacy explicit.

As has been suggested, all three documents have at their heart the recognition of the interactive nature of the literacy process. This process is described below.

A researcher and literacy specialist, Marilyn Jaeger Adams (1990), was commissioned by the American government to review all the recent psychological research into the development of reading. Adams has described the literacy task as having several different processes that operate together in order for the individual to be able to read a text. There is evidence that children who experience teaching that plans to develop holistically both the 'top-down' (i.e. the meaning-making) and the 'bottom-up' (i.e. the decoding) skills of print and sound identification in a balanced programme learn to read and write more successfully and quickly than those who do not. We suggest that practitioners who are aware of the multifacetedness of the literacy process are more able to provide a variety of appropriate teaching approaches for their pupils.

The literacy process

Figure 3.3 shows clearly the way in which different aspects of the literacy process inter-relate so that fluent reading will occur. This is a helpful model for the adult to bear in mind when working with and supporting young children. From the diagram it can be seen that at the centre of the reading act lies meaning, which is the whole purpose of the activity. The context of the story or sentence allows the reader to support the task of decoding in order to predict what the words might be in the search for meaning. Illustrations have a hugely supportive role in this aspect of the processing. The use of context is described as the 'top-down' process of reading, and this can be encouraged when an adult reading a story to a child asks, for example, 'What do you think is going to happen next?' or 'What is he going to say to the Mother Bear when he gets home?'

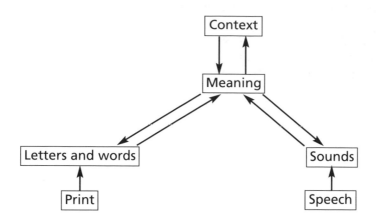

Figure 3.3 *'Top-down' and 'Bottom-up' processing skills*
Source: Adams (1990: 158)

The use of context cues also includes a prediction of what kind of word might be expected in the text according to the rules of language or grammar. In this instance, the adult might ask the child when she comes to an unknown word, 'What do you think will make sense here? What sort of a word will fit here?' This way of working, even with very young children, encourages them to realize the meaning-making activity that reading is. This modelling demonstrates to children what has to happen in the reader's own head when he or she is reading.

To learn to read, the child also has to be able to hear and distinguish between the different, individual sounds in words and to map them on to letters and groups of letters on the printed page (phonemic segmentation). Increasingly, this is recognized to be a crucial ability: it is an essential element of reading and writing that can be enhanced by practising breaking words into their component sounds, in different and fun ways. This aspect of reading is demonstrated in Figure 3.3 – which shows that awareness of both the visual aspects of print and the aural sounds of spoken language develop side by side and that they complement each other and are interrelated. The two processes are referred to as the 'bottom-up' or decoding skills. These skills can be developed not only through the adult sharing picture books with children and showing how meaning is made from the printed text and illustrations but also by directly pointing to words as they are read aloud, occasionally distinguishing between different words and pointing out those that are high frequency (i.e. key words), distinctive or highly patterned (for example, words that begin with the same letter and sound as a child's name and are therefore most easily identified by her).

Emergent literacy

There is research evidence that shows the extent of the rich store of knowledge about literacy the child acquires before schooling begins. This fascinating work demonstrates the understandings that children develop (from about the age of 6 months) incidentally and naturally from living in a print-filled world. Such learning is often shown most clearly through their writing or mark-making. The role of the adult in early years settings in the Foundation Stage through to Key Stage 1 is to capitalize on this early learning: to be sensitive to the stage that each child has reached and to be aware of the learning that has to occur for progress towards conventional literacy to take place.

Understanding the 'big picture' of literacy and the first steps on the path to fluent reading

Until very young children are aware of both the nature and purpose of literacy very little progress towards reading and writing can be made. This concept (referred to by researchers as understanding the 'big picture' of literacy) is key and is not referred to in the *Curriculum Guidance for the Foundation Stage* (DfEE/QCA, 2000). Great emphasis is placed on the code aspect of literacy at the expense of the fundamental, essential and motivating understandings. Acquiring the concept of the 'big picture' of literacy will ensure that a child has a positive attitude towards the meaning-making, enjoyable and purposeful aspects of books and print.

Alongside this, children need to understand and know the day-to-day uses of literacy. This can only be done by observing more experienced readers and writers who show how a text is used within the child's particular context. It is important, too, for educators to be aware that there are different ways of making meaning from texts, and the ones with which the child is most comfortable may be different from those presented in the setting in which a child is placed (see Heath, 1983).

Concepts about print

Many practitioners working with young children are familiar with the work of Marie Clay. Clay emphasizes that an essential step on the path towards reading is an understanding of the communicative function of print and, also, within that the realization, that text has its own conventions of format and layout (concepts about print). These understandings are often not given as much emphasis as the research evidence suggests. They might perhaps, therefore, be placed higher up on the list of Early Learning Goals. 'Concepts about print' are mentioned in the *Curriculum Guidance* (Early Learning Goals section) document where it is simply suggested that children, by the end of the Foundation Stage, will be able to: 'know that print carries meaning and, in English, is read from left to right and from top to bottom' (p. 62).

Concepts about print develop slowly during the early years through children being engaged in meaningful reading and writing activities that arise naturally at home, at pre-school or in the nursery, and often from the age of a few months old. Sharing books and stories is, of course, central to this process, as is making books and writing (and observing others writing) letters, cards and notes. When young children jointly use print with adults for various purposes, this constantly reinforces the need to be able to read and write in order to function effectively in the world. The use of commercially produced large texts and home-made 'big books' is invaluable for demonstrating to a small group of children that spoken language can be written down, that the marks and squiggles on the page always stand for the units of speech which can be read out and which always remain constant, and for demonstrating where the print starts and ends and the direction in which it runs. The essential understandings needed by children in order for them to be able to benefit from the more formal teaching of literacy are usefully listed by Hall (1987: 32–3). These are as follows:

- When we read we rely on print to carry the message.
- Print is different from pictures.
- We read and use books in a particular order – from front to back.
- We follow the print in a certain order: line by line, word by word.
- Books and print have a particular orientation.
- Print is made up of letters, words, punctuation and spaces.
- There are relationships between the words spoken and the print observed.
- There is a language associated with the activity of reading books: front, back, page, word, letter, etc.

Early childhood practitioners, as suggested earlier, are in an excellent position to support the development of these understandings whenever they work with children and so fully to use the many situations that naturally occur in the nursery, reception or Year 1.

The symbolic nature of the alphabet

The next intellectual leap that the child makes is the understanding that the letters of the alphabet are symbols and that they stand for the individual sounds that one can identify within words. Through many pleasurable encounters with print the child's awareness becomes further developed to appreciate that these letters (or groups of letters) not only represent the sounds in speech but can also be put together to make up words and that these, in turn, form sentences which can then be read to say something meaningful, or better still, interesting! This ability is an important indicator of success in reading once the child starts formal schooling. In fact, in a study that was conducted on 191 new school pupils, it was possible to predict with 80% accuracy which children would be reading by the end of their first year in the reception class from their assessment on entry to school (Riley, 1996). This skill is referred to in another of the statements under Early Learning Goals in the Curriculum Guidance document: 'link sounds to letters, naming and sounding the letters of the alphabet' (p. 60).

This is a hard-won understanding to develop and only a rich, varied and meaningful programme of literacy activities will ensure that the child's knowledge of the alphabet is a genuine one (rather than rote learned) and is secure enough to support the early stages of fluent reading. It is now recognized that simply teaching the alphabet to children is not an effective way to develop these understandings. It would seem that young literacy learners develop this knowledge most successfully when making their own connections, supported sensitively by an adult, in the task of reading and writing. Direct instruction is useful only when it is matched closely to the child's developing capability and it is grounded in stimulating, meaningful activity.

The teaching of literacy through writing activities, books and stories

The environment

A stimulating nursery or classroom environment provides a host of opportunities for the adult to model the use of written language as this naturally arises from activities and conversations. Every early years setting and classroom should include designated spaces for the teaching of literacy. A writing area shall be equipped with all types of writing and mark-making implements (pens, pencils, papers, envelopes, card and ready-made blank booklets) for writing stories and poems, and these should be enticingly presented and be accessible at all times to the children. A quiet area should also be provided that is furnished with cushions and a carpet and that contains a range of high-quality books for browsing through and sharing with adults.

Book-making

Adults need to demonstrate clearly the 'encoding' of speech into print by making books with and for children on current interests or topics – writing letters, notes, lists, news, messages, rhymes and stories on white boards, 'smart boards' or on easels, in notebooks and on paper. After modelling (either shared or guided) writing follows the explicit 'decoding' back to the children, pointing to each word (with clear emphasis) as the message is read and reread to make obvious the link between speech and text, sound and symbol.

When presenting books to the children, it is preferable to have a frequently changing display of high-quality, interesting and challenging texts that are in prime condition. These should have been chosen to represent a range of content, text features, illustrations and styles of writing. Large texts (both commercially produced and 'setting or class-made' big books) should be included. These books allow small groups of children to have a literacy learning experience every time books are shared, as they can be clearly seen and the way that print and its conventions work can also be shown. Any confusions that have arisen can also be clarified. Pointing to the words as they are read aloud takes practice but is so valuable that, after a couple of readings, the children will join in with the memorable phrases. Drawing attention to distinctive print features (e.g. 'Can anyone see a word that has the same ending/rhyme as this word?') highlights the important difference between a letter and a word, and frequently repeated words focus the children on the aspects of print to which they need to attend in order to read and write as their understanding gradually deepens. These teaching approaches mirror reading that is done at home and should be undertaken with as much pleasure, support and satisfaction.

Sharing story or non-fiction books provides an opportunity for the adult to monitor this developing awareness of text and print. For example, adults will note whether the children:

- listen attentively;
- talk and discuss effectively;
- follow the story line;
- ask questions about the text;
- listen to and add to the contributions of others;
- show ability to predict what might happen next;
- offer alternative endings; and
- have a growing appreciation of character and plot.

Shared reading using a large text: *Ten in a Bed* by Penny Dale

The use of the delightful book *Ten in a Bed* (written and illustrated by Penny Dale) enables both aspects of the literacy process to be learnt, the 'top down' and 'bottom up' processes, in a meaningful context. And of course, it demonstrates to children the pleasure and purpose of reading. Shared reading can occur with a small group (which is most likely in an early years setting) or a whole class as pupils move through their Reception Year. The teacher begins with the 'big book' placed next to her on a stand. She points to each printed word as she reads aloud using a pointer.

Before beginning the story, she introduces the book to the children, saying, for example: 'Look . . . this is the cover of the book. This is the picture and here's the title *Ten in a Bed* they both give you a clue about the story. Here's the name of the author, Penny Dale. She wrote the story.' The teacher may ask the children to speculate about what might happen in this story, reinforcing the idea that readers come to a text with expectations of content. This enables the children to make sense of the text, to anticipate vocabulary and to predict both the sentence structures and the vocabulary. By turning over the pages to the beginning of the story and commentating on what she is doing, the teacher continues to reinforce basic bibliographic understandings of how books work.

Concepts about print

The conventions and concepts about print are demonstrated as the story is read. The repetitive and rhythmic aspects of the language combine to aid aural and visual memory and invite the children to join in: 'There were ten in the bed . . . They all rolled over. Ted fell out.' This reinforces the message that it is the print which is read and that the pattern and structure of the words suggest the way the next few sentences will run. It also indicates what the next word in the sequence is likely to be (i.e. the text teaches readers how to use semantic cues). Pupils develop the concept of one-to-one correspondence – that language is made up of separate words and that words are made up of groups of letters on a page.

Developing the use of semantic cues

Semantic or meaning cues are developed through talking about the content of the text. The teacher, perhaps, may pause and ask questions, such as:

- 'Who's left in the bed?'
- 'Who do you think will fall out next?'
- 'What do you think will happen when they've all fallen out of the bed? Let's read on and see, . . . shall we!'

Demonstrating the importance and use of phonic cues

The ability to identify and distinguish different sounds within words is aided by taking a simple consonant/vowel/consonant ('cvc') word from the text, such as *ten*. The children read the word and their teacher reminds them that the word can be phonemically segmented into three separate sounds and then blended back together. Why this ability is so important in reading is then shown by asking the children to generate words which rhyme with ten (e.g. *men, hen, pen, then, when*) and, by using magnetic letters, how new words are created by changing of the first phoneme and its associated grapheme. Knowing how to use detailed knowledge of the English alphabetic system is an essential step if pupils are to read and spell independently – it is in this way they become successful users of written language.

Establishing sight vocabulary

A key sight vocabulary of high-frequency words, particularly those which are not phonically regular, can be focused upon in the context of the book as they arise (e.g. *one, said, out*). If written on separate pieces of card and identified both in and out of context, they are made more memorable.

Linking reading to writing

Finally, the text is used as a model for shared writing. The same textual and sentence structure will be used as in *Ten in a Bed* but this time it is the class members who will be falling out of bed. The production of a class book, written and illustrated by the pupils themselves and integrated into the reading resources of the classroom, is the final outcome of the teaching sequence.

Using environmental print to support print awareness

Environmental print can be capitalized upon to teach pupils the value of literacy and how print works. The adults need to draw the children's attention to:

- labels;
- notices;
- instructions;
- packages and labels in the class shop or play corner;
- charts of helpers, days of the week, equipment;
- the words printed on the walls that are personally meaningful to individual pupils; and
- the print in the outside environment by going for a 'looking-for-print walk'.

Environmental print, with its mysterious, anonymous author, can be puzzling. Children need to understand that print in a setting is composed and written by a writer just as it is in stories. This awareness can be developed when practitioners and children compose together the environmental print for their own classrooms – for example, deciding how to label cupboards, what titles to put on class displays and instructions over the sink for washing up paint pots.

The use of children's names can assist print awareness

The adults in the playgroup or nursery can teach letter recognition in the ways shown in Figure 3.4.

Providing opportunities to write enables children to appreciate the links between speech and print

Staff in early years settings can encourage the early writing of their pupils by the methods shown in Figure 3.5.

Developing sound (phonological) awareness

Developing the youngest children's phonological awareness is encouraged in the Curriculum Guidance (DfEE/QCA, 2000: 60): 'hear and say initial and final sounds in words, and short vowel sounds within words.' In their observations, adults need to identify those children who are demonstrating the ability to 'segment phonemically' – i.e. those who are able to distinguish sounds within

- Substituting the names of characters in stories with the names of the children in the group.
- Encouraging children to identify words that begin with the same letter of the alphabet, as Darren's name, etc.
- Writing captions under paintings (e.g. 'Amanda has drawn her cat' or 'Bill has painted his fire engine').
- Drawing children's attention to their friends' names with labels (e.g. on coat pegs, shelves, pictures, models and belongings).
- Displaying a photograph of each of the children, with his or her name and what he or she likes doing.
- Making books about the pupils and their favourite foods, toys and activities (e.g. *William likes Cocoa Pops for Breakfast, Sally likes Weetabix* and *Khadia likes Shreddies*, etc.).

Figure 3.4 *Teaching print awareness*

- Recognizing when children demonstrate that they know the difference between drawing and writing.
- Responding to children's writing, making it explicit what they know (e.g. 'You are clever – you know that "bus" begins with a *b*').
- Celebrating children's efforts by displaying their attempts.
- Sharing real writing with children (e.g. letters, cards, notes, lists).
- Suggesting that children write for genuine purposes (e.g. make a card for someone who is ill or for a birthday, or a list of cooking ingredients).
- Discussing the writing with children, pointing out print details and encouraging them to read it.
- Retelling by drawing and/or writing a story.
- Making a class story for the wall – the children do the illustrations and the adult writes the text.

Figure 3.5 *Methods to encourage early writing*

words. Children who are in the early stages of acquiring this important skill are able to distinguish aurally words that rhyme from those that do not (e.g. *h-at, c-at, r-at, h-ad*). In the next stage they are able to supply a rhyming word for a word (e.g. *h-en* with *p-en*). Next in the sequence, the children are usually able to

- A variety of rhymes and verses, learning them by heart and matching the spoken word to the printed word.

- A poem or rhyme of the week printed on the easel, for reading, rereading and chanting.

- Sharing 'big books' with distinctively patterned and rhyming text. Several readings are a valuable reinforcement and provide the opportunity to join in.

- Strings of words that rhyme with particular words during writing or reading activities (e.g. *rod, pod, cod, tod, hod*). Even thinking of nonsense words can be fun and emphasizes that language is a flexible system.

- Opportunities to break words into the beginning and end sounds (e.g. *M-um, b-ook*), particularly when writing.

- Activities such as the game 'I spy' and 'All those with a name beginning with *T* can fetch their snack'.

Figure 3.6 *Developing children's phonological awareness*

differentiate those words which begin with the same sound from those that do not (e.g. *m-an, m-ad, m-en* but *p-en*). Finally, and after some experience of reading, the child can split a word into all its component sounds or phonemes (e.g. *ch-i-ck-en*). To develop their phonological awareness, children in early years settings need to experience those things listed in Figure 3.6.

The following stage of print and sound awareness is developed through activities such as the adult explicitly mapping the sound (phoneme) on to the written symbol (grapheme) when writing the daily message or sentence for the group. Children are able to learn about the inconsistencies of the English alphabetical system if given the appropriate experiences, support and encouragement. The wise use of praise will encourage early attempts, will make explicit to the learners what they know and will provide further opportunities for them to progress. Very young children working and playing in this type of setting will be 'scaffolded' into developing as speakers and listeners, readers and writers.

Provision which aims to develop the concepts, understandings and skills essential for progress in language and literacy in the Foundation Stage

Enabling young children to become fluent communicators in both spoken and written language is enhanced when they are taught by adults who have a sound grasp of the underlying processes involved and who are able to integrate these into a coherent and developmentally appropriate programme. The planning framework in Figure 3.7 aims to help adults do this. With it is given an example of a reception teacher's planning for speaking and listening, reading and writing, for one morning.

Planning framework

Within the THEME or TOPIC there need to be opportunities for:

- speaking and listening;
- understanding the 'big picture' of literacy;
- acquiring 'concepts about print';
- consolidating letter identification;
- developing phonological awareness; and
- developing grapheme/phoneme (letter/sound) association.

A worked example: the theme or topic of nursery rhymes

Mary, Mary, Quite Contrary – a large poster of nursery rhyme is on the easel. Role-play area converted into a 'garden centre' following a visit to the local one – this has a sign outside. One table consists of children decorating large/jumbo-sized seed packets (8 or 9 inches) with silver cockle shells and pretty maids. Display area/nature table of a garden with different varieties of flowers. Children working in shallow sand trays making gardens with shells and twigs.

Opportunities for speaking and listening
Discussion about planting primulas in pots, sowing seeds and what plants need to grow.

Opportunities for understanding the 'big picture' about literacy
Display of gardening books/stories about growing. One enlarged text (*Jack and the Beanstalk*) is on a stand with a pointer for children to 'read' to each other.

Opportunities for acquiring 'concepts about print'/one-to-one word matching
Smaller versions of the *Mary, Mary, Quite Contrary* rhyme (A4 size) are in book corner for children to listen to on tape, pointing to words as it is sung. These also go home for practice and keeping. Children decorate the black and white versions.

Opportunities for consolidating letter identification
As children come into the classroom they put their names into two hoops for registration or 'Who is here?'. One hoop has a notice 'All those whose names begin with *m*'. And another hoop has 'All those whose names don't begin with *m*'. Parents/carers help children to select if necessary.

Opportunities for developing phonological awareness
Shared reading occupies 5 or 6 minutes reading/singing the nursery-rhyme poster on the easel with different children finding the rhyming words. Children identify the onset and rhyme, hearing and looking at the letter patterns.

Opportunities for developing grapheme/phoneme (letter/sound) association
A group of six children working with the teacher 'write' descriptions of the flower their seeds will grow into on the back of the decorated seed packets (decorated the day before). Much support is given/much is discussed about the kind of things which are on the back of packets. The teacher/child scaffold writing. Some are at a very early pre-communicative stage, some are further along. They are given appropriate help with phonemic segmentation and then with mapping the sound on to the symbol.

At the end of the hour some children show their packets and 'read' their descriptions. The teacher points to some of the more conventional attempts and makes explicit what is accurate. Much is praised.

Figure 3.7 *Planning framework for language and literacy in the Foundation Stage*

Drawing the strands together in Key Stage 1: writing a caption book about favourite toys

The following example demonstrates how a class teacher draws together all the separate but inter-related understandings and skills involved in the literacy process into a lesson at Key Stage 1. Not only does the practitioner take into account the concepts, understandings and skills but also the specific teaching objectives and range of text types stipulated in the *National Literacy Strategy Framework for Teaching*. The following is a detailed description of a lesson in the first term of Year 1.

Before the lesson

A literacy lesson does not exist in isolation; it is built upon previous learning and is related to what has gone before and leads on to what will follow. The Literacy Hour in a Year 1 classroom described here is located in a concrete and real experience.

Creating the context

The theme of 'Toys' was used by one teacher to plan work across several curriculum areas. Although the following account is focused on literacy, the theme of 'Toys' also provided the basis for her art, mathematics and technology teaching. Non-fiction texts, non-chronological reports and captions, in particular, have been used in a sequence of literacy lessons over a period of two weeks. The differences between these non-fiction texts in function and form from narrative texts have been discussed. The central focus for the sequence of work (and to which most of the teaching and learning relates) is a display of 'Our Favourite Toys'. The children each brought in a favourite toy (or a picture of one), as has the teacher.

Shared reading

In the first week of this sequence of work, shared reading has taken place. The teacher and the children have been reading information texts about toys, with a particular focus on one – *Toys around the World* (Longman Book Project). The content and the structure of the book have been explicitly discussed in order to show how these can be used for information retrieval, along with the reasons why contents, indexes, page numbers and page headings are necessary features of a non-fiction text.

The children have been introduced to the idea that the book will be used as a model for their own writing of picture captions. Their awareness has been raised about the function of picture captions and about the fact that in *Toys around the World*, they generally consist of two sentences. The first sentence tells the reader what is in the picture and the second sentence gives the reader some extra information.

Planning for the lesson

The previous day the children carefully completed an observational drawing of their favourite toy. It was intended that these drawings would be made into the class book entitled *Our Favourite Toys*, along with the accompanying captions. The teacher has three literacy-teaching objectives in mind for the next session:

1 *At text level* – to structure and compose picture captions using two related sentences.
2 *At sentence level* – to write and punctuate two simple sentences, each sentence containing one main idea.
3 *At word level* – to support pupils' competence in using phonic strategies for spelling.

The teacher chooses two groups to work with for focused guided writing. Before the lesson, all the necessary resources are collected together: the shared reading book, a flip chart and pens, the teacher's own favourite toy (a teddy bear) and paper and pencils for the pupils. Finally, she briefs the classroom assistant who will support some of the pupils during the lesson.

The lesson itself

Introduction – recalling previous teaching and learning At the beginning of the lesson, the teacher introduces the session to the children. She reminds them what has happened in previous lessons and refers to the big book. In particular, they review what they have learnt about picture captions. She makes explicit the teaching objective and the practical outcome expected by the end of the lesson. They read again examples of picture captions and discuss simple sentences and the way that sentences are punctuated. The teacher reinforces the idea of a simple sentence through the repetition of the words 'one idea equals one sentence'. The first half of the lesson is spent with the whole class working with the teacher.

Teacher demonstration of writing The teacher shows the children her favourite toy and explains that she will write two sentences for a caption for this toy whilst they watch and listen. As she writes her sentences, she gives a commentary explaining the thinking and the decision-making that a writer needs to undertake:

> My first sentence needs to tell the reader what my toy is so I'm going to write 'This is my teddy bear . . .' No, I think I need to say whose teddy it is rather than *my*. I'll write 'This is Ms Smith's teddy bear'. That's my first idea so it's my first sentence. I'll just read it again to make sure it makes sense. Now I'm going to write my second sentence which needs to give some important extra information about my toy. What I really like about my teddy is it's lovely soft fur so I'm going to write 'It has soft, brown fur'. Right, that's my two sentences. Do they do what I want them to? Let's read them together and see. Have I remembered to put in two capital letters and two full stops? Good.

During this process the teacher is demonstrating how the whole text is built up through composing the sentences and is helping the children to understand what the writer has to do in order to make the meaning clear to an intended and absent reader. She may also stop to ask the children to help her with the spelling of one or two of the words to reinforce phonic strategies:

> This word 'soft'. Who can help me to spell it? Let's count the phonemes that we can hear: s . . . o . . . f . . . t. How many is that? Five? Let's count them again together to check, shall we? How many do you think there are now James? Four? Good. What are they again? Now which letter do we use to write each one?

Teacher scribing and shaping of children's ideas The teacher then selects another toy to give the pupils a chance to compose two sentences about it before they compose their sentences for their own toys. To help them do this she first uses paired discussion: 'I'd like you to turn to the person sitting next to you and decide on the two sentences we could write for this toy. Let's read mine first again to help you.'

The pupils talk in pairs to assist in the composition of a caption. This gives the teacher and the classroom assistant an opportunity to support those pupils who need it; all pupils have now become actively involved in embedding the learning. After a short time the teacher chooses one or two pairs to report on what they have decided. The teacher writes another picture caption on the flip chart based on their suggestions, and she is able to pick up any errors or misconceptions. For example:

Jack, you said 'This is Ahmed's football and you kick it to play football'. That's one long sentence with two ideas in it. We need one sentence for each idea. What's the first one? 'This is Ahmed's football.' Good, let me write that down. What do we need to show that is the end of the first sentence? So the second sentence will be . . .? Yes. Let me write down what you said – 'You kick it to play football.' That's the second idea so that is the second sentence. We now need to make sure that both sentences have a capital letter and a full stop.

There are opportunities for demonstrating how redrafting can occur. Again, one of the examples is reread and the pupils consider if it can be improved by adding or changing a word, or whether there are any technical (features such as spelling or punctuation) to be addressed.

Supported composition The teacher now asks the pupils, again in their pairs, to decide on the two sentences they will write about their own favourite toy. Their partners listen carefully and check whether they have composed a picture caption that consists of two simple sentences. Again, the adults present can use this as an opportunity to support particular children in their oral composition. Some of these are shared with the whole class and problems are dealt with or used as the basis for further teaching, if necessary. By this time the children have had the opportunity to see and compose several captions and have a sense of what they are going to write. There have been opportunities to show how phonic strategies for spelling can be used as the children are writing. The considerable emphasis on oral composition before writing ensures that the majority of children will be able to approach the writing task confidently and independently.

Independent and guided practice The teacher invites the children to write their own picture captions. Most write these independently and share them with their original partner to see if improvements might be made. During this time the teacher gathers together a smaller group of five children who she knows need additional work to transform their ideas into simple sentences. The first guided writing group is encouraged to do some more oral work on composing sentences so that they are confident about what they want to say before putting pencil to paper. She leaves them to work independently and she works with three other children. They each compose sentences but need support in order to represent the sounds they can hear in words as they spell them. This is the second guided writing group.

During this time the classroom assistant is ensuring that other pupils in the class who need support receive it. This prevents interruptions as the teacher works with the guided group.

Plenary: reflection and evaluation Ten minutes before the end of the lesson, the pupils gather together as a whole class. The teacher has chosen two or three children to read aloud what they have written and to explain why. This is a regular part of the classroom routine and it enables pupils to deepen their understanding of their learning through discussion with their peers – in other words, this provides an opportunity to embed learning by talking and listening. The teacher reinforces the teaching objectives and the class are able to reflect on their own written drafts in the light of hearing other examples. Later, in a handwriting lesson, they make a fair copy and arrange their pictures with the accompanying captions. The completed book is enjoyed during shared reading and placed on display next to the toys. It will be read by every class member and to every visitor for the foreseeable future!

In this lesson we have shown how a skilled teacher engages children in a demonstration of the way language is used for specific purposes. The practitioner has taken her young pupils forward to become producers of language in the context of a rich, oral exchange. This is, at heart, practical – it is focused on a purposeful task with a defined, if general, audience. As a more experienced language user, the teacher models and talks through the act of writing. The pupils are shown clearly what writers do and, in time and after practice, they will add this to their own linguistic repertoire.

Conclusion

Increasingly, research findings indicate the importance of the first years of education. Children's ability to use spoken and written language fluently and with confidence and for a range of purposes enables them to access at an early age what education has to offer. The adults working in early years settings and classrooms have both the opportunity and responsibility to affect the future learning of their pupils in a far-reaching and powerful way.

Suggested further reading

Riley, J.L. (1999) *The Teaching of Reading at KS 1 and Before*. Cheltenham: Stanley Thornes.
Riley, J.L. and Reedy, D. (2000) *Developing Writing for Different Purposes: Teaching about Genre in the Early Years*. London: Paul Chapman Publishing.

References

Adams, M.J. (1990) *Beginning to Read: Thinking and Learning about Print*. Cambridge, MA: MIT Press.
Brooker, E. and Siraj-Blatchford, J. (2002) 'Click on Miaow!', How children aged 3 and 4 experience the nursery computer', *Contemporary Issues in Early Childhood*, 3(2):251–72.
Clark, M.M. (1976) *Young Fluent Readers*. London: Heinemann Educational.

Clay, M.M. (1998) *By Different Paths to Different Outcomes*. York, ME: Stenhouse Publishers.
Crystal, D. (1987) *The Cambridge Encyclopaedia of Language*. Cambridge: Cambridge University Press.
Cummins, J. (1978) 'Linguistic interdependence and the educational development of bilingual children', *Review of Educational Research*, 49: 222–51.
Cummins, J. (1984) *Bilingualism and Special Education: Issues in Assessment and Pedagogy*. Clevedon: Multilingual Matters.
Dale, P. (1998) *Ten in a Bed*. London: Walker Books.
DES. (1989) *Aspects of Primary Education: The Education of Children under Five*. London: HMSO.
DfES/QCA (2000) *Curriculum Guidance for the Foundation Stage*. London: QCA.
Hall, N. (1987) *The Emergence of Literacy*. Sevenoaks: Hodder & Stoughton.
Halliday, M.A.K. (1975) *Learning How to Mean. Explorations in the Development of Language*. London: Arnold.
Heath, S.B. (1983) *Ways with Words: Language, Life and Work in Communities and Classrooms*. Cambridge: Cambridge University Press.
ILEA (1990) *Language and Power*. London: Harcourt Brace Jovanovich.
Raban, B. (2000) 'Talking to think, learn and teach', in P.G. Smith (ed.) *Talking Classrooms: Shaping Children's Learning through Oral Instruction*. Newark, DE: International Reading Association.
Riley, J.L. (1996) *The Teaching of Reading: The Development of Literacy in the Early Years of School*. London: Paul Chapman Publishing.
Rosen, M. and Oxenbury, H. (1989) *We're Going on a Bear Hunt*, London: Walker Books.
Siraj-Blatchford, I., Sylva, K., Muttock, S., Gilden, R. and Bell, D. (2002) *Researching Effective Pedagogy in the Early Years. DfES Research Brief* 356. London: DfES.
Snow, C.E. (1991) 'The theoretical basis for relationships between language and literacy development', *Journal of Research in Childhood Education*, 6: 30–46.
Wells, C.G. (1987) *The Meaning Makers: Children: Learning Language and Using Language to Learn*. London: Hodder & Stoughton.
Whitehead, M. (1997) *The Development of Language and Literacy*. London: Hodder & Stoughton.
Wilkinson, A. (1982) *Language and Education*. Oxford: Oxford University Press.

Useful Addresses

Books for Keeps (children's book magazine. Published six times a year, purchased by subscription only): 6, Brightfield Road, Lee, London SE12 8QF.

Madeleine Lindley (books for children and their teachers): Book Centre, Broadgate, Broadway Business Park, Chadderton, Oldham, Greater Manchester OL9 9XA. Tel: 0161 683 4400; fax: 0161 682 6801.

Language Matters (journal of the Centre for Language in Primary Education. Published three times a year. Subscription includes CLPE library membership): CLPE, London Borough of Southwark, Webber Row, London SE1 8QW.

4

Mathematical development and education

Carol Aubrey and Patti Barber

> *Developing mathematical ideas and methods to solve practical problems.*
> (QCA/DfEE, 1999: 31)

> *. . . empirical investigation of young children's constructions of mathematical knowledge provides both a starting point for designing an appropriate curriculum and a means of critical analysis of existing curricula based on logical analysis of subject content. It remains now for us to consider the development of instruction by the creation of a curriculum content and sequence that both reflects and advances the structure of children's existing forms of representation, problem-solving and knowledge.*
> (Aubrey, 1997: 88)

Introduction

Since September 2000, for the first time early years practitioners working with 3–5 year-olds have been directed towards a more subject-orientated curriculum and they are asked to consider the *Curriculum Guidance for the Foundation Stage* (DfEE/QCA, 2000) as they plan the provision for their young pupils. With regard to promoting the child's development and mathematical thinking in particular, this document suggests that practitioners should give attention to:

- many different activities, some of which will draw out the mathematical learning in other activities, including observing numbers and patterns in the environment and daily routines;
- practical activities underpinned by children's developing communication skills;

- activities that are imaginative and enjoyable;
- help for those children who use a means of communication other than spoken English in developing and understanding specific mathematical language;
- opportunities to observe, assess and plan the next stage in children's learning;
- relevant training to improve practitioners' knowledge, skills and understanding. (DfEE/QCA, 2000: 68)

We go on to discuss the extent to which these Early Learning Goals issued to all early years settings are in concert with the thinking in the field. Accordingly, what we propose to do first is to examine current research on young children's early mathematical development and, secondly, to consider the basis and framework of the early mathematics curriculum, which might be constructed on the basis of this. This chapter focuses on the learning and teaching of mathematics across the early years from birth to around 7 years. In order to do this, we examine the evidence concerning young children's mathematical experiences in the home and in out-of-home settings, through the pre-school years and into the first stage of formal schooling, as well as providing telling examples of those experiences, both formal and informal.

How Children Begin to Think Mathematically

Desforges (2000: 2) has proposed that educational research should be judged, first, in terms of its disciplined quality and, secondly, in terms of its impact. He suggested that teachers want from research:

- standard and stable models of learning;
- coherent, organized, well-established findings;
- vibrant working examples of success; and
- research results converted, as far as possible, into the technologies of education – that is, into curriculum or other pedagogic materials.

Our intention here is to present the reader with robust models of mathematical learning which are based on sound evidence, supported by exemplar vignettes, as well as to consider the implications for practice.

Desforges (2000: 6) goes on to suggest that the intention of research should be to solve immediate practical problems whilst, at the same time, seeking to obtain basic understanding of fundamental processes. The research method of choice is the so-called 'design experiment', collaboratively planned and progressively adapted to meet desired goals through partnership between teachers and researchers. Such interventions are pursued in the authentic settings of classroom life, and practices are validated through observation and the collection of quantitative and qualitative data. We hope, therefore, that this chapter will serve as a stimulus to practice in this way.

Reforming teaching practice, we think, is taken to result from transformations of the participant's understandings of the basic assumptions of teaching and learning. Research assists in identifying principled ways of accomplishing these transformations. The role of theory, in this case, is to assist in clarifying alternative practices (Greeno *et al.*, 1996: 40). One of us tried out this way of working with a reception class teacher (for 4–5-year-olds), using Dutch realistic mathematical theory as a source and a starting point for the construction of an early mathematics curriculum. This seemed to work very well.

Background

As detailed elsewhere, one of us (Aubrey, 2001) has suggested that much research on young children's early mathematical development has used experimental approaches which may have ignored or at least underemphasized the context of the young child's learning as a source of knowledge and undervalued the extent to which mathematics is a socially defined and constructed activity. The way children respond to the mathematics presented to them will be influenced by the way they define and respond to the social situation in which it is presented. As Nunes and Bryant (1996) have argued, the challenge for us, as teachers, is to help children form a view of mathematics that will enable them to bring their rich understanding of mathematical experiences into the classroom. 'Doing maths' from this perspective means that we have to take as much account of *how* children learn mathematics as *what* they learn. This constitutes a new way of thinking about what mathematics is and how children acquire it. It means that we have to try to uncover and document the social processes collectively produced by children with adults in the many different and interwoven contexts of their lives. It also suggests a number of principles which, in fact, have been derived from Dutch realistic mathematics educators (Treffers, 1991):

- Formal knowledge can be developed from children's informal strategies.
- Teaching in formal contexts should not be isolated from the real world but should relate to that world by using the knowledge and experience children have of all kinds of mathematical problems.
- This process should be as natural as possible and children should contribute to the teaching/learning process.

- Allowing children to come up with their own informal mathematical tools to help organize and solve a problem located in a real-life situation helps to lead them from their perceived world to the world of formal mathematics.
- Assisting children to establish strong and meaningful 'models' of the real-world contexts in their lives, which can create a bridge to their informal knowledge and a point of departure to a more formal, standardized manner of operating through constructive contributions of the children themselves.

This means that we shall need to do a number of things:

- Look at the nature of young children's mathematical experience right back to the start of life.
- Take note of the way adults support children's mathematical development in different kinds of learning environments and what we can learn from it.
- Tease out the salient features of mathematical learning environments for children under 3 who may be either in the home or in alternative, out-of-home provision; for children of 3–5 years who are working through the Foundation Stage; and for children of 6–7 years who are in the first stage of formal learning.
- And, perhaps, most important of all, pay particular attention to the *transitions* between these contexts of learning and, hence, their 'match' from the child's point of view.

Right back to the start

To capture the child's point of view, it is essential to go right back to the start of life. Psychologists such as Alison Gopnik, Andrew Meltzoff and Pat Kuhl (1999) have shown that sophisticated technology can vastly improve the quality and amount of observational research that has been carried out with even quite tiny babies (Jeni Riley has discussed this work in more detail in Chapter 1). Let us just say here that, by using video recording and computers, researchers can exploit what babies do naturally – looking and sucking – as well as watching, moving, imitating and emphasizing, to enrich our knowledge of the earliest preverbal stages of development. This suggests that, right from the start, babies are thinking, observing and reasoning, building models which are then refined in the light of subsequent experience.

An American researcher, Karen Wynn (1998), for instance, has gathered a significant amount of evidence to support her view that babies come into the world already equipped with number concepts and that they can represent number across a range of different kinds of entities, physical objects and patterns, regardless of colour, size or configuration and perceived through visual or auditory modes. Using what people call the 'habituation method' she noticed that infants 'habituate' – that is, get bored and lose interest in a changing but predictable array of Mickey Mouse puppets but look longer at unpredictable changes. For instance, if infants were shown an enactment of one mouse added to another mouse which, after being hidden from view, unexpectedly 'becomes' one mouse or three mice, they stared longer than if the quantity of mice remained as expected – in this case, two mice. At around 5 months, infants can only manage quantities of no greater than two or three but some time between 8 and 13 months this will increase to four or five. Wynn argued that infants are able not only to represent the number in small arrays but also to engage in a process of numerical reasoning to determine the numerical relationship that holds between different quantities.

Others, such as Catherine Sophian (1998), have not accepted this interpretation which amounts to a preverbal counting mechanism and argued for a more general processing or 'subitizing' model by which adults, as well as children, are observed to enumerate small arrays of objects. Whatever the mechanism, what is important for early maths educators to note is that even quite small babies are able to 'recognize' or otherwise determine the quantity of small amounts and that this capacity is distinct from the verbal or 'rote' counting which is a mark of the early language acquisition stage. Importantly, it means not only that we need to take care *how* we map counting words on to these previously established, infant numerical abilities but we need to take very great care of the way this early quantitative thinking is represented with fingers, structured mathematical apparatus or, indeed, any intermediary physical objects, lest we confuse and impede learning. Children's early visual recognition of small configurations can be later exploited, however, through the use of dice and dominoes for children's board and card games, as well as playground equivalents, which provide a real, game-like context for tapping, counting and otherwise mapping on to children's existing early enumeration strategies. But that is running too far ahead with the story. Next, it is important to look closely at children's early linguistic and interactive experience with adults, as Riley and Reedy have already done in Chapter 3. If we are to understand early mathematical learning we need to examine the social and discursive practice of the home and early out-of-home setting.

When we were very young: an awareness of number

In order to investigate the toddler's evolving experiences of learning and behaving in respect of mathematical activities and, especially, at key times of transition, very detailed observations of young children and the contexts in which they interact, including speech, activity and specific resources, must be carried out. In general, such studies are small scale yet time-consuming. They can demand a timescale which occupies many months and sometimes years of working within the contexts being examined. They may require gathering data from different sources (for instance, audio-tape, video-tape, parental diary and detailed field notes) in order to capture the different perspectives of parent, child and researcher, and to do justice to the complexity of the enterprise. Even so, there is always the element of luck or opportunism on the part of the researcher. The 21-one-month-old grand-daughter of one of us raced into the sitting room with an 'Emu' puppet, shouting 'one, two, nine . . .' giving little clue as to where and in what context she had acquired this string or what it meant to her. Yet, the following day at tea-time, she sat silently pushing banana pieces on to her fork and then, triumphantly, held up the fork, squealing 'two 'nanas!' showing clearly that she was able to map the number words she had learnt to the quantities that she was manipulating. Her sister, at a similar time, was observed racing around the garden grabbing strawberries from a basket her mother had left carelessly on the garden table, shouting 'two strawberries!' What was going on here? How has this early mapping of number words on to small quantities come about?

Durkin et al. (1986), in a longitudinal study of ten infants' spontaneous reference to numbers and very early counting, watched their conversational turn-taking with adults, at monthly intervals from 9 to 24 months and, thereafter, at three-monthly intervals until 36 months. Below 2 years, the age of the little girls described above, number words were used either singly in conversation or as part of standard expressions, such as 'one, two, three, go . . .' Between 21 and 30 months recitation of the number sequence in the context of turn-taking was observed to constitute a substantial proportion of number word utterances. In the second and third year, young children used number words incidentally or in conversation rather than in the context of generating a number string. Counting expanded at this stage but only one set of objects at a time. The most frequently produced words were 'one', 'two', 'three' and 'four', and mothers used these more often than their children so they had many opportunities for exposure to the first four numbers and, occasionally, to larger numbers. This is an interesting finding given our earlier examination of infants' preverbal 'counting' of small amounts. Numbers were being used:

- in nursery rhymes, stories and songs (in expressions such as 'ready, one, two, three . . .');
- in the recitation of number strings ('count them, look, one, two, three . . .');
- in the repetition and clarification of cardinal number (how many cakes . . . one, two, three . . .');
- in alternating strings between mother and child ('let's count again, one, your turn, two . . .'); and
- in incidental uses (such as 'How old are you?' and 'What is the number of the house that you live at?').

The Nature of Effective Support from Adults

This study revealed that children encountered numbers and counting in the course of their interactions with their parents from before the emergence of language and through the period of early language development. Interestingly, these young children encountered number and counting routines in a number of ways but these declined considerably in the child's third year. At the same time as the mother's number and counting interactions declined, however, the number of words used by the child increased with age.

Others have found little evidence of mathematical conversation between young children of 3–4 years and their mothers, which may tie in with Durkin's finding that mothers' interventions diminish at this age. Martin Hughes (1986) concluded that there were relatively few conversations in the Tizard and Hughes (1984) transcripts, where mothers were explicitly using the language of arithmetic. Valerie Walkerdine (1982; 1988) also drew upon the Tizard dataset in order to compare the social discourse practices of home and pre-school setting and noted marked similarities. She classified certain sorts of tasks in relation to practices involving number as *instrumental*, where the mother's main goal was the accomplishment of a task in which numbers were an incidental feature; and *pedagogic*, where number was the explicit focus of a purposeful activity to teach and practise counting. Both these main parental activities have been identified by the Durkin study. Walkerdine went on to distinguish between formal teaching situations where the adult adopted a pedagogic role and the more participative role observed to be taken by a mother, as helpmate and equal participant, in which the adult both joined in and extended the child's knowledge, thus recognizing the pedagogic importance of the activities.

Matthews and Matthews (1978) emphasized that such practices were embedded in activities involving active manipulation of objectives which provided opportunities for classification – to take a different example, using such terms as 'big', 'little', 'small', 'bigger', 'smaller' or 'biggest'. This reminds us to take a broad social perspective, taking account not just of the language being used but the social practices themselves and the materials or 'tools' which embody them. Walkerdine also recognized that mothers engaged in pedagogic discourse which involved size relations but, as in the case of number, she stressed that discrimination of size might not be the main objective but simply the focus for imparting information relating to size. Furthermore, like Durkin, she drew attention to the fact that discourse practices in the home might not always be adult-initiated, as children themselves also initiated counting sequences quite

Learning Story 4.1 Child of 21 months, playing in sand

Mother to child: 'You put that in and count . . . one.'
Child to mother: 'Two.'
Mother to child: 'What comes after? Eh?'
Child to mother: 'Three.'
Mother to child: 'That's right. One, two, three.'
Child to mother: 'Two.'

Learning Story 4.2
Child of 30 months creates repeating patterns whilst mother prepares tea

Child to self: 'Two, three. Two, two, three. No. Two, two, three. Two, two, three . . .'

spontaneously – another important point to be borne in mind by early educators who may be thinking of setting up both adult- and child-initiated mathematical activities in the pre-school context.

In Chapter 3 Riley and Reedy have already drawn attention to the importance of Gordon Wells' (1976–1982) study of mother–child conversations in the home and the lessons to be drawn for early educators. One of us (Aubrey et al., 2000) was recently involved in an examination of the Wells' transcripts from a mathematical point of view which correspondence with the author established had not been done. The interest in this dataset for us was its potential in generating evidence of home influences on the course of numerical development. Interestingly, an initial scrutiny of a set of transcripts for 39-month-old toddlers in conversation with their mothers showed mothers supporting children's counting of objects, pictures and playing cards – again, most commonly, to four but sometimes to six, seven and eight and even, in one instance, to twelve and above. There were also instances of children counting themselves, though usually from only one to three and with one or two references to shape and position. Mathematical references to 'in front of', 'bigger/smaller than', 'less' and 'more' to describe position, size and quantity were extracted, as were references to comparing, sorting, matching, ordering and sequencing, as well as counting familiar objects, recognizing and recreating patterns, nursery rhymes, songs, counting games and activities. Recognition and use of numbers, practical problem-solving and evidence of the number operations of addition and subtraction and related language were also sought.

As Hughes had established, there were relatively few 90-second samples of approximately 36 minutes, in which reference was made to mathematics. There was some variation between children and some indication of a slight increase in incidence with age. Overall, 2.1% of samples made reference to number and/or mathematical experiences. Most relevant references were made to number and counting, with one or two references made to shape and block-fitting activities in the field notes, unaccompanied by speech. In terms of frequency, reference to shape and measure was second only to number and counting and, most frequently, this occurred in the context of a single utterance, which received no response. The most frequently occurring exchange was the two-word utterance which comprised, most commonly, a short comment, request or question and a response. Adult-led exchanges provided examples of a pedagogic style in which number words and counting were reinforced in a didactic manner, as well as a more supportive and discursive style in which children might be tutored and guided, as Walkerdine had found. Children practised counting by themselves, from one to three, and also talked about size relations, predominantly 'big' and 'little' (see Learning Stories 4.1–4.4).

Learning story 4.3 Child of 30 months talks to television

Television: '. . . Four. One, two, three . . .'
Child to television: 'Man.'
Television: 'Four boys and a man.'
Child to television: 'Four boys . . . a man [whispering] . . . Four boys and a man.'
Mother to child: 'Mm' [agreeing].
Child to mother: 'Four boys.'

Learning story 4.4
Child of 42 months and mother doing child's hair

Mother to child: 'Get a big ribbon.'
Child to mother: 'Got to get one.'
Mother to child: 'Yes, um.'
Child to mother: 'Two ones we got [ribbons], isn't it? 'That two rib . . . Black ribbons, isn't it?'
Mother to child: 'Blue.'
Child to mother: 'Blue?'
Mother to child: 'Two blues, aren't they?'
Child to mother: 'Um, yes.'

Young (1995) kept a personal diary record over a 21-month period of home mathematical experiences, as well as collecting diaries from six other families, concerning children from 2 to 4 years. Home as well as playgroup or nursery video-recordings were made, and nursery staff and parent interviews were also carried out. Hour for hour, the average pre-school setting carried a higher number of numerical mediations with adults, although the nature of home and pre-school experiences was similar, as shown above. Young maintained that being able to recite to 20, count in one-one correspondence with small quantities up to ten and, possibly, recognize the first ten digits was thought to be all children needed or would be expected to show. Once these expectations were met, mathematical support seemed to subside. Practitioners may be interested, at this point, to compare these expectations with the Early Learning Goals for mathematical development (DfEE/QCA, 2000).

No purpose or use was seen by adults for large numbers, number recognition or sums which, in any case, were regarded as unnecessary for children's play and their daily routines. *Number mediation always took place in the context of the adult's involvement in a child's activities, such as counting buttons whilst dressing, or when a play situation was developed to mediate aspects of number, such as playing dominoes.* Parents indicated that they began to mediate number sequences and one-one correspondence counting to young children from 1 to 2 years of age and that children usually developed these skills a year later. Common home activities included songs, verses and rhymes, using counting books, playing with bricks and toys, counting up and down stairs, finger counting and other body parts, as well as discussion about this. This suggested a form of apprenticeship relationship in which children engaged with adults in social practices which had numerical meaning. As the previous studies we have introduced had previously shown, varying rates in the quantity and quality of number-mediated interactions were thought widespread and young children's accomplishments with number seemed to be linked to the quality and quantity of mediated interactions with the caregiver. Two children, for instance, did develop the use of sums, subitizing and number recognition after adult mediation of these aspects of number. Whether it comprised playing with dominoes, jumping off a trampoline or counting buttons whilst being dressed, successful mediation was characterized by its focus on the child's interests and needs, as well as adult participation.

As part of a wider, multi-method and longitudinal study of Gill Bottle (1999) which has tracked the home mathematics of nine young children from the age of between 1 and 2 to 5 years), we examined an in-depth observation and discourse in the home of two of these small children, Child H and Child L (Aubrey et al., 2001). Margaret Clark (2001) has argued that it is possible to pinpoint contexts in homes and pre-school settings from research evidence which are most likely to stimulate learning in young children and to lay effective foundation for literacy and numeracy.

With ages centred on 30 months to match the presentation of the Wells' analysis, on average, the children in the Wells study appeared to start with a much lower incidence rate of mathematical dialogue than Child H or Child L but ended up in a position comparable with Child H, suggesting no noticeable increase in the amount of discourse in English homes over the intervening 30 years. Child L seemed to have a fairly constant input of mathematical dialogue over the period of observations, whereas Child H received markedly more input with increasing age.

Both children experienced activities during observation which were adult-initiated and mathematically related, though the relevant experiences of Child L were shorter in duration, less frequent in incidence and less varied in range. These activities tended to be quite formal occasions and covered a narrow range of card-matching games, puzzles, drawing and counting. Opportunities to exploit ongoing, informal household activities did not seem to occur to the mother of Child L. By contrast, the parent of Child H demonstrated her awareness of the importance of time spent in such activities as well as her positive ability to develop mathematical experiences with her child. What, perhaps, best distinguished the two sets of experiences was the response of the two children. Whilst Child H was actively engaged, Child L clearly was not. There were occasions where Child L even appeared to be actively subverting her mother's attempts to secure her engagement. In fact, what marked out the experience of Child H was her mother's skill, not only in capturing and holding the young child's interest but also in her ability to encourage, support and even challenge the little girl mathematically. The quality of the interaction seemed to lie in the mother's capacity to establish joint participation, to use the child's ideas and extend these, as noted in a preliminary analysis of data by Gill Bottle (1999; see also Learning Story 4.5).

Learning Story 4.5
Mother and child engage in make-believe play

The mother 'pump-primes with ideas':

Child H: 'I'll give it to the McDonald's lady.'
Mother: 'Who's the McDonald's lady?' (Child H brings a doll.) 'What do you normally have at McDonald's?'
Child H: 'Put the money in there. I'm going to have two of these plates. One plate, two plates.' (Gives one to self and one to mother.) 'I can have two pieces of sandwich.' (Puts food on one plate and passes it.) 'And that one and that one . . . Some cups . . .' (Gets out two cups. Gives one to mother.) 'That's yours . . .'

The mother of Child H seemed to recognize that talking and communicating were important and saw mathematics as part of everyday experience. Learning for Child H arose from play activities chosen mainly by Child H herself. Her mother did not believe that she should 'school' Child H in any formal way, although she did indicate that she thought other parents often did so. The mother of Child L, by contrast, saw mathematics in the home in terms of discrete activities where the goal was the acquisition of counting and arithmetic skills and in which the adult might assume a directing role. These two parental styles had much in common with Valerie Walkerdine's typifications of mother–child conversational practices as *instrumental*, where the mother's main focus was the practical accomplishment of a task in which mathematics was an incidental feature, and *pedagogical* where mathematics was the explicit focus of a purposeful mathematical activity. Durkin et al. (1986) had drawn attention to the effective adult strategy of directing a child's attention to the co-ordination of manipulation of objects with verbal control of the activity. This, somehow, captured the essence of skilful adult support which exploited children's own interests and activities in order to identify and draw attention to important mathematical relationships.

Key Principles

A number of key principles have emerged from the investigation of home mathematics which have relevance to early years practitioners:

- Meaningful mathematical experiences appear to take place in the context of the adult's involvement in a child's interests and activities.
- Common home practices include songs, verses and rhymes, counting books, playing with toys, bricks, sand, cards, dominoes and board games, as well as dressing and grooming routines, walking up and down stairs and television watching.
- An effective caregiver style seems to be one which establishes joint participation in play activity or routine social and domestic practices, in order to use and extend children's own intuitive mathematical ideas.

Learning and Teaching in the Pre-school Setting

If lifelong learning is to be a steady incremental process of building a body of knowledge, skills and attitudes, the importance of drawing upon children's learning characteristics on entry to their first pre-school education setting can hardly be over-stressed. Examination of the experiences of Child H and Child L suggests that they may have entered their first formal learning setting with very different expectations of adults' pedagogical styles, as well as different valuations of particular types of mathematical activity.

In tune with children's early mathematical experiences in the home, Jozsef Nagy (1989) has drawn particular attention to the importance attached in Hungarian pre-school preparation to things being recognized and understood by their relations in space, time, quantity and extent, as well as the treatment and transformation of these relations, before formal teaching is begun. For Nagy, small children first learn to recognize, sort into order and manipulate the range of relations which can be perceived in objects by handling them continually for two or three years, between the ages of 3 and 6 years. Then they get to know the terms of the relations through the acquisition of language and, after that, the terms for more complicated relations, such as 'equals' and 'equivalent'. These relational terms, Nagy has argued, form the basic set of 'operators' in a language. Knowledge of them is presumed in every language, and they are used as a device in teaching children when they later enter school. Counting forms another prerequisite skill. This means rote counting, which involves enumerative knowledge of the number terms and pattern finding, which means the mastery of counting in a way which leads to an understanding of the structure of the numerical system.

This view of early mathematical development is entirely consistent with practices we have already examined in which adults direct attention to children's own manipulations of material, as well as the co-ordination of these with language relations in space, size, quantity and time which lead, in time, to the establishment of conceptual understanding which underpins longer-term mathematical development (see Learning Story 4.6).

Learning story 4.6 Three-year-olds in a Hungarian nursery

The teacher, as leader of the group, drags out a carpet to set the scene for an imaginative experience which she and the children jointly construct and act out:

'This is a magic carpet . . . we are sitting on the carpet. Here are the woods . . . This is where the bear lives. A wonderful bear's cave . . . Knock, knock . . . [The teacher gets out a bear puppet. She speaks for the bear.] I am sleeping. Why are you waking me? We are on a journey. We have brought you honey . . . Let's dance together. Put your hands on your hips and dance . . . Bear, bear, jump, turn, clap. [The children join in.] Now will you help? One, two, three. Three, two, one. Start again. Who volunteers to count alone? One, two, three . . . three, two one. [The teacher asks a boy to count back.] What is this? See how angry the bees are . . . *zzz* in bee language. Don't go too close to the bees! Count the bees. [One child counts.] One, two, three, four . . . Now altogether . . . How many white flowers? How many red flowers? Who can count how many altogether? One, two, three, four, five, six [and so on].'

This entire activity extended children's language and vocabulary through drawing on familiar story traditions and characters. It involved the children in purposeful counting, both forwards and backwards, combining small sets of objects, as well as using the language of measure. It reinforced colour recognition as well as set the scene for creative activity at the end of the scene. It engaged the children socially and emotionally in imaginative play. They worked co-operatively in a group with the teacher, as leader of the group, demonstrating action rhymes, songs and movement.

This skilful Hungarian kindergarten teacher was able to manage with a large group of children what a sensitive parent in a one-one situation could achieve. Like the skilful parent who was able to use mathematics incidentally to accomplish a practical task, the kindergarten teacher involved children in an imaginative experience in which language, make-believe, movement and mathematics all contributed to the experience she had created. In less skilful hands this might not have been the case. Munn (1997), for example, was able to show that pre-school children's numerical goals might not be the same as their adult partners where, for them, early counting seemed essentially imitative of the social practices and playful in intent rather than quantitative, with little sense of adult-imposed definitions. For her, shifts towards a greater self-consciousness occurred around school age, at 5 years, which might be accounted for in terms of changes in the child's environment.

And so to School

Once at school this is where the curriculum is underpinned by the *Curriculum Guidance for the Foundation Stage* (DfEE/QCA, 2000: 74, 76, 80).

- Say and use number names in order in familiar contexts
- Count reliably up to 10 everyday objects
- Recognise numerals 1 to 9
- Use developing mathematical ideas and methods to solve practical problems
- In practical activities and discussion begin to use vocabulary involved in adding and subtracting
- Use language such as 'more' or 'less' to compare two numbers
- Find one more or one less than a number from one to ten
- Begin to relate addition to combining two groups of objects and subtraction to 'taking away'
- Use language such as 'greater', 'smaller', 'heavier' or 'lighter' to compare quantities
- Talk about, recognise and recreate simple patterns
- Use language such as 'circle' or 'bigger' to describe the shape and size of solids and flat shapes
- Use everyday words to describe position.

Counting

By the time Child H left playgroup a record of her mathematical attainment was reporting that she could compare size and quantity, understand position language, sort and match a variety of objects by colour and size, and name and recognize shapes such as a circle, square and triangle. She could count objects to ten, match objects one to one and copy a simple pattern. She was aware of number in relation to her own experience, such as her house and telephone number, was also aware of mathematics in other areas of learning and could use mathematical language.

Child H was 4 years and 4 months when she entered the reception class at school. In the baseline assessment carried out in the first six weeks of schooling, it was reported that Child H could recognize the numerals '1', '2', '3', '5' and '8' but was not able to identify the amounts of '6', '7', '9' and '10'. She was aware of addition in practical terms and knew that '1 more than 4' was 5. She could not do 'addition in the abstract'. She understood positional language such as 'in', 'on' and 'under' and could compare size to say which was 'bigger' and 'smaller'. She was able to match one to one and to sort. The report of Child H's rich mathematical understanding was entirely compatible with the observed home experiences of this child which had not placed emphasis on the sums, subitizing and symbol learning that the mother of Child L valued. The challenge for the reception class teacher of Child H would be to value the way this young child approached mathematics, build upon her practical problem-solving skills and *not* confound this with too early an introduction to formal, symbol-dominated methods.

Judith Adelsberg was just such a reception teacher. She saw her challenge to design curriculum tasks which evolved from her 4–5-year-olds' own informal ideas, in a learning process which started with a situation in which the mathematical model was a bus (van den Brink, 1991). This provided her children with a realistic situation in which counting, number recognition, addition and subtraction could emerge naturally from the ongoing changes in the number of passengers, or compare bears, getting on and off a bus. In this case the bus was a Pixie robot (see below) which moved along a Pixie number track and a description of these quantitative changes in passengers in an informal 'arrow language'.

The Dutch mathematics educator, Treffers (1991), described various forms and functions of counting as follows:

- *Acoustic* counting, which involves reciting the numbers in an ordered line.
- *Synchronous* counting, with accompanying rhythmic movements and one-one touching.
- *Resultative* counting, or otherwise determining amounts or quantities.
- *Abbreviated* counting, taking structured amounts of different size (for example, twos or threes) with ordered and unordered sets of objects, visible or only partly visible.

Children, it was thought, needed to learn that numbers could be used for naming – for example, 'bus number 2' – as a measure 'I am four years of age' or for amounts ('there are three blue compare bears and two red compare bears on the Pixie robot'). The challenge for Judith was to teach the subskills of counting, at the same time easing children gradually towards an understanding of their function in determining the sum of two, separate numbers or amounts or, indeed, splitting an initial amount into two, smaller ones.

In order to do this, Judith exploited the basic idea of the board game, in this case, a number track marked 0 to 10, attached to a portable board with 110-millimetre squares and an animal symbol in each square, 10 being the farm and represented by a cow. At the same time, the Pixie robot served as a bus, lending itself to picking up and setting down teddy bear passengers as it moved along the track (see Figure 4.1). This combination of developing basic counting subskills and number recognition with van den Brink's notion of the passengers getting on and off the bus provided a context in which we hoped a curriculum could be designed which fulfilled the key objectives of the National Numeracy Strategy (1998), constituting the Early Learning Goals for mathematics (DfEE/QCA, 2000) but which took better account of children's own informal knowledge. Dutch realistic mathematics development work has led to the construction not only of a curriculum which is also founded upon the principle of reinvention, allowing children to build their own mathematical ideas, but one which is also embedded within rigorous analysis of psychological theories and ideas (see Learning Story 4.7).

0	1	2	3	4	5	6	7	8	9	10

0	1	2	3	4	5	6	7	8	9	10

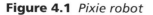

(i.e. to go from 0 to 4 needs 4 moves)

Figure 4.1 *Pixie robot*

Learning Story 4.7
Planning for the development of mathematical thinking

Ellie's teacher had planned a structured activity where children were encouraged to make collections. She had decorated match boxes in attractive ways and put numbers on the top. The children were asked to go out into the nursery garden or in the classroom and collect that number of things. Ellie had ten on her box. She went into the garden and came back with her ten objects. As she counted she put one thing on each finger. She then realized that she had ten fingers and exclaimed that she would always remember the number ten because of her fingers. She was delighted with her discovery.

Judith had encountered one of us in the context of her professional development work in reception classes. This work had introduced a fundamental principle of Dutch realistic maths, which is to take children's informal ideas as a starting point in order to help them 'reinvent' the formal mathematics curriculum. This coincided with her being lent a robot Pixie by the local maths adviser and created the stimulus for her to appropriate the bus context in designing a curriculum for her class. Judith took the lead in the innovation, whilst one of us provided additional background information on the original Dutch project (described more fully in Aubrey, 1999a) and made termly visits. Thus, the 'design experiment' described earlier in this chapter was begun. As a follow-up to initial in-service training which introduced realistic mathematics philosophy, theory and basic concepts, Judith was supplied with an information pack related to realistic maths for young children. This material was already available for practitioners in published form (Aubrey, 1999b). The basic ideas were then adapted by the practitioner to take account of the Early Learning Goals, which set out key mathematical objectives for the school year (see Learning Story 4.8).

Learning Story 4.8
At the start of reception year: the practitioner's tale

My first impressions of the Pixie robot when it arrived in September were that, although very simple to operate, it looked very fragile. Now, six months later, we have ordered a machine for the school – it's been fantastic!

From the first day my 4-year-olds were captivated. They were immediately curious to explore the functions of each button and soon extended their vocabulary to include 'clear the memory', 'forwards', 'backwards', 'turn', 'wait' and 'go'.

We soon graduated from pushing a few buttons at random to guessing where it would finish and then trying to estimate which buttons we needed to press in order to reach a specific point. It amazed me how quickly the children became quite proficient in programming the machine and how supportive they were of one another. An activity which started with two children soon gathered an audience of four, five or more . . . The children quickly learnt to count to five and then to match their counting to the action of pressing the arrow keys. Even the child to whom the concept of counting had no meaning began to see some relevance to the process. Now it was time to formalize the control process and relate it to a number line.

All even numbers were orange and odd numbers yellow. The majority of my class, however, were not confident in reading the numbers to 10, so we decided to add a farm animal to each number to give another dimension to the position of each square within the whole track. This was now more inspiring to use and fitted in well with numeracy aspects of the Reception curriculum. Simply moving about the track gave lots of opportunities to work with the numbers but once we had hit on the idea of using a compare teddy bear as the driver of the Pixie, it wasn't long before Pixie became a bus, the empty track became the bus lane and passengers appeared at bus stops! Now the possibilities for mathematics became endless.

Initially each child in a group of six chose one passenger bear and placed their own bear at a bus stop and the 'driver' was then given accurate instructions for picking them all up. This gave scope for working with counting different combinations of bears as passengers joined the bus. Naturally, this progressed to dropping specified passengers off at various destinations.

As the children became more confident and the bus proved powerful enough to carry more bears, the numbers of passengers grew, giving opportunities to deal with larger numbers, to sort them by colour and size. We would collect all the blue bears, for instance, and take them to see the cows in the field at bus stop number 10 or we might pick up all the little teddies, who were off on a trip together. Sometimes we had to go back for someone we'd missed. This allowed the introduction of the reverse movement and counting numbers backwards.

Children progressed to programming the bus to move forward to collect the first passenger, wait while he got on, move forward for the next one, wait again and so on. Soon children were able to predict how many moves were needed from one stop to the next and were ready to relate this to addition. Consequently, we introduced arrows to represent the transition from one number to its adjacent number or from one square in the bus lane to the next, and were working towards recording it together:

$$0 \rightarrow \rightarrow \rightarrow \rightarrow 4$$
$$0 + 4 \rightarrow 4$$
$$0 + 4 = 4$$

To develop the ideas of counting on and counting back further, we also made some lucky-dip cards to see where the bus and passengers should start, as we explored addition and subtraction in a practical scenario. There was even the possibility of extending this to a 6×6 grid for a treasure island, to place objects within the grid or make an obstacle course to introduce the notion of turning with, possibly, the earliest idea of co-ordinates being incorporated (see Figure 4.2).

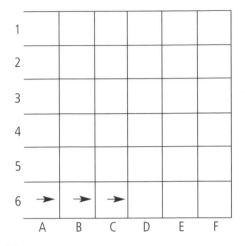

Figure 4.2 *6 × 6 grid*

I feel that the only areas of the Early Learning Goals which are not naturally addressed in using the Pixie are the concept of weight and the exploration of 2D and 3D shapes . . . although with a little bit of connivance, anything is possible!

In order to build upon and extend children's existing number concepts at the beginning of the reception year, Judith used the Pixie bus theme in order to elicit children existing knowledge of counting subskills, numeral recognition and their understanding of the value of these numbers on the Pixie number line. She had been exploring the patterns of adjacent numerals and the meaning of 'more' and 'less', 'bigger', 'smaller' and so on. This provided endless opportunities for practising counting and for considering the difference between two number positions on the board to determining quantities of compare bears (see Learning stories 4.9 and 4.10).

Learning story 4.9
At the beginning of the year: the researcher's tale

Children decided for themselves at which 'bus stop' the teddies would wait, as well as considering how many spaces the bus would need to travel between the 'stops':

Judith: 'Choose a teddy and decide which bus stop he will wait at . . . number 4 . . . number 2. Is that more or less than 4? How many spaces? Count . . . 1, 2. What number is between 2 and 4? 3 . . . Well done! Ah, which teddy is on the highest number? How many passengers to pick up altogether?'

Whilst a teddy was placed on the Pixie robot as driver, one child was elected to carry out the programming of the Pixie robot to go forwards or backwards, according to the instructions of the group:

Judith: 'Tell me, how many is zero? . . . Yes, nothing at all . . . Who's going to be bus driver, red teddy or yellow teddy?'

Throughout she promoted counting subskills – reference number according to the 'stop' where the teddies were waiting, acoustic number through reciting the number string, synchronous number with the rhythmic movements associated with tapping the forward and reverse arrow on the Pixie robot, with accompanying flashing lights, and resultative counting of the teddy bears, which combined subitizing and counting.

Questions which were not correctly answered were repeated and children invited to compare different responses to check accuracy. At the same time, children learnt the language of number ('more' and 'less'), the language of position ('forwards' and 'backwards'), as well as experiencing the turning of the Pixie robot through 90 degrees and clearing its memory – 'it means to lose the instructions'. Moreover, the learning of numerals took place in a meaningful context. Finally, structuring of quantity was stimulated when all the teddies were gathered altogether:

Judith: 'How many passengers picked up, altogether? How many red teddies? 4 . . . And how many left [when the total passengers were split]?'

In the post-video discussion, Judith stressed that the transition from concrete manipulation of the Pixie robot to a more abstract understanding of increasing and decreasing numbers along the Pixie number line was assisted with 'arrow language' – one arrow provided for each square the bus travelled over. Most children soon learnt to count and to recognize the numbers 1–12 at the beginning of the year and were beginning to count in 10s and 2s. Most challenging of all was the organization such intensive group teaching in the classroom situation involved at a stage when children were working entirely through activity and oral-mental methods, and before recording of their own ideas was established.

Learning Story 4.10
At the end of Reception Year: the researcher's tale

By the end of the year, children were counting and carrying out simple 'bare' arithmetic problems through the combining and splitting of small amounts determined by the throwing of two dice, as well as recording these moves. They were counting confidently in 2s and 10s and using the language of 'doubling' and 'halving', explaining their methods and reasoning orally. At this stage, the Pixie robot was being used to check their calculations and the arrow language maintained to check the difference between two numbers:

Judith: 'What happens when we roll two dice? . . . A number pattern.' (Throws the first die.) 'Louis [SEN child] . . . Count the spots for me . . . Find 5 on the number line ... Louis have you found . . .? Second is number 1 . . . How many

▶

altogether? 1 add 5 equals 6 . . . How did you know that, Michelle? Six comes after 5 . . . Can you show me on your fingers now? 1 finger with one hand, 5 fingers with the other hand . . . count them. How many? Is that the same as 5 add 1? It's still 6! This is how you write it . . . Well done!'

Judith: 'What am I doing now? This time it's take away.' (Throws a number 2.) 'Right, number 2.' (Throws a second die.) 'Right, number 2, take away 2. Write it down for me . . . 2 take away 2 . . . What comes next? Equals, good. 2 . . . take away 2? Put your answer down . . . What's left? Zero! Were you right? I'm going to get the Pixie number line in a minute to check these sums. We're going to check . . . How many places do we have to move Pixie? Remember to clear the memory. Press! Say "forward". OK!'

In summary, the children had learnt to:

- say and use the numbers in order in familiar contexts;
- recite number names in order, continuing the count forwards and backwards from a given number;
- begin to recognize none and zero when counting;
- count in 10s and 2s;
- estimate a number in the range that can be counted reliably, then check by counting;
- recognize numerals 1–9, then 0–10 and beyond;
- begin to record numbers;
- use language such as 'more' or 'less', 'greater' or 'smaller', to compare two numbers and which lies between two numbers;
- begin to use vocabulary involved in adding and subtracting;
- relate addition to counting of doubles and to counting on; and
- separate (partition) a given number of objects into two groups.

As seen at the beginning, these are closely aligned with many of the Early Learning Goals for mathematics (DfEE/QCA, 2000).

The strategies used showed that children's everyday knowledge could be recast in mathematical terms and could lead to a more abstract manipulation of 'bare' problems. This is in line with the van Hieles' (1959) 'level' theory (see also Learning Story 4.11):

- At ground level, numbers were attached to observable quantities of bear passengers and bus movements.
- At 'first' level, relations between numbers and quantities were being investigations through the die throwing (1 + 5 = 6).
- At the 'second' level, the relations themselves were the subject of investigation (1 + 5 equivalent to 5 + 1; 10 – 4 = 6 as inverse of 6 + 4 = 10).

Learning Story 4.11
The use of technology and supporting mathematical thinking

Jamie was playing with a calculator left on the table by the class teacher. One of us was sitting with him and he asked the name of the number 10. He then added another nought and asked the name of 100. He kept on going and was fascinated by the number of noughts. He kept asking about the names as the numbers grew bigger.

The Key Principles of Realistic Mathematics Education

From the practitioner's point of view, it is important to note the following:

- The first learning principle of realistic mathematics education is that learning mathematics is foremost a constructive activity. This was clearly visible at the beginning of the year with children being given the opportunity to construct counting principles themselves through the concrete orientation of the Pixie line presented to them.
- The second learning principle is that learning of mathematical skills is stretched over a long period time and moves at various levels of abstraction. This was demonstrated over the school year with children first using the context-bound bus models yet later carrying out actions, which could be understood within the number system. To achieve this, children were provided with the tools of the arrow language and the manoeuvres of the Pixie robot to help bridge the gap between concrete and abstract. Visual models, model situations and symbols thus served in a progressive schematization, whilst the arrow language continued to constitute a concrete basis for the learning process.
- The raising of the level of the learning process through reflection, as children compared responses of themselves with others, constitutes the third principle of learning.
- Finally, the fourth principle – learning is not a solo activity but occurs in, and is directed and stimulated by, the socio-cultural context.

For these children 'doing mathematics' was embedded in a realistic context and situationally accomplished. Specific artefacts and procedures for doing mathematics, in this case, the Pixie robot and the Pixie number line, were part of the resources used to organize the specific class context. Thus, according to a situated view of learning, decontextualized skills and knowledge had no place.

Learning skills and knowledge cannot be separated from learning to organ-ize a context, according to Ueno (1998). Learning maths in the classroom also includes learning about context, just as is the case for other everyday social and cultural context:

> School learning of concepts of counting and calculation cannot be separated from learning to organise a context with a teacher in the classroom. Understanding maths concepts is always accomplished by organising a specific context or a specific language game . . . the meaning of calculation, number, maths concept, and measurement . . . [lies in] . . . the mastery of the practices required to use those signs, tools and procedures competently within a relevant language game. (Ueno, 1998: 128)

Transition issues from the Foundation Stage to Key Stage 1

Our account of the nature and social contexts of young children's early learning will already have alerted the practitioner to the importance of a smooth transi-tion period between the Foundation Stage (for 3–5-year-olds) and Key Stage 1 (for 5–7-year-olds) which constitutes the first stage of formal learning. Galton et al. (1999) have pointed to the importance of giving special attention to transi-tions between key stages of learning. In a recent telephone survey of the implementation of the Foundation Stage in reception classes (Quick et al., 2002), however, nearly three-quarters of headteachers interviewed felt that the transi-tion of children to Key Stage 1 had not been a problem since the introduction of the Foundation Stage. Perceived problems were generally associated with con-cerns over adjusting to a more formal teaching method and academic demands required by Key Stage 1. Curriculum organization, in any case, tended to be adjusted towards the end of reception year in order to increase the differentia-tion and formality, making the end of reception year more like Key Stage 1. In general, headteachers and reception class teachers did not regard implementa-tion of the National Numeracy Strategy as a problem (Quick et al., 2002). The majority of reception class teachers delivered the National Numeracy Strategy flexibly in term one though, by term two, most were teaching a daily mathemat-ics lesson with three elements: oral work and mental calculation, using whole-class teaching; main lesson for new topics and consolidating previous work; and plenary session to draw together what had been learnt.

Obviously, there are similarities and differences between the Foundation Stage and Key Stage 1 and, indeed, Galton et al. (1999: cited in DfES, 1998: 38) recommended that 'schools need to consider the possibility of providing flexible teaching which takes account of differences in pupils' preferred learning styles'. In terms of similarities, there seems no reason why the play-based mathematics curriculum that is a feature of the Foundation Stage curriculum cannot be a powerful vehicle for learning mathematics in Key Stage 1, too. Structured play experiences can work well in Key Stage 1 – for example, finding out which of three bowls belongs to the giant by comparing capacity or shopping in the role-play corner using prices and real money.

The teaching ethos that is promoted in the Foundation Stage (DfEE/QCA, 2000) is easily transferable to Key Stage 1 – for example, as we have seen, fostering an atmosphere where mistakes are valued as learning experiences. Holton et al. (1999) suggested that mathematical play not only creates such an atmosphere but that the teacher also has a direct role in asking questions, making the misconceptions clear and providing further scaffolding to focus 'play' in a more productive direction.

Similarities in the approach to problem-solving and collaborative learning can be fostered across these two key stages, too. The daily mathematics lesson encourages the use of flexible groupings, and activities can be planned to promote collaboration – for example, where a group of children has to come up with one agreed strategy for building a tower with boxes. In both key stages children can be encouraged to share jokes about mathematics and their sense of enjoyment (see Learning Story 4.12).

Learning story 4.12 Researcher to young child

Researcher: 'I remember you telling me something about pairs – you said there were pairs of buttons. Can you remember telling me that?'
Nicky: 'Ya.'
Researcher: 'What did you tell me? What is a pair?'
Nicky: 'Not an apple!' (Wood and Bennett, 2001: 7)

Differences in teaching approaches can be minimized for young children. There is the difference between the formalized numeracy lesson and a more integrated/informal numeracy session in the Foundation Stage and, indeed, reception teachers in the telephone survey recognized the importance of child-initiated and spontaneous learning. The mental/oral starter can easily be integrated throughout the reception year with an emphasis on number rhymes, clapping games and stories. The children will then be more familiar with the structure when they begin the three-part lesson. Reception children can also be introduced to the wide variety of mathematical resources used in the numeracy lesson so that they are familiar with these. These can then be introduced within contexts that they know already. Carr (1994) suggested that children are able to use more complex mathematical skills when the context is familiar and, for an experience to become familiar, it needs to be available for exploration and repetition.

Children can be given time to play with the resources first. Whiteboards can be used in the role-play area for writing down lists and appointments in a health clinic/doctors surgery. Calculators can be integrated into role play in shops and banks.

Key Stage 1 (for 5–7-year-olds)

By the time children have reached the end of the Foundation Stage, as noted above, it is assumed that they will have the capacity to:

- participate in an oral-linguistic approach to teaching;
- engage in appropriate co-operative behaviour; and
- have conceptual understanding of quantity, time, size and space which underlies later mathematical understanding.

It is common at this age that children may be using a range of distinct strategies for solving simple number operations of addition and subtraction:

- Counting the actual objects in the problem, using manipulatives or other concrete aids.
- Finger counting.
- Verbal counting without concrete material.
- Recalling a number fact.
- Transforming one or both quantities (or numbers) to make an easier sum.

Understanding of whole–part relationships in numbers provides the basis for learning number facts – 0 to 5; 5 to 10; 10 to 20 and so on – as well as place value and basic operations in number. Early understanding of the base-ten system is derived from counting. Thus, an important part of understanding two-digit numbers, first to 20 and then beyond, is counting and number names. The Pixie bus which allowed children's existing counting strategies to be mapped on to early arithmetic and problem-solving can be developed into a double-decker city bus context to show 'doubles', such as 5 + 5 passengers or 'near doubles', such as 5 + 6 passengers and, hence, the 'crossing ten' strategy. The power of the bus model is that children are aware of what is happening and are able to imagine or reinvent the real-life context from more formal notation as it is introduced. Whilst children are using real-life problems they are also being inducted into the logical properties of number (see Learning Story 4.13). The Pixie bus track can be increased to 20 to help visualizations of the number line, though it is likely to be superseded by other working models, such as a bead string or abacus, with a five or quinary structure. Indeed, the abacus can serve as a parallel model to the double-decker bus. Hence, it forms a bridge between the bus model and the Dutch empty number line which, in turn, can serve as a model for addition, subtraction, multiplication and division, as well as fractions, decimals and ratio.

Learning Story 4.13
The importance of practitioners' subject knowledge and the curriculum

As referred to by Jeni Riley in the Introduction and Chapter 1, we cannot underestimate the importance of the subject knowledge of adults in the teaching and learning of mathematics.

Kerry was a primary student teacher working with a Year 1 class on addition. Her learning objectives were to provide opportunity for the pupils to understand counting on both 1 and 10. Using the 1–100 square they were tossing a coin; if it fell on 'heads' the children could add 1 and if it fell to 'tails' they could add 10. Kerry discussed which direction they were entitled to move on the 100 square depending on what had been thrown – namely, they could move across if it was a 1 and down if it was a 10. She failed to explain the reason. No discussion took place regarding a pattern or what was different about the numbers. It was hard to see the value of this activity and what the children might learn through it. If Kerry had used her subject knowledge to explain the principles of place value, the dienary system and, perhaps, had made connections between these and the learning activity then genuine mathematical understanding might have taken place.

The National Numeracy Strategy, indeed, incorporates the realistic empty number line as a transition paper-and-pencil procedure which links children's mental calculation to the formal written algorithm. In this context, it provides the first stage of recording calculations for larger numbers with 'informal jottings' in which teachers guide pupils to more efficient and reliable methods. In general, what we are suggesting here is:

- flexible, 'bottom up' problem-solving;
- reflection on the learning path of individual children through their own constructions and productions; and
- the use of the support provided by the realistic context or 'model' situation.

In this context, assessment itself becomes a teaching tool. Through a variety of means – observation, questioning, varying the problem, offering assistance and encouraging reflection by modelling talk-aloud strategies – teachers can investigate children's existing knowledge or access informal strategies, which can be exploited in the next stage of learning. Planning and assessment, in this context, will form a crucial part of the transition process. Central to this process will be the new Foundation Stage profile (see Learning Story 4.14).

Learning Story 4.14
The importance of understanding what children know about mathematics

A situation highlighted the importance of assessment of children's understanding of mathematics when another trainee primary teacher was observed 'teaching ways to count on 9', as a counting strategy, to a group of Year 1 children.

Samantha demonstrated 'count on 10 and take one away' as a quick method for adding 9. The problems occurred when many of the children were unable to count on 10 automatically so were forced to go through a laborious system of counting on ten in ones and then taking off one. When asked about her lesson afterwards, Samantha realized that she had forgotten a vital bit of information about the group before her lesson, which was whether these pupils were able to count on in tens.

Conclusion

Throughout this chapter we have stressed the need to:

- build on the knowledge children already have;
- relate school learning to the real world by exploiting their everyday knowledge and encouraging active learning; and
- lead children gradually from real-world problem-solving to the more abstract world of mathematical logical properties.

Early childhood education has undergone rapid change over the last few years. We now have an appropriate Foundation Stage curriculum for young children of 3–5 years, marked by its 'informality, child-centredness and practicality' (Quick et al, 2002), and the bridge it provides to Key Stage 1. The challenge now lies with us to provide the mathematical opportunities which are appropriate to motivate, support and extend our young children.

■ Suggested further reading

Anghileri, J. (ed.) (2001) *Principles and Practices in Arithmetic Teaching*. Buckingham: Open University Press.

Gifford, S., Barber, P. and Ebbutt, S. (1998) *Number in the Nursery and Reception*. Oxford: BEAM.

Thompson, I. (ed.) (1997) *Teaching and Learning Early Number*. Oxford: Oxford University Press.

Williams, H., Skinner, C. and Barber, P. (2000), *Teaching the Early Years*. Oxford: Rigby Foundation Mathematics.

■ References

Adelberg, J. (2000) Using Pixie in a reception class (unpublished report). St Crispin's Infant School, Westgate.

Aubrey, C. (1997) 'An investigation of the mathematical knowledge and competencies which young children bring into school', *British Educational Research Journal*, 19(1): 19–37.

Aubrey, C. (1999a) 'Maths for the millennium', *Special Children*, 122: 1–8.

Aubrey, C. (1999b) *A Developmental Approach to Early Numeracy*. Birmingham: Questions Publishing.

Aubrey, C. (2000) 'Towards a realistic solution?', *Educational and Child Psychology*, 17(3): 70–85.

Aubrey, C. (2001) 'Early mathematics', in T. David (ed.) *Promoting Evidence-based Practice in Early Childhood Education*. London: Elsevier Science.

Aubrey, C., Bottle, G. and Godfrey, R. (2001) 'Early mathematics in the home and out-of-home contexts', Paper presented at the European Association for Research on Learning and Instruction conference, Switzerland, University of Fribourg, August.

Aubrey, C., Godfrey, R. and Godfrey, J. (2000) 'Children's early numeracy experiences in the home', *Primary Practice*, 26: 36–42.

Bottle, G. (1999) 'A study of children's mathematical experiences at home', *Early Years*, 20(1): 53–64.

Carr, M., Peters, S. and Young-Loveridge, J. (1994) *Early Childhood Mathematics: Finding the Right Level of Challenge*. Wellington, New Zealand: Wellington College of Education.

Clark, M.M. (2001) 'Challenges and changes in pre-school education', *Primary Practice*, 28: 42–7.

Desforges, C. (2000) 'Familiar challenges and new approaches: necessary advances in theory and methods in research on teaching and learning.' The Desmond Nuttall/Carfax Memorial Lecture, British Educational Research Association conference, Cardiff, September.

DfEE (1998) *National Numeracy Strategy*. London: DfEE.

DfEE/QCA (1999) *Early Learning Goals*. London: QCA.

DfEE/QCA (2000) *Curriculum Guidance for the Foundation Stage*. London: QCA.

DfES (2002) *Teaching Mathematics in Reception and Year 1*. London: DfES.

Durkin, K., Shire, B., Riem, R., Crowther, R.D. and Rutter, D.R. (1986) 'The social and linguistic context of early number word use,' *British Journal of Developmental Psychology*, 4: 269–99.

Galton, M., Gray, J. and Ruddock, J. (1999) *The Impact of School Transitions and Transfers on Pupil Progress and Attainment. Research Brief* 131. London: DfEE.

Gopnik, A., Meltzoff, A. and Kuhl, P. (1999) *How Babies Think*. London: Weidenfeld & Nicholson.

Greeno, J.G., Collins, A.M. and Resnick, L.R. (1996) 'Cognition and learning', in D.C. Berliner and R.C. Calfree (eds) *Handbook of Educational Psychology*. New York, NY: Macmillan.

Hiele, van P. and Hiele, van M. (1959) La pensée de l'enfant et la géométrie', *Bulletin de l'Association des Professeurs de Mathématiques de l'Enseignement Publique*, 38: 199–205.

Holton, D., Ahmed, A., Williams, H. and Hill, C. (1999) 'On the importance of mathematical play', *International Journal of Mathematical Education in Science and Technology*, 32(3): 401–15.

Hughes, M. (1986) *Children and Number: Difficulties in Learning Mathematics*. Oxford: Blackwell.

Matthews, G. and Mathews, J. (1978) *Early Mathematical Experience*. London: Addison-Wesley.

Munn, P. (1997) 'Childen's beliefs about counting', in I. Thompson (ed.) *Teaching and Learning Early Number*. Buckingham: Open University Press.

Nagy, J. (1989) *Articulation of Pre-school with Primary School in Hungary: An Alternative Entry Model*. Hamburg: UNESCO Institute of Education.

Nunes, T. and Bryant, P. (1996) *Children Doing Mathematics*. Oxford: Blackwell.

Quick, S., Lambley, C., Newcombe, E. and Aubrey, C. (2002) *Implementing the Foundation Stage in Reception Classes*. London: DfES.

Sophian, C. (1998) 'A developmental perspective on children's counting', in C. Donlan (ed.) *The Development of Mathematical Skills*. Hove: Psychology Press.

Tizard, B. and Hughes, M. (1984) *Young Children Learning: Talking and Thinking at Home and at School*. London: Fontana.

Treffers, A. (1991) *Three Dimensions. A Model of Goal and Theory Description in Mathematics Education: The Wiskobas Project*. Dordrecht: Reidel Publishers.

Ueno, N. (1998) 'Doing mathematics as situated cognition', in C. Donlan (ed.) *The Development of Mathematical Skills*. Hove: Psychology Press.

van den Brink, F.J. (1991) 'Realistic arithmetic education for young children', in L. Streefland (ed.) *Realistic Mathematics Education in the Primary School. On the Occasion of the Opening of the Freudenthal Institute*. Utrecht: CD-B Press.

Walkerdine, V. (1982) 'From context to text: a psycho-semiotic account of abstract thought', in M. Beveridge (ed.) *Children's Thinking through Language*. London: Edward Arnold.

Walkerdine, V. (1988) *The Mastery of Reason. Cognitive Development and the Production of Rationality*. London: Routledge.

Wells, G. (1982) 'Language at home and school', *Newsletter of the Child Development Society*, 30.

Wood, E. and Bennett, N. (2001) ' "I know what I've got better at": young children's understanding of progression in their learning.' Paper presented to the European Association for Research on Learning and Instruction conference, University of Fribourg, Switzerland, August.

Wynn, K. (1998) 'Numerical competence in infants', in C. Donlan (ed.) *The Development of Mathematical Skills*. Hove: Psychology Press.

Young, J. (1995) 'Young children's apprenticeship in number.' Unpublished PhD, University of North London.

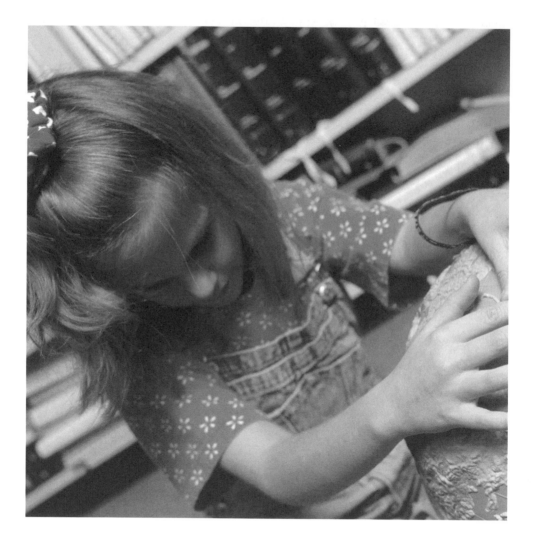

5

Knowledge and understanding of the world

Esmé Glauert, Caroline Heal and John Cook

> *What is our knowledge worth if we know nothing about the world that sustains us, nothing about natural systems and climate, nothing about other countries and cultures?*
>
> (Jonathon Porritt, Forum for the Future, 1999)
>
> *In my ideal school, respect for people and the world around you, would be taught before anything else.*
>
> (Angela Gillen, aged 15, *Guardian Education*, 2001)

Introduction

Those children who are starting school now will live well into the latter part of the twenty-first century and their children will have every chance of continuing their journey way beyond 2100. It becomes an awesome responsibility to help shape these young minds and enable them to come to terms with a rapidly changing and highly technological world. They need insights into its complexities and contradictions, the fragility and balance of the world's resources. Children need plenty of opportunities to gain wider knowledge, experience and understanding of the world in which they live and to appreciate the difference in the ways of thinking, working and viewing the world.

This chapter draws on recent research evidence and examples of classroom practice to discuss ways in which children begin to learn about the world around them. In particular, the focus is on the understandings and skills associated with geography, history and science with reference to the Early Learning Goals for knowledge and understanding of the world

(DfEE/QCA, 2000) and the National Curriculum requirements for Key Stage 1 (DfEE, 1999). The chapter is divided into three parts, one for each subject. Each part follows a common format in which we:

- review what is known about young children's learning;
- consider the nature of the subject and key areas of development;
- indicate suitable content and contexts for learning;
- discuss appropriate teaching and learning approaches and range of experience; and
- examine issues associated with the transition from pre-school settings to more formal compulsory schooling.

Finally at the end of the chapter we highlight the importance of a partnership with parents in supporting young children's learning.

Science

This part deals with the strand of knowledge and understanding of the world that is concerned with science.

Growing evidence of young children's capabilities

From their earliest years young children observe and interact with their immediate physical environment. They follow the movement of toys as adults play with them or reach out and feel objects. As their motor skills increase they push and pull things, make sounds by banging or shaking, splash in the bath or become aware of small creatures around them. Through these early experiences children build up patterns of expectation about the physical and biological world. Even young infants show an awareness of differences between animate and inanimate objects recognizing that animate objects can move by themselves whereas inanimate objects need to be pushed or pulled by an external force. Their responses in experiments suggest early development of expectations about how objects should move and behave – for example they are aware that objects continue to exist when out of sight, that objects cannot pass through a solid barrier or that objects cannot remain suspended in mid-air without support. If something unexpected happens they seek out a cause or mechanism to explain it (Baillargeon, 1994). With greater mobility and the development of language children can pursue interests further and draw adults into their inquiries (see Learning Story 5.1).

Learning Story 5.1 May

May is 2. Her parents report she is very interested in small creatures, particularly the snails and spiders she watches in the garden and coming into the house. She asks lots of questions about what they are doing and why. Why is the spider making a web? Why is it climbing up and down? Where is it going? Spirals and web shapes frequently appear in her drawings. She also has the idea that batteries can make things work. When a flash light was not working she suggested 'put batteries in'.

Studies of young children's explorations over time often show persistent concerns (see, for example, Navarra, 1955). Children return frequently to an area of interest, refining and developing their knowledge and ideas. Learning Stories 5.2 and 5.3 give two examples. These examples illustrate both the strengths and limitations of young children's explorations. Both children sustained interest over long periods of time. They developed and made explicit their knowledge of life-cycles and electrical circuits. Darren showed an ability to classify animals and order the stages in the duck life-cycle. Omar moved from just making circuits work to seeking to understand *how* they work. In hospitable circumstances like these, research increasingly shows that, with time and a rich environment, children can begin to form theories and develop their own investigations (Brown et al., 1997). However they will need support in developing their ideas. Without further help Darren did not resolve why a chicken did not come out of the egg. His comments suggest he associates growth with getting bigger, lacking knowledge about the remarkable transformations that take place inside the egg. Omar was unable to make the buzzer work because he did not know (or discover accidentally) that it only works if connected one way in the circuit.

Learning Story 5.2 Darren

Following a cooking session in a nursery class Darren showed an interest in eggs. He was very disappointed that a chicken did not come out when the egg used in cooking was cracked open. On several different occasions he sorted a set of small toy animals into those that lay eggs and those that do not. He checked those he was not sure about with adults around and asked if the eggs would turn into baby animals. Later he found a puzzle in which each piece represented a different stage in the life-cycle of a duck from the egg to an adult duck. Eventually he decided: 'If you get eggs from the shop they have runny egg in it. If you had it from the chicken it will have chicken in it. A chicken can be in it because it is small.'

Learning Story 5.3 Omar

In a reception class Omar explored making electrical circuits over several weeks. At first he made circuits with bulbs. Then he managed to make a motor work using the same circuit model. However he failed to make a buzzer function despite repeated attempts. This resulted in a detailed study of circuit connections needed. After this he became interested in the effects of adding more batteries in a circuit. He commented: 'I did it with two – look it's going to get brighter [and] should be two connections [on battery] . . . they should be there and there . . . the battery's got power.'

None the less what emerges from studies of young children's learning is their active concern to make sense of the world around them. Their early knowledge, curiosity and search for causes provide important foundations for future learning. Given these promising beginnings, how best can we promote learning in science in the early years?

The nature of science

First of all what is meant by science and what are the key areas of development in the early years? These are important issues because educators' views of science will influence the provision they make for children's learning. Having a framework of the kinds of skills, processes, attitudes and understandings that are important is helpful in identifying the scientific potential in activities, resources and children's interests.

Science with young children is about a search for explanations for phenomena in the biological and physical world. Through experiences both in and outside school children can begin to appreciate that explanations need to be developed and tested drawing on evidence. They can start to recognize the impact of science on our everyday lives and appreciate that science is a worldwide human endeavour. They can begin to think critically about science-based issues that may affect their lives and the local environment.

As well as learning about the nature of science itself, learning in science will involve the development of the following:

- *Concepts* – words such as dissolving, animal, shadow or life-cycle, or relationships such as 'a complete circuit of conducting material is needed for a current to flow'.
- *Skills*, such as measuring, using equipment or constructing charts.

- *Processes*, including questioning, observing, predicting, communicating, hypothesizing, interpreting and investigating.
- *Attitudes* – both positive attitudes to science and scientific attitudes, such as curiosity, respect for evidence, flexibility or sensitivity towards living things and the environment.

These elements are commonly reflected in science curricula across the primary school. For example, the Early Learning Goals (DfEE/QCA, 2000: 86, 88) highlight processes used in science:

Investigate objects and materials by using all of their senses as appropriate.

Find out about, and identify, some features of living things, objects and events they observe.

Look closely at similarities, differences, patterns and change.

Ask questions about why things happen and how things work.

National Curriculum requirements (DfEE, 1999) make reference to children's understanding of the nature of science and the investigative skills and processes associated with scientific inquiry and their conceptual development in the areas of life processes and living things, materials and their properties, and physical processes.

Selection of content

In selecting suitable scientific topics and activities a key consideration is the opportunities they might offer for the different areas of learning listed above. Historically practice in the early years has tended to focus on skills, processes and attitudes, many of which are employed across the curriculum. But the concepts and the messages you convey about the nature of science matter too. Often concepts will be embedded in the vocabulary you introduce or the phenomena or relationships you hope to highlight. The contexts chosen for science and the approaches adopted with children will give important messages about the nature of science. Taking advantage of incidental opportunities for learning science and encouraging children to begin to think about their impact on the environment can help reinforce connections between science learning and everyday life. Adults can act as important role models in showing interest or in referring to evidence in reviewing ideas.

There are many possible starting points for science topics. Some of these are shown in Figure 5.1. All of these would provide meaningful opportunities for science learning linked to children's everyday experiences. What is important is that there is a balance of opportunities over time for the

- General provision for indoor and outdoor play, such as sand and water, large toys, role play or cooking.
- Children's interests shown in the classroom or communicated by parents.
- Resources in the local environment, such as parks, building sites and shops, or the expertise of adults in the community, such as health visitors, cyclists or musicians.
- Familiar stories or events.
- Interactive displays of objects (for example, puppets or fruits and seeds).

Figure 5.1 *Starting points for science topics*

development of skills, processes, attitudes and concepts and a wide range of content related to living things, materials and physical processes.

Challenges in learning science

As suggested at the start of this chapter, studies of young children increasingly indicate young children's capabilities, but they also highlight some of the challenges in learning science. We need to identify and build on young children's capabilities but an awareness of the potential difficulties children may encounter is also important in planning learning experiences (Driver, 1983; Osborne and Freyberg, 1985).

First, the ideas children develop through their everyday experiences may not be in accord with scientific views although they may be logical from the child's perspective. This is hardly surprising as children have limited experience to draw upon. Many scientific ideas, such as the earth is a sphere or 'down' is towards the centre of the earth, can seem to go against common sense and cannot be easily derived from direct experience. Children's ideas are influenced by the surrounding language and culture. Take animals for example: 'No animals in this shop' does not mean that humans cannot enter but in science children need to begin to recognize that humans are animals. Comics often show light shooting out of the eyes of characters whereas scientific explanations talk about light travelling to the eye. Learning in science will therefore often involve not just taking on new knowledge but changing ideas and recognizing the differences between everyday and scientific ways of thinking. Extensive international research has revealed common 'misconceptions' held by both adults and children in different concept areas and it is very helpful to be aware of these, both in supporting the children and in avoiding unwittingly reinforcing misconceptions. The SPACE research reports (1990–8) and Nuffield Primary Science (1985) provide useful summaries of key concepts, common misconceptions and teaching strategies for changing ideas related to different content areas in science.

Secondly, although many young children spontaneously ask questions, make observations and look for explanations, scientific ways of working do not necessarily come naturally. Teaching and support will be needed to enable children to carry out investigations in a systematic and scientific way (Feasey, 1998; Goldsworthy, 1998). Children may need encouragement to articulate their predictions or explanations. Helping children talk and think about the strategies they are using, introducing skills and processes such as measuring and fair testing or asking children to evaluate their own investigations will all be important in developing children's abilities to understand and carry out scientific procedures.

Thirdly, despite growing evidence of young children's capabilities, their skills and understandings can be fragile and fleeting. Performance may be inconsistent or ideas not generalized or applied across different contexts. Ensuring children encounter ideas in a variety of contexts, providing different opportunities to develop and utilize skills and processes and helping children to make connections between one situation and another will all therefore be important.

Finally, learning in science will inevitably involve being prepared to make mistakes, take account of evidence that goes against your preconceptions and change ideas. This is not something that children or adults find easy (or even scientists!). Developing a supportive classroom climate will help children feel able to take risks. Acting as a role model, valuing children's learning from their mistakes and increasingly discussing the ways in which scientific ideas have changed can all be helpful.

Teaching and learning approaches and range of experience

Given what we know about children's capabilities and the challenges posed in learning science, what sorts of teaching and learning approaches are effective in promoting scientific development? Exploratory play and practical experience have always played a key role in early learning and can have a variety of purposes (see Figure 5.2).

However, direct practical experience is not always possible or effective. There are limitations in how far some areas of science can be explored practically (for example, earth in space or health and the human body) and a range of approaches is important to accommodate different learning styles. Finding information in second-hand sources such as videos, CD-ROMs or non-fiction books, exploring ideas through story, drama and role play or hearing about science from educators or visitors are all valuable.

Finally, while activity is important so too is the thinking, imagining and talking associated with it. Talk with peers and other adults plays a powerful role in

- Providing experiences of a range of scientific phenomena, such as the behaviour of magnets, the changes that take place in cooking, shadows in the environment or the needs and behaviour of small animals.

- Offering opportunities for sorting and classifying to support the development of scientific concepts, such as magnetic, transparent or hard.

- Demonstrating or illustrating scientific concepts, such as burning or light travelling (particularly if there are safety issues involved).

- Developing skills such as measuring or using a chart to record observations.

- Encouraging and building on children's explorations or problem-solving activities to help them develop their skills and understanding related to investigations.

Figure 5.2 *The value of exploratory play and practical experience*

Learning Story 5.4 Bones

In a nursery class a table had been set up with toy animals and picture books about animals. On the shelf nearby were a selection of animal bones and a book about bones. As children came to the table an adult engaged them in discussions about the names of animals and parts of their bodies.

Samuel picked up a skull, turning it over and making comments as he pointed to different features: 'Used to be gums like that . . . and take some of the teeth out . . . these are pointy ones, like vampire teeth . . . eye goes in there . . .'

He then took the conversation further. Here are some extracts to indicate the direction:

'Got bones inside' [bending his knuckles] there's my bones . . . when you starting to grow bones grow, get stretched . . . if you die bones only left. The rest goes away all the blood and skin goes away. Vampires come down and scoop up the blood and drink it up.'

The adult asked: 'how do you know?' Samuel said: 'I've seen a skeleton vampire', and he pointed to the bones book. For some time following this exchange the child and the adult looked through the book together. It contained pictures of the skeletons of different animals. Samuel said: 'These are all dinosaurs.' The adult suggested they look to see what the book said. She pointed out the skeletons of a fish, a duck and a dog. Samuel asked: 'When I die will I look like this?' They discussed the different bones in the skeletons and compared the skull from the classroom with the illustrations. This discussion continued for some time and other children were drawn into the process.

helping children to make their ideas or strategies explicit and available for change and development as they offer predictions and explanations for phenomena, articulate questions, discuss how they might tackle investigations or review their learning. Recording and reporting of activities through discussion, displays of drawings, photographs or models can help promote reflection and reinforce learning.

Learning Stories 5.4–5.6 illustrate a range of approaches to science and highlight the role of the adult in supporting learning. In each of these examples children's ideas and suggestions were taken seriously, allowing time for them to develop. In particular the adult in the 'Bones' example did not dismiss talk about vampires. She gradually elicited the child's connections between dinosaurs, vampires and skeletons and supported him in the process of thinking about his own skeleton and those of other animals. All three explorations built on children's ideas and responses and connections were made between home and school experience. Adult intervention helped to extend and sustain explorations in a variety of ways by providing additional resources, encouraging children to talk about what they were thinking and doing, setting new challenges or encouraging children to share and discuss findings with the class. The adults had a significant role too in highlighting key observations and drawing attention to the scientific knowledge and concepts that might be developed.

Learning Story 5.5 Making houses for the three pigs

Camilla came to school with a house she had made for the three pigs out of small boxes. She had cut out holes for the windows. It had a door on a Sellotape flap and a chimney. Her mother said she was always improvising houses out of whatever was available. The nursery teacher decided to use this as a theme for model-making in the construction area. She provided a variety of resources, boxes, plastic bottles and tubs, paper straws, lollipop sticks, newspaper and card with glue, string and Sellotape and watched to see what they would do. The children made houses and put them out on a nearby display table. Later when the class were together she read the story of the three pigs. Then they tried blowing the houses down with a balloon pump. Some blew sideways, the roofs came off a couple and one that was made out of a tall plastic bottle fell down. The class discussed how the houses could be made stronger. One child suggested that the tall bottle house needed to be 'big at the bottom'. The house was modified to have a bigger base and it worked. Over the next couple of weeks the children explored different ways of making strong and stable structures and then extended this testing different materials to see which would make their houses waterproof.

Learning Story 5.6 I spy on my way to school

At the start of the day Syreeta said she had seen a snail on the path on her way to school. On the following day Jack said he saw spiders in the garden. The teacher decided to build on these observations by asking the children to draw pictures of their animals and where they found them. He put them on a noticeboard labelled *I spy on my way to school*. He invited contributions from other children and their parents. This started with animals but began to include plants too. Children brought in drawings, writing and even photographs. The noticeboard offered rich opportunities for discussing the variety of life in the local environment and for similarities and differences between animals and habitats.

Transition from Foundation Stage to Key Stage 1

There is much still to be learnt about the development of children's capabilities in science but there are some features of progression that educators can observe. As children gain in experience they may increasingly:

- ask questions and suggest ideas;
- offer predictions and explanations based on previous knowledge and experience;
- tackle explorations and investigations more systematically, beginning to use measurement and to recognize the need for a fair test;
- notice patterns in observations;
- be able to communicate in a variety of ways;
- make links between one situation and another and begin to apply ideas in new situations; and
- show confidence and independence in their approach to science activities (Glauert, 1998).

The kinds of teaching and learning approaches suggested throughout this section will continue to be relevant as children enter the more formal stages of compulsory schooling. However pressures of time and prescribed curriculum content can make it more difficult to take account of children's ideas and interests, offer opportunities for children's own explorations and maintain a focus on developing children's skills and understanding as well as their factual knowledge. Here are some suggestions about how this might be achieved.

First of all, even if science topics are more frequently initiated by adults and determined by curriculum requirements, the contexts and direction for activities can still draw on children's ideas and interests. This need not be restricted to the start of the topic. Developing displays as in the examples described above, collecting children's questions over time, involving parents and having incidental discussion about the progress of topics are all ways of sustaining interest and dialogue across sessions and encouraging children's ideas and suggestions.

Carrying out background research into the topics you are teaching will be helpful in determining priorities. This will enable you to identify the most important teaching points or the particular concepts that children are likely to find difficult and will need to be the subject of your time and attention. Keeping these in mind may help maintain focus on the development of children's understandings in science.

Although it may not be possible to have extended periods for practical exploration, allowing time for play with new materials is important for learners of all ages. This can enable children to become familiar with the area of study and begin to formulate their ideas and questions. Coming up with ideas and questions is often hard to do immediately or in the abstract. In addition, leaving equipment or displays available for further study after activities can provide valuable opportunities to consolidate and extend learning.

If children are to develop the skills and understandings associated with scientific investigations they need both focused teaching of relevant skills and open-ended opportunities to make decisions for themselves in their own investigations. Whilst building these kinds of activities into curriculum planning is vital and is often neglected it is important to recognize that not all science needs to be approached in this way.

The organization of the timetable may not allow much time for visits outside the classroom but even short explorations in the local area can be invaluable. They can be used to highlight the ways in which living things colonize the built environment, changes across the seasons or the use of different materials for different purposes. Indeed the fact that you can return to places easily can be very useful in following up ideas.

Finally, science can provide a rich context for developing children's skills in literacy, numeracy and ICT through carrying out research using CD-ROMs or non-fiction texts, measuring and data handling, using models and simulations to develop ideas or recording in a variety of ways. Capitalizing on these connections across the curriculum makes learning more meaningful and can enhance opportunities for science learning.

There are many reasons for supporting science in the early years. It can capitalize on children's ideas and interests as they seek to understand the natural and made world and their place within it. There are opportunities to share in the wonder of all around us and the 'explanatory stories' (Millar and Osborne, 1998) scientists tell. It provides a rich context for developing skills and attitudes across the curriculum. Finally, science experiences can foster critical thinking, respect for evidence and a concern for the environment that will inform future decision-making as a person and as part of a wider local and global community.

History

This part of the discussion deals with the strand of knowledge and under-standing of the world that is concerned with time and with the past – what will later be called 'history' in the curriculum for older children.

Growing evidence of young children's capabilities

History has been thought of as a particularly difficult area of learning for young children, but as we are coming to understand in a more subject specific way about how children learn in different areas, we are refining our ideas about what their capabilities are and how they can be sensitively extended.

'Time' is a tricky business. You can't see it or touch it. Children need to develop 'a sense of time', but how does this happen? The young child who asks 'Have I had my lunch yet?' or 'Is it home-time?' is not showing us that she does not have a sense of time but precisely that she does! She knows that time is passing and that patterns can be seen in it. Markers can be used to divide it up. This is the beginning of progress towards the grasp that will be needed eventually of all the conventional ways of measuring time and the specialized vocabulary for talking about it. As we shall see later, language is particularly important in learning about the past. Chris Husbands (1996: 36) has said: 'Historical description is drenched in linguistic convention.'

In early childhood education, talk and activity related to morning, after-noon, yesterday, today, tomorrow, seasons, birthdays and festivals, last year, next year and so on are important gradually to build up an understanding of the way the passing of time can be described. The work of Pat Hoodless (2002) shows how very young children can understand how time is repre-sented and are aware of complex features of temporal narratives. Using story books such as *Where the Wild Things Are* (Sendak, 1963) and *Come away from the Water, Shirley* (Burningham, 1977), she gives examples of very young chil-dren confidently interpreting the ways in which writers present 'time' aspects in a narrative. These include recognizing 'jumps' in time, parallel story lines and the idea of subjective time.

Very young children can also surprise us. Consider the question a 7-year-old put to his parents, as shown in Learning Story 5.7. This is exciting because there is clear evidence here that this child is moving far beyond simply remembering things he has seen, done or been told. He has been putting things together in his mind and making something new.

Learning Story 5.7 The Victorians

An infants school had been working on a term-long topic on the Victorians that had involved every class in the school and most curriculum areas. As part of this they had also been looking at family trees and discussing family relationships in their own households, and in the past, including those of the royal family. Josh understood that people living during the reign of a particular monarch are sometimes known by a collective name. His parents were not a little startled to be asked: 'Did the Edwardians have children whose grandparents were Victorians?'

A second challenging aspect of understanding the past is to do with the fact that the past has, by definition, 'gone'. If we want, in some way, to 'know' about the past we cannot go back and experience it directly. We are dependent (for clues?) on the 'traces' of the past that have been left behind, so it is of *these* that the children should have first-hand experience. We will return to a discussion of this when we look at teaching and learning approaches. For the moment the important point about this way of thinking about the study of the past is that it always involves the interpretation of evidence – the detective work of history.

Finally, a third challenge comes from the fact that history is sometimes seen as a 'grown-up' subject, involving the grasp of complex concepts and necessarily dealing with the actions and concerns of adults, which young children are too inexperienced to understand. However, if the adults working with them are sufficiently aware of what this range of concepts and concerns are and can recognize and structure opportunities for children to build on their existing knowledge and experience, then children can grow in understanding. For this to happen, however, it is vital that practitioners in the early years have sufficient subject knowledge in history so that they can shape appropriate learning experiences for the children.

The nature of history

So what kind and level of historical knowledge do early years practitioners need in order to maximize learning for children? This is an interesting question, not least because, in shaping new school curricula for history, fierce debates have raged about the nature of history as a subject. Some of these have centred round the selection of historical content to be included. What should young people be taught about the past? Which people and events should children learn about?

Which time periods should be included? Other arguments have been about the relative balance of (and the relationship between) knowledge and skills – between knowing some historical 'stories' and being able to evaluate sources.

Are these debates relevant to early years educators? The guidance for the history National Curriculum for younger children at Key Stage 1 (DfEE, 1999) focuses on children exploring their own past and that of their carers, families, friends and neighbours and emphasizes the *recent* past – within living memory – so that the children can talk with people who remember. There are good reasons for this. The assumption is that this kind of focus is particularly meaningful to young children because it is a focus on a familiar world and about people they know. In these circumstances, it is reasonable to ask: 'What, then, is the early years practitioner expected to know? Surely it is just a question of being interested to find out, alongside the children?'

On the other hand there is also a requirement in Key Stage 1 to introduce children to 'significant people and events', but since the choice of these is left to teachers to determine, surely teachers can just choose people and events that they already know about. This spirit of inquiry – exploring together – and the retelling of stories about the past are important aspects of learning about the past but they are not enough. It is necessary to understand something more about the concepts and skills that are developing and to identify these we must return to ideas about the nature of history as a subject.

Concepts are important in learning in all curriculum areas, so what are the concepts that are special to history? It is useful to think of at least two types of concept. First, there are concepts to do with the 'stuff' of history – concepts (among many) like 'government', 'trade', 'technology', 'castle', 'battle', 'priest', 'slavery', 'migration'. These concepts might not seem relevant to the youngest children but they are among the many ideas that early experiences should lead towards. A child coming to understand the difference between, say, a castle and a palace, or learning about the possible meanings of a word like 'court' (royal or law), is grappling with sophisticated ideas to do with form and function. Additionally how some of these kinds of labels are applied can subtly depend on the perspective of the user – consider, for instance, the words 'settler', 'refugee', 'asylum-seeker', 'immigrant' – or 'mutiny', 'uprising', 'rebellion', 'revolution'.

Secondly, there are concepts like 'cause', 'consequence', 'change', 'continuity', 'interpretation' and 'evidence', which are crucial in learning in history and which transcend the particular circumstances we might be trying to understand. If children are to begin to do real historical thinking rather than just 'remembering', then they have to be introduced to this range of ideas. This applies even to the youngest children.

Selection of content

So, bearing in mind what we have said so far, what criteria should determine the choice of content for this aspect of the curriculum in early years settings? We have noted the good sense of starting from what children are most familiar with – their own lives and the lives of carers, families, friends and neighbours. But what aspects of these lives are 'historically' significant? What should we be drawing attention to in the learning opportunities we provide?

The children's own personal sense of time past may not stretch very far – they certainly remember things, but their ability to locate them on a personal time line will be undeveloped. Most children are also told stories at home about their own earlier lives and their sense of having a personal biography lengthens. This extends further as they come to understand that the older people around them have their own biographies that go further back in time.

Exploring this in a variety of ways is important, not just because it is personally meaningful to the child but because the birth and care of children are universal human functions. Focusing on them and developing the concepts and the vocabulary to think and talk about them make it possible then to look at the birth, growth and life experience of other children and other families in other places and times. This extends to all aspects of family life. How do we live? How is it similar and different for people in different places and at different times?

It is important to note, at this point, that attitudes to difference can be positive or negative and cultural sensitivity is vital. This applies to sensitivity to differences within the class as well as to sensitivity about the lives of people in other places and times. We know, for instance, that children often think that ways of life other than their own are odd or wrong and sometimes our teaching can inadvertently feed these views. The Romans were not, for instance, too stupid to invent electricity.

Notice that we refer to different places as well as different times. This is important because it draws attention to the fact that place is an important aspect of understanding the past. The links to the geographical aspects of the curriculum are very strong. The environment of the school and home, usually in the same neighbourhood, again will be a personally meaningful place to start. Some families stay put, others make long journeys. They travel different distances and do so for different reasons. Again this is historically significant because journeying is a universal human activity.

I am trying to explain that through a focus on the lives of the children and their families, links can be made to more general historical phenomena. The rather loose additional requirement at Key stage 1 to study people and events can then be linked to these – for instance, it would be appropriate to introduce children to a significant local figure or event from the past.

Teaching and learning approaches and range of experience

We have said that one of the main challenges of teaching and learning about the past is that the past cannot be experienced directly; we can only learn about it from the traces of it that have been left behind. The kind of teaching and learning experiences that will be vital, then, are those that bring children into contact with these traces.

So what is left over from the past? Different kinds of traces have different potential for learning.

Objects

Working with objects from the past is frequently suggested as a particularly rich way of learning (Durbin et al., 1990). The presence of a historical object in the classroom allows children to use their senses, to observe, describe, compare and contrast, speculate and so on. The range of objects that are useful is wide and includes, of course, modern objects for the purposes of comparison. Close observation is very important; however, too often work with objects goes no further than this. Objects that are made and/or used by human beings have historical significance because they are examples of material culture. Children in the Foundation Stage and Key Stage 1 are not too young to be encouraged to ask what something is made from and how it might have been made, as well as what it might be for and who might have used it. The environment, of course, is full of objects that can be explored in the same way, including buildings and monuments of all kinds.

Pictures

Picture sources similarly provide evidence about the past. A picture *is* an object, of course, and has been made using a particular technology. In this way it can be related to the time and circumstances of its production. But it is also a representation *of* something – its maker intended to convey something through its making. This is a particularly powerful aspect of work with pictures because it opens up the way for the discussion of 'interpretation'. How do you think the picture-maker wanted to make this subject look? And so on.

Written sources

Written sources are also very important, though some will be too difficult for children to access without help. Diaries, letters, inscriptions, inventories, census returns and surveys are all written sources that offer rich possibilities.

Stories

Finally, we must reserve a special place for 'stories'. This is a broad inclusive category and a crucial one. Indeed, one definition of history is that it is the 'stories that we tell ourselves about the past'. This description is helpful because it highlights the narrative aspect of history and alerts us to the fact that there can be many stories and many story-tellers. For instance, a child explaining how she has changed since she was a baby, an elderly visitor to the classroom describing her childhood and a writer describing the events of the Gunpowder Plot are all building a story. And all these stories can be subjected to the questions: 'What does this tell us?' and 'How could we tell if it is true?'

So if these are the kinds of traces of the past that children can be brought into contact with, what forms can that contact take? What practical activities will be valuable? There is currently a great deal of interest in different modes of learning and these suggest a range of learning experiences. In history language is vitally important. Exposure to stories and opportunities to make their own stories must be a central part of the curriculum – stories in books, stories told by visitors to the classroom and by the teacher, stories stimulated by other sources and including those told by the children themselves. Links to language development are inextricable. Then these stories need to be evaluated, compared and contrasted and these evaluations justified: 'I think this because . . .' Talk will be crucial for young children. 'Writing down' is of secondary importance.

Kinaesthetic modes of learning will be important – for instance, making things, dressing up, role play, using different technologies and talking about who uses them, where and when – the conditions of life and how people solve the problems that they face (see Learning Story 5.8).

Learning Story 5.8 Kinaesthetic learning

In a school undertaking a whole-school topic on the Tudors, the nursery children and their teachers turn the role-play area into a 'Tudor' kitchen. They have visited Queen Elizabeth's hunting lodge in Epping Forest and looked at pictures of Tudor buildings and interiors. The corner is relined with plain sugar paper with dramatic oak beams applied with paint. An open hearth is built and a cooking pot suspended. A spit is improvised. Only simple furniture is left and bright colours are eliminated with brown paint. Cooking implements are researched from pictures in books – bowls and wooden platters, knives and spoons, and the food items are meat and vegetables. Herbs are on display. Outside a knot garden is planted. Clothes to dress up in have been made and are well used. On other occasions the children have the opportunity to hear Tudor music played and see Tudor musical instruments. Throughout the school there are displays that reflect the whole-school involvement. There is constant talk about Tudor times that extends throughout the school and overflows into the home.

Transition from Foundation Stage to Key Stage 1

There is no need for abrupt changes in approach as children get older. As with all learning, the important thing is that the learner can make sense of new experiences by relating them to what is known already. The Key Stage 1 curriculum for history in England and Wales does not specify very particular content to be taught and this is helpful. It enables teachers to shape experiences for the children that will connect with what they understand already.

History *is* a demanding subject because there is a limit to what young children can do on their own. They can be encouraged to pose historical questions, but they will need careful support in pursuing their inquiries. Planning the curriculum for history requires knowledge and skill. Choosing topics and finding appropriate sources will be vital. It will always be important, also, to be aware of children's interests and take up opportunities for historical inquiry that arise from them. Learning in history does not have to be limited to occasional stories or projects. It should be ongoing and cumulative so that interest and curiosity are sustained.

As they get older children will be able to ask more sophisticated questions and make connections. They will develop a deeper grasp of chronology and of the nature of historical explanation. These are processes that are not confined to learning in school, of course. It is very clear from the steady increase in the numbers of visitors to museums and sites of historical interest, the sales of books and magazines with historical content and the range of broadcasting devoted to history that there is a deep and widespread interest in it. Young children at home and at school are joining this community of interest.

Geography

Here we consider the aspects of knowledge and understanding of the world that are to do with geographical skills, knowledge and understanding.

Growing evidence of young children's capabilities

From an ability to follow simple plans to talking with some understanding about far-away places, these talents have time and again surprised those who have conducted research into younger children's views of the world around them. They appear to know so much. At one time it was thought that little was worth teaching to younger children beyond topics which centred on the local area and immediate environment. Although this is still clearly relevant we now know much more about children's views and interests to alter our thinking. Educators should not underestimate the children's competencies and need to take a wide approach to their ongoing geographical learning.

Care and concern for the environment

One of the most significant findings (Palmer 1994; 1995; 1998) shows that children as young as 4 have gained considerable knowledge about the world around them and are capable of sophisticated thinking and feeling about environmental issues. Pictures and photographs were shown to young children of cold places, tropical rainforests and recycling of rubbish. Researchers conducted interviews to find out just what the children knew and understood. For instance:

> 95% of the children made a valid observation when shown pictures of the rainforests such as *lots of trees* and 50% were able to give a name such as *rainforest, jungle, forest or wood*. About one third of children were able to give at least one accurate fact about climate or atmosphere, 18% regarded forests as dangerous or frightening places (Palmer, 1994).

Of course, the children's ideas were at times incomplete or blurred. However, Palmer's work highlights the fact that teachers need to be aware that their children will have ideas about the environment, that misconceptions do exist and through this they can help to develop future learning. They need to accept that the children are active thinkers in the area of environmental issues and are constantly trying to relate the ideas they encounter to their own experience.

An experience of a range of different environments

It is an interesting phenomenon that in some western countries children in their early years are being exposed less to their local area whilst at the same time journeying further away and more often to distant environments through holidays. Parents more than ever are placing restrictions on children 'playing out' because of their fears about busy and polluted roads and 'stranger danger'. Children in fact need access to their local surroundings in order to develop a sense of personal identity, to learn to follow routes and to build up a sense of direction. Also, they need to be able to make decisions when on their own and learn how to act responsibly.

A knowledge and understanding of their own environment is essential when it comes to making comparisons with other places and in more distant parts of the world. Mayer Hillman (1998), who has researched the long-term consequences of reducing children's freedom to explore in their local area, argues very strongly for a rethink on public policy to embrace the full spectrum of children's lives to spend more of their leisure time in the outdoor environment. Home zones are already being experimented with in some British cities in an attempt to provide safe areas for play in the close community. What it does mean is that educators of young children need to plan carefully in order to build in the experiences of the very local, at the same time still recognizing that children may well be knowledgeable about other countries or places through personal travel, story settings they encounter in books or from watching films and television. It has been shown that many British 4-year-olds have heard of France and Spain and that 7-year-olds frequently add Greece and Italy to their repertoire (Weigand, 1993).

Using or making simple maps, plans and diagrams

Geographers use the term 'graphicacy' to describe the ways in which we locate and position ourselves in the world through maps, plans and diagrams. It is a world of visual images now further enhanced through the use of computer technology. Like print literacy it employs the processes of identifying, decoding and interpreting symbols. In developing their graphicacy skills children may be using computer software, signs, symbols, diagrams, photographs, maps, atlases or globes in the context of their learning. There is plenty of evidence from research studies to show that working with these sorts of resources can still come within the remit of younger-aged children. For instance, a project led by Blades and Spencer (Plester, 2000) found that both 4 and 5-year-old children are capable of using both oblique and vertical aerial photographs as navigation aids in the familiar territory of the school playground. They had considerable success in both naming features on the photographs and in using the photographs to locate Easter eggs hidden in four places in the area.

Children have had similar successes when using a scale model or very simple plan to find the 'treasure' or teddy hidden in the nursery classroom (e.g. Blades and Spencer, 1986; Perry and Campbell, 1999). Similarly they show some ability to follow routes and recognize especially designed symbols on a map for roads, rivers, parks and even the use of simple co-ordinates. Classic Piagetian approaches questioned the notion that children were capable of understanding these more 'abstract' mapping concepts. This does not appear to be the case. In fact the question now worth asking is: 'How are the children doing it?'

Support and help in order to foster cultural development

Children's images of and attitudes towards other countries and the people living there are of huge importance in today's multicultural and interdependent world. Even before they reach school age children are developing attitudes, beliefs and values about other people and places. Some of these may be positive but it is also a fact that stereotyping and expressing negative reactions to other ethnic groups can be found in children as young as 4 (Aboud, 1988). It has also been found that 5 and 7-year-old British children expressed a liking for the French and Spanish (countries about which the children were best informed). They expressed negative views about the Germans, even though they had little knowledge of them.

It would appear, though, that at a young age these ideas are superficial and are relatively easy to counter or change. Harrington (1998) quotes a small-scale student study where 6-year-olds changed their images of Africa as a result of a short teaching programme whilst 10-year-olds tended to retain their negative attitudes. It all argues very strongly for an inclusive approach in which very young children are given opportunities to experience other communities both in their own and other localities. Connections to other places help children understand both themselves and those places in meaningful ways and to imagine the kind of world they might want to construct.

The nature of geography

Children, then, are natural geographers with a desire to explore their surroundings. They become aware of places and have experience of investigating them from the moment they begin to move around. They are keen to explore and search for meaning from their immediate environment. By the time children go to school they are aware of the world around them and have acquired a notion of their own identity. The phrase 'knowledge and understanding of the world' is a particularly appropriate one and describes an early year's approach which leads on to the teaching of geography during formal schooling. The central purpose of a geographical education is to continue to give children a fuller, more rounded, structured opportunity to view, perceive, understand and respond to the world in which they live (Smeaton, 1998). This is absolutely vital because it will ultimately be their decisions which will determine the well-being or not of the earth's environments and its future resources.

The subject helps children to develop an informed concern about the quality of the environment and the future of the human habitat. Geography describes our world and geographers seek to understand and explain the interaction of people with their environment. Geographers try to describe the patterns and processes involved and suggest and use key geographical questions to study places and aspects of the environment. The sorts of questions which might be asked of children between 5 and 7, for instance, are as follows:

- Where is this place?
- What is this place like?
- What do you like/dislike about it?
- How do you think it became like this?
- How could it be improved upon?
- How is it similar or different from other places that you know?

Starting with what is called an 'inquiry' approach should lead into creative, motivating and questioning situations for children to pursue their studies. Young geographers are taught the skills of fieldwork and the use of maps, atlases, globes and diagrams. They are introduced to simple geographical terms and use the scientific principles of how to describe, explain and predict. Their work often crosses the boundaries with other subjects. They use their emerging literacy, numeracy and ICT skills to support their learning. They also find that the subject encourages debate and the need to see a situation from a range of opinions and views. Even the youngest children will have their thoughts about how perhaps their playground environment could be improved upon or made more attractive. This leads on to knowing about how decisions are made in school and how they can contribute to the decision-making process. They might work in groups and so recognize the importance of working with others.

Geography also features strongly in the new models for citizenship education (DfES, 2002). Through the subject children develop skills of questioning and communication, which helps them to reflect on and discuss issues, problems and events. The focus on environmental issues means that the links between geography and education for sustainable development are clearly very strong. Geography gives opportunities for children to learn that resources can be allocated in different ways and that the nature of these choices can affect individuals, communities and the sustainability of the environment. Similarly as they learn about their own locality and distant places they come to appreciate the diversity of cultures and identities. The connections with other countries in the world begin to become apparent. With this in mind the children begin to develop skills of empathy, learn to respect diversity and understand the need for racial harmony.

Selection of content

The curriculum and content for children in the Foundation Stage have always emphasized beginning from where the children are and the use of first-hand experiences. It is assumed that practitioners are fully aware of the potential of their children in all the areas of learning and have a good knowledge of the possibilities of working in the local environment. This may not always be the case. Teachers in the early years still need to draw upon and keep up to date with 'subject' knowledge, pedagogy and current research in all the areas of learning just as teachers in Years 2, 6, 9 or 11 need to update their knowledge of the subjects of the curriculum.

Young children need opportunities and space to explore and discover, observe and record. They also need opportunities through play to develop and make sense of their ideas and views of the world. Hence in a general sense teachers plan for a wide variety of activities both indoors and outdoors to help their children make progress through the Stepping Stones and Early Learning Goals provided in the *Curriculum Guidance for the Foundation Stage* (DfEE/QCA, 2000). In terms of a sense of place these are more specific:

- Observe, find out and identify features in the place they live and in the natural world.
- Find out about their environment, and talk about those features they like and dislike. (p.96)

It presupposes a range of activities which will not only develop this but which will obviously overlap into other aspects, such as:

- Begin to know about their own cultures and beliefs and those of other people.
- Look closely at similarities, differences, patterns and change. (pp. 88, 98)

Two extracts from 2002 OFSTED school inspection reports, in which the children make very good progress, highlight the sort of approach and content areas that can be provided (see Learning Stories 5.9 and 5.10).

Learning Story 5.9
Learning about the world in a south London primary school

The children learn about the world in and around the school, making good use of the school's site and further afield, on numerous visits to widen their horizons. They receive good direct teaching on the use of computers. They develop an awareness of past times from events they recall in their family lives, and from looking at the life cycles of insects and frogs. They talk about the seasons, the changes in weather and the passage of time. The teachers introduce the children well to the cultural richness of various faiths and nationalities in the locality.

Learning Story 5.10 A geographical perspective at an infant and nursery school in Liverpool

In the reception classes, the work on 'Our World' has resulted in a sound understanding of what can be found in the locality and on children's journeys to school. They can describe their route well and draw it as a simple plan. In another class children use travel brochures to select places they would like to visit. This work is illustrated with cut out pictures and the children are able to explain why they choose certain places. For example, one boy was able to explain his love of mountains.

The core content of the National Curriculum for geography (DfEE, 1999) for 6 and 7-year-olds comprises five elements:

1 Geographical inquiry and skills, which includes asking questions of a geographical nature, recording and communicating in a variety of ways.
2 Developing geographical skills, such as the use of geographical terms and vocabulary, fieldwork skills, using maps and plans, atlases and globes.
3 Knowledge and understanding of chosen places both local and distant.
4 Beginning to see and recognize some of the more obvious patterns and processes involved in change in the landscape and in towns and cities.
5 A developing knowledge and understanding of environmental change and sustainable development.

The QCA geography schemes of work (DfES, 2000) comprehensively translate these broad areas into themes and units of work. Schools rightly adapt them according to their circumstances and resources. Once again, a good glimpse of how this is achieved is provided by a south London school (see Learning Story 5.11).

Leaning Story 5.11
Translating the QCA geography scheme of work into themes and units of work

Geography is mainly taught within topics for the younger pupils in the school, which is often when pupils begin to think about the wider world. The topic on transport in Year 1 is associated with travelling to places outside the pupils' immediate locality. The pupils in Year 1 identify features they see on the way to school. The pupils in Year 2 talk in detail about Catford. Many visits provide valuable opportunities for fieldwork. Catford is used a great deal by the school for local studies.

Using and making maps is a strong aspect of the pupils' learning. The pupils develop the ideas of position and direction – when in Year 1 the pupils make simple maps of the way to the park and in Year 2 the pupils learn about compass directions. They improve mapping skills by making a map of a Treasure Island.

The pupils develop a good knowledge and understanding of characteristic features of other places. The pupils in Year 2 begin to appreciate wider geographical location and improve their cultural development when they learn about St Lucia as a contrasting locality. (Adapted from an OFSTED school inspection report, 2002).

Another interesting point made about the school is the use of the work in geography to support teaching and learning in literacy and numeracy as is also the good progress made by children with special educational needs and English as an additional language because of the quality of resources and the help that is given by support staff.

Teaching and learning approaches and range of experience

The teaching of geography in England is seen as lagging behind other subjects and a 'cause for concern' (OFSTED, 2002). Although inspectors found a great deal of satisfactory teaching they said that the expectations of teachers were still too low and the quality and range of learning opportunities limited. Effective teaching has to provide opportunities for a variety of teaching and learning strategies because children learn in different ways and have different learning needs. Also, some geographical themes lend themselves to particular approaches – for instance, debate, discussion and role play often help children understand environmental issues better. Fieldwork is a characteristic feature of many geography units of work. A continuum of approaches relevant to the teaching of the immediate local area for early years educators and teachers of 6 and 7-year-olds is shown in Figure 5.3

And, of course, good teachers are not frightened to incorporate the unexpected – see Learning Story 5.12.

Learning Story 5.12
Kite-flying at a south London primary school

The reception teaching ranges from good to excellent. On occasions, it is inspired. For instance, on a windy afternoon, when the children were not too interested in phonic sounds, the teacher took them out kite flying. Their intense concentration proves once again that learning is best when it is relevant and fun. Consequently they [the children] love coming to school, and work well throughout the busy day. (OFSTED, school inspection report, 2002)

- Direct teaching of knowledge and skills – showing how an aerial photograph can be used to identify, record and label features of the landscape.

- Fieldwork activities – go for a walk in the local area and identify features, take photographs, follow a simple map, observe and describe a local landmark, talk about likes and dislikes.

- Using the outdoor setting or playground environment to develop treasure hunts, recreate the local street layout, learn about direction and use simple maps and plans.

- Other practical activities which stimulate curiosity and interest – introduce children to a character such as a toy bear (for example, Barnaby in the geography schemes of work) and take photographs of him in the local community. Where else could he visit?

- Quality interactions with each other and with adults through play – what do we need for, and how can we set up, the park keepers' hut or the nearby garden centre as a role play area?

- Carefully framed questions, posing problems – what does this picture show? Where is it? What are the people doing? What should people not do there? Is it a safe place?

- Gathering information – do a traffic count identifying the colours, number or type of vehicles, using a range of methods to count and display the results.

- Strategies which build on the children's knowledge and achievements – provide play maps, home-made and commercially produced, to show roads and rail tracks. These can be used for younger children to create their own townscapes. In this way children can learn to follow routes and to locate and construct buildings in sensible places.

- Using displays to interact with and enhance learning – make a display of vehicles, including the children's own paintings and drawings, and label these with inquiry questions such as 'Who travels in this?' 'How many people could travel in this car?'

Figure 5.3 *Teaching the local area*

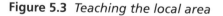

Transition from Foundation Stage to Key Stage 1

One of the biggest issues facing geography and other foundation subjects in Key Stage 1 is the competition for available time and the heavy emphasis that is placed upon English, mathematics and science often at the expense of other subjects: 'In a significant minority of schools pressure on the primary curriculum has reduced the breadth and depth of the geography curriculum' (OFSTED, 2001). A year later things were no better: 'In a significant number of schools, insufficient time and resources are allocated to geography' (OFSTED, 2002). Improving pupils' work in geography and putting geography back on the map were still seen as the key issues for schools to address. Improving subject leadership in geography is also recognized as an area for development. The OFSTED subject report gives some clues as to the way forward. In more and more lessons, particularly in Key stage 1, literacy is being used to enhance geographical learning. Increasingly, good use is being made of ICT applications in geography. So subjects overlap and the nature of learning becomes more holistic. With this in mind and in order to account for a citizenship curriculum the question of time, balance and purpose needs to be revisited. Schools need to see their pupils as confident future citizens with attendant hopes and aspirations for the world they live in. If these pupils are viewed as having creative minds capable of making decisions about their world, the way forward is to have reinstated a curriculum which is genuinely broad and balanced in order to develop the whole person.

Partnership with parents

Parents are the children's first and most enduring educators. When parents and practitioners work together in early years settings, the results have a positive impact on the child's development and learning (DfEE/QCA, 2000). Clearly, a successful partnership with parents requires a two-way flow of information, expertise and ideas. Schools can help parents support their teaching and curriculum development in this area of learning in a number of ways.

The knowledge and expertise of parents and other family adults can be used to support the learning opportunities (see Learning Story 5.13). Information about children's preferred activities or interests at home can also be used as a starting point for school-based learning. The two science activities discussed earlier ('Making houses for the three pigs' and 'I spy on my way to school') developed from interests children had shown at home. Experiences at home can be used to develop learning at school – for example, visits, celebrations or journeys (see Learning Story 5.14).

Learning Story 5.13
Using the knowledge and expertise of adults

Children have a good awareness of their local area and can draw picture maps talking about the hills, trees, woods, railway line and fence. This was in the context of a lesson in the school grounds where the children tried to draw a map locating where they would build a house. Part of the inspiration for this came from the visit of a parent who was a mapmaker herself. (1999 OFSTED School Inspection report of a Church of England primary school, Burnham on Crouch).

Learning Story 5.14 Experiences at home

Visits and celebrations
Children develop their investigational skills well and the wide range of visits enhances their knowledge of the local and distant communities. On special days, particularly birthdays and celebrations from the wide range of cultures and religions in school, pupils increase their knowledge of different cultures by joining in the celebrations. (2000 OFSTED school inspection report of a primary school, Balham).

Journeys
Hazareesingh et al. (1994) describe a whole-school topic on 'journeys' which involved children and their families and the teachers at the school in describing and mapping important journeys in their lives, recording stories of past experiences, translating them into other languages and making them available to the school community through assemblies and displays.

Expeditions into the local environment – special expeditions and ordinary ones – can all be occasions for developing a curiosity about the way the environment and the lives of different members of the community are changing. The increasing range of educational opportunities offered by places children may visit on family outings (such as parks and museums) provides invaluable experiences to support learning across the curriculum. Teachers can also help by suggesting relevant learning and play activities for parents to follow with their children.

The reading and sharing of books is widely promoted, and positive help and encouragement to look at the story setting and picture images supports the development of early geographical, historical or scientific vocabulary (see Learning Story 5.15). Any journey, visiting friends, going shopping, the way to school, gives parents the chance to talk about directions and places. The preparations for journeys and experiences during family holidays are obviously a rich source of early geographical learning for the children.

Learning Story 5.15 Baby Bird

In the *Maths Together* series (Walker Books, 1999) a selection of picture books includes *Baby Bird* who has only one thing on his mind: he wants to fly into the sky and nothing is going to stop him. The notes for parents, which come with this series, highlight how the book gives the child a gentle introduction to the difficult concepts of position and direction. Ideas given to support the learning include a picture map to trace Baby Bird's journey from the nest and a tree of words that are used to explain where something is or the direction in which it is going.

Schools may suggest activities that children and adults can carry out together at home linked to topics addressed in school. For example, the materials produced by the School Home Investigations in Primary Science Project (1991 onwards) provide useful examples of science activities that can be carried out at home with everyday materials. They were designed to link school and home in supporting children's learning and increasing children's enjoyment in science.

Educators can communicate with parents about the aims and purposes of the curriculum and the kinds of approaches adopted in their settings. Open evenings where parents have opportunities to engage in the kinds of experiences provided for their children can be one of the most successful ways of achieving this.

In these and other ways the close partnership can be built between educators, parents and children that is so important in learning.

Endnote

As the sections in the chapter indicate, we should not underestimate young children as they seek to make sense of the world around them. The world is vast, complex and full of wonder and excitement. Young children are entitled to a broad curriculum that recognizes this – a curriculum that draws on their interests as well as providing a foundation for their future lives and lifelong learning.

Suggested further reading

Cooper, H. (1995) *History in the Early Years* (2nd edn). London: RoutledgeFalmer.

de Boo, M. (ed.) (2000) *Science 3–6: Laying the Foundations in the Early Years*. Hatfield: Association for Science Education.

Heal, C. and Cook, J. (1998) 'Humanities – developing a sense of place and time in the early years', in I. Siraj-Blatchford (ed.) *A Curriculum Development Handbook for Early Childhood Educators*. Stoke-on-Trent: Trentham Books.

Palmer, J.A. (1994) *Geography in the Early Years*. London and New York, NY: Routledge.

References

Aboud, F. (1988) *Children and Prejudice*. Oxford: Blackwell.

Baillargeon, R. (1994) 'Physical reasoning in young infants: seeking explanations for impossible events', *British Journal of Developmental Psychology*, 12: 9–33.

Blades, M. and Spencer, C. (1986) 'Map use by young children', *Geography*, 71: 42–52.

Brown, A.L., Campione, J.C., Metz, K.E. and Ash, D.B. (1997) 'The development of science learning abilities in children', in H. Kjell and B. Arnold (eds) *Growing up with Science*. London: Jessica Kingsley.

Burningham, J. (1977) *Come away from the Water, Shirley*. London: Random Century Children's Books.

DfEE (1999) *The National Curriculum at Key Stage 1 and Key Stage 2*. London: DfEE/QCA.

DfEE/QCA (2000) *Curriculum Guidance for the Foundation Stage*. London: QCA.

DfES (2000) *Primary Geography: Schemes of Work*. London: DfES.

DfES (2002) *Citizenship a Scheme of Work for Key Stages 1 and 2. Teachers' Guide*. London: DfES/QCA.

Driver, R. (1983) *The Pupil as Scientist?* Milton Keynes: Open University Press.

Durbin, G., Morris, S. and Wilkinson, S. (1990) *A Teacher's Guide to Learning from Objects*. London: English Heritage.

Feasey, R. (1998) 'Scientific investigations in context', in R. Sherrington (ed.) *ASE Guide to Primary Science Education*. Cheltenham: Stanley Thornes.

Glauert, E. (1998) 'Science in the early years', in I. Siraj- Blatchford (ed.) *A Curriculum Development Handbook for Early Childhood Educators*. Stoke-on-Trent: Trentham Books.

Goldworthy, A. (1998) 'Learning to investigate' in R, Sherrington (ed.) *ASE Guide to Primary Science Education*. Cheltenham: Stanley Thornes.

Goldsworthy, A. and Feasey, R. (1997) *Making Sense of Primary Science Investigations*. Hatfield: Association for Science Education.

Harrington, V. (1998) 'Teaching about distant places', in S. Scoffham (ed.) *Primary Sources: Research Findings in Primary Geography*. Sheffield: Geographical Association/Thanet Press.

Hazareesingh, S. with Kenway, P. and Simms, K. (1994) *Speaking about the Past. Oral History for 5–7 Year Olds*. Stoke-on-Trent: Trentham Books.

Hillman, M. (1998) 'Neighbourhood safety', in S. Scoffham (ed.) *Primary Sources: Research Findings in Primary Geography*. Sheffield: Geographical Association/Thanet Press.

Hoodless, P. (2002) 'An investigation into children's developing awareness of time and chronology in story', *Journal of Curriculum Studies*, 34(2): 173–200.

Husbands, C. (1996) *What is History Teaching? Language, Ideas and Meaning in Learning about the Past*. Milton Keynes: Open University Press.

Millar, R. and Osborne, J. (1998) *Beyond 2000: Science Education for the Future*. London: Kings College London, School of Education.

Navarra, J.G. (1955) *The Development of Scientific Concepts in a Young Child*. New York, Teachers College Press.

Nuffield Primary Science (1985) *Nuffield Primary Science Teachers' Guides*. London: Collins Educational.

OFSTED (2000–2) *Primary Subject Reports (Geography)* London: OFSTED.

Osborne, R. and Freyberg, P. (1985) *Learning in Science*. London: Heinemann Educational.

Palmer, J.A. (1994) *Geography in the Early Years*. London and New York, NY: Routledge.

Palmer, J.A. (1995) 'Environmental thinking in the early years: understanding and misunderstanding of concepts relating to waste management', *Environmental Education Research*, 1(1).

Palmer, J.A. (1998) 'Environmental cognition in young children', in S. Scoffman (ed.) *Primary Sources*. Sheffield: The Geographical Association.

Perry, V. and Campbell, R. (1999) 'The development of young children's understanding of the relationship between a model and the room it represents'. Paper presented at the British Psychological Society Development Section conference, September.

Plester, B. (2000) 'Young children using aerial photographs in a treasure hunt', in *Raising Achievement in Geography Occasional Paper* 1. London: Register of Research in Primary Geography.

Sendak, M. (1963) *Where the Wild Things Are*. New York, Harper & Row.

Smeaton, R. (1998) In *Handbook of Primary Geography*. Sheffield: Geographical Association.

SPACE (1990–8) *Research Reports*. Liverpool: Liverpool University Press.

Weigand, P. (1993) *Children and Primary Geography*. London: Cassell.

6

Physical development and physical education

Richard Bailey, Jonathan Doherty and Russell Jago

> *Physical Education makes me feel as if I could fly away!*
> (Primary school pupil from Leeds, quoted in Talbot, 2001: 47)

Introduction: Movement in the Lives of Children

Movement plays a central role in children's development and learning. Observe almost any infant, in almost any setting, and you will see ample evidence of this: through movement, children learn about their bodies, their physical and social environments; they try out different roles and rules; they test themselves. Indeed, it might be claimed that movement, action and play make up the 'culture of childhood' (Bruner, 1983).

What recognition is there that movement is so important in children's learning and development in their early education? Jan-Roar Bjorkvold (1989) has suggested that there is too frequently a clash between 'child culture' and 'school culture'; between children's natural and spontaneous way of learning and the approach to learning offered by schools (see Table 6.1). Readers might like to reflect for a moment on the school experiences of the children they know or teach. Do they build on 'child culture'? Are they playful, sensory and dynamic? Do these children approach the activities presented to them with a sense of joy and passion? For many children, one of the most likely contexts for these types of feelings and experiences is physical activity. We suggest that this fact is of enormous significance to parents, carers and teachers seeking to provide genuinely child-centred and child-respecting experiences. Movement experiences, such as physical education lessons, playground games and informal physical activities, are among the most obvious and appealing ways of keeping in touch with 'child culture' and giving them experiences of delight and pleasure that may be missing

Table 6.1 *The clash between child and school culture*

Child culture	School culture
Play	Study
Being in	Reading about
Physical proximity	Physical distance
Testing one's own limits	Respecting boundaries set by others
The unexpected	The expected
Sensory	Intellectual
Physical movement	Physical inactivity
I move and I learn!	Sit still!

from other parts of their daily lives. As such, there is a strong case for considering movement at part of the true 'core' curriculum for young children.

A movement education

In presenting 'The case for physical education' at the World Summit on Physical Education, Margaret Talbot (2001: 39) lists six distinctive features of movement-based activities which no other learning or school experiences share:

1 They are the only educational experiences where the focus is on the body, physical activity and physical development.
2 They help children to develop respect for the body – their own and others.
3 They contribute towards the integrated development of mind and body.
4 They develop understanding of the role of aerobic and anaerobic physical activity in health.
5 They positively enhance self-confidence and self-esteem.
6 They enhance social and cognitive development and academic achievement.

There are many different ways of thinking about the content and character of physical education. For present purposes, we are going to draw upon a useful model for understanding the different elements of the experiences (Arnold, 1979; Bailey, 1999b). The model conceives of physical education in terms of three general themes:

1 Education *about* movement.
2 Education *through* movement.
3 Education *in* movement.

Education *about* movement

This aspect stresses the value of introducing pupils to a range of physical activities, as well as the concepts, rules and procedures associated with them. Of course, there are many activities that pupils might experience, and each can make a contribution to their development and education. The National Curriculum (DfEE, 2000), for example, states that all children from 5 years should experience a broad and balanced range of movement experiences, including the following:

● Dance activities.
● Games activities.
● Gymnastics activities.

Of course, there is no suggestion that these three types of activity represent the totality of children's movement experiences. Rather, they are the minimum expected content during timetabled lessons.

In learning about movement it is important that children come to know the range and character of the activity areas. Performance of these activities constitutes a vital aspect of this knowledge. By taking part in different structured activities, children can come to know how to move in particular situations to achieve certain outcomes. At the same time, they also need to come to know that some ways of moving offer success or are more aesthetically pleasing than others.

Different children enjoy and succeed in different activities, and the breadth of the physical education curriculum is a recognition of this fact. A narrow emphasis on competitive team games threatens to alienate a large proportion of the school population, as well as rob them of valuable learning experiences. An adequate education about movement, therefore, introduces the full range of movement experiences and offers each pupil the opportunity to excel.

Education *through* movement

This aspect of the physical education curriculum refers to the use of physical activities as a means of achieving educational goals which are not necessarily part of those activities. An important aspect of this concept, and one that is particularly significant during the early years, is the contribution physical education can make to work in other areas of the curriculum. Movement is particularly well placed to act as a vehicle for learning across the whole curriculum since, as we have argued above, it plays so fundamental a role in children's general learning and development.

Movement experiences can create a learning environment that is enabling and fun, which allows pupils to relax and enjoy learning. By presenting learning situations as games and play, teachers can encourage pupils who may have built up resistance to lower their defences, frustrations and anxieties, and develop their skills and understanding almost incidentally as they engage in physical activity. Also, as physical activity and play are universal to all children around the world, pupils become involved in experiences that bridge differences in social or cultural background or intelligence (Bailey, 1999b).

Nowhere is the potential for education through movement more apparent than in the area of language. Hopper and her colleagues (2000: 91) suggest that 'translating movements into spoken language in a variety of contexts offers a treasure chest of descriptive, directional and action words for children to explore and experience'. The scope of language usage implicit within physical education is vast, and cutting across the activity areas is a language of description, quality and expression. Simply participating in physical education lessons provides an environment in which pupils are led to use language naturally and purposefully. They read instructions on work-cards, record scores and devise notation systems and routines and, in each case, the activity occurs in a meaningful context (see Figure 6.1).

run	jump	twist	turn	rock	roll
stop	start	wobble	balance	be still	
catch	throw	kick	hold	drop	
under	over	through	between	against	
straight	round	curved	zigzag		
quickly	slowly	smoothly	quietly	loudly	

Figure 6.1 *The language of movement*

Education *in* movement

If we believe in the value of education in physical activity for the . . . child then we believe that, by giving the child the experience (and skills necessary for the experience) of movement activities, we are introducing him/her to a 'physical' dimension which should be included in education for its intrinsic value and for the satisfaction which such movement experiences can bring. (Williams, 1989: 21)

Education *in* movement is the most fundamental dimension of the physical education curriculum. Through engaging in physical activities and through exploring the possibilities and the limitations of those activities, pupils come to experience them from the 'inside' rather than as disinterested observers. An important function of physical education lessons must be to build on children's love of formal and informal physical activities. To do so, teachers must realize that physical education is much more than a collection of strategies for keeping pupils fit and healthy or useful tricks through which to teach less palatable parts of the curriculum. They are activities and experiences that are valuable and worth while in their own right. Of course, there are powerful extrinsic benefits to be gathered from participation in physical activities, too, but the ultimate importance of these activities lies in their intrinsic worth.

So, the ultimate justification of physical education rests with the distinctive nature of movement and its great importance to the lives of pupils. Games, dance and other forms of activity represent experiences that are valuable aspects of our culture. If pupils cannot come to see the activity from the perspective of an 'insider', they will never recognize the true appeal or beauty of that activity. If they are denied the opportunity of these experiences, their education would not be complete. They are part of the process of becoming a civilized human being (Bailey, 1999b).

Physical development and physical education

The Early Learning Goals in the *Curriculum Guidance for the Foundation Stage* (DfEE/QCA, 2000) define six areas of learning for children (aged 3–5 years). These are personal, social and emotional development; language and literacy; mathematical development; knowledge and understanding of the world; physical development; and creative development. The goals establish the educational expectations that most children will achieve by the end of the Foundation Stage. The goal concerned with 'physical development' seeks to support and promote 'opportunities for all children to develop and practise their fine and gross motor skills and to increase their understanding of how their bodies work and what they need to be healthy and safe' (DfEE/QCA, 2000: 10). It is concerned with improving children's co-ordination, control, manipulation and movement skills. In addition, it recognizes that gains can also be expected in levels of confidence and self-esteem and in developing a positive sense of well-being.

The Early Learning Goal for physical development is made up of eight statements that most children ought to be able to achieve by the end of the Foundation Stage:

- move with confidence, imagination and in safety
- move with control and coordination
- travel around, under, over and through balancing and climbing equipment
- show awareness of space, of themselves and of others
- recognise the importance of keeping healthy and those things which contribute to this
- recognise the changes that happen to their bodies when they are active
- use a range of small and large equipment
- handle tools, construction objects and malleable materials safely and with increasing control. (DfEE/QCA, 2000: 104–35)

The importance of physical education is also recognized as a foundation subject within the National Curriculum. During Key Stage 1 (ages 5–7):

> pupils build on their natural enthusiasm for movement, using it to explore and learn about their world. They start to work and play with other pupils in pairs and small groups. By watching, listening and experimenting, they develop their skills in movement and coordination, and enjoy expressing and testing themselves in a variety of situations. (DfEE, 1999: 130)

The Programmes of Study at Key Stage 1 require that pupils are taught knowledge, skills and understanding through *dance*, *games* and *gymnastic activities*. These are the core areas of activity for the key stage and activities in these areas define the mandatory physical education experiences of children from 5 to 7 years old. There is also a possibility that children will be introduced to swimming activities and, of course, they are all likely to experience regular outdoor play.

As a highly valued aspect of our culture, by adults and children alike, it is vital that all children come to understand the range and importance of these purposeful physical activities. It is also essential that professionals remember that their roots lie in naturally occurring childhood games. Those who build upon children's natural playfulness and physicality are likely to find learners who are enthusiastic and eager to learn.

Dance

Dance plays a number of significant roles in cultures throughout the world as people everywhere love to dance and they dance for many reasons. Children should be exposed to as many different forms of dance as possible, as participants and as spectators. In this way they can appreciate dance for its own worth and make informed choices about engagement in it in later life.

Learning Story 6.1 Fireworks

In the autumn term a Year 2 class have been following a unit of work in dance on 'Fireworks'. Over a few weeks the children have explored the qualities of different types of firework and have interpreted these in movement. One group has been practising turning and spiralling actions to represent Catherine wheels, whilst another group has worked together to show the powerful explosive characteristics of rockets. It is their intention to present their firework dance extravaganza to parents and other children in a class assembly.

Through dance they communicate understanding not only of cultural heritage but also of their lifestyles and, in doing so, they are led to understand dance in both artistic and social contexts. Or, as Brinson (1993: v) put it, 'dance has always been a means of knowing oneself and others, of understanding the society around one and fitting into it'.

Above all else, the contribution of dance remains in its unique capacity for self-expression. It allows the communication of moods and feelings that go beyond the confines of words. To children, it is often their most natural form of expression. As a primary art-form it uses the body as the instrument of expression requiring no equipment or facilities other than an awareness of what the body can do. It provides a foundation for other movement responses and develops a fuller range of physical skills. Participating in dance exercises the whole body and the effects of it can be seen in increased strength and stamina, better posture and more graceful movements.

Whilst other areas within physical education are concerned with more functional movement, many writers on the subject stress dance's contribution in assisting in children's aesthetic development. For example, Joan Russell (1975) claims that, since dance and drama are expressive of inner life and involve mood and feelings, children should be given opportunities to experience dance that grow from their personal movement expression. In this way children use their bodies to express the language of movement expressively and creatively.

Alongside the physical dimension, dance has an important role to play in fostering personal and social skills and in building self-confidence, co-operation, tolerance and leadership skills through participation. Dance stimulates sensory awareness, developing awareness of others' movements, and in the appreciation of sound, phrasing and rhythm in movement. Laban (1975) spoke of kinaesthetic learning and developing a 'sense of movement' through dance. This is only possible through a conscious process of understanding the elements of dance and requires intellectual engagement with the activity. This cognitive dimension provides the context for creative thinking and imagination, emphasizes making dance decisions individually and solving problems with others.

Finally, dance is able to inform and illuminate other areas of the curriculum. Cross-curricular links improve children's understanding of a whole curriculum, and dance offers great potential to link with all area of the curriculum, and collaborations between drama, music, art and language offer excellent opportunities to consolidate and deepen learning (Arts Council, 1993).

The medium of dance

> Dance can spring from anything in human experience. The basis of dance is broad and far-reaching but the *expression* is always in terms of movement. Rhythmic movement is the raw material of dance: the rhythms arise out of the movement and the impulse to dance. A dancer uses rhythms and shapes in the same way that a painter might use colours and textures. (Shreeves, 1990: 12)

Three inter-related processes of *composing*, *performing* and *appreciating* provide one useful framework for dance education. Children between 3 and 7 years should have opportunities to be involved in the activities shown in Figure 6.2.

Teaching dance

The National Curriculum Programme of Study for dance for pupils in Key Stage 1 (DfEE, 1999) states that:

> Pupils should be taught to:
>
> - use movement imaginatively, responding to stimuli, including music, and performing basic skills
> - change the rhythm, speed, level and direction of their movements
> - create and perform dances using simple movement patterns, including those from different times and cultures
> - express and communicate ideas and feelings.

Using movement imaginatively, responding to stimuli, including music, and performing basic skills. Basic skills include travelling actions employed in moving from point A to point B, such as walking, jumping, galloping and skipping. Jumping from one or both feet and turning movements of the body around an axis should be used along with gestures such as waving, punching and reaching and controlling the body in stillness. Changes in body shape add a further dimension to children's work. Children should also be encouraged to include more imaginative movements in their dances. The examples given in Table 6.2 are illustrative of creative movement in the different movement categories.

Stimuli can be used at the start of a session to generate ideas around a theme and also to provide an accompaniment to movement. The most

Composing
- Moving freely to different musical stimuli.
- Exploring ideas through movement.
- Solving problems showing variety in movement.
- Experimenting to find new movement responses.
- Creating short movement phrases with a beginning, middle and end.
- Repeating and improving movements selected.
- Sharing ideas with others about planning dances.

Performing
- Showing increased control in movement skills.
- Co-ordinating physical actions involving the whole body and parts of the body.
- Performing single actions (such as jumping, turning, skipping).
- Performing simple combinations of actions.
- Using appropriate movements to express a mood or idea.
- Showing expression in movement.
- Working both individually and with others.

Appreciating
- Viewing a range of dance styles.
- Noticing differences and similarities between types of dances.
- Using appropriate language to describe dances.
- Reflecting on the quality of their own/others' dance.
- Begining to make judgements based on the quality of the movements observed.
- Appreciating the role of music and other resources as part of the dance performance (see, for example, Smith-Autard, 1995).

Figure 6.2 *The inter-related processes of composing, performing and appreciating*

Table 6.2 *Creative movements*

Travel	Turn	Jump	Gesture	Stillness
Amble	Spiral	Pounce	Wave	Pause
Slither	Wheel	Swoop	Tremble	Freeze
Soar	Circle	Fly	Wiggle	Hover
Strut	Twirl	Zoom	Flutter	Perch

common form of stimulus for dance is music, but there are many other sources available which promise new ideas and interest, like percussion, poetry, stories, nature, photographs, artefacts and festivals.

Changing the rhythm, speed, level and direction of their movements. Spatial and dynamic aspects of movement are addressed under this objective. The former refers to where the movements take place, which may be in personal or general space. Movements may also be performed at high, medium or low levels or in forward, backward or sideways directions. Children may also take straight, angular or zigzag pathways on the floor or in the air. The dynamic qualities of movements refer to how the movements are performed: in terms of speed, force and fluidity.

Creating and performing dances using simple movement patterns, including those from different times and cultures. Children should be given opportunities to see and take part in traditional dances that include prescribed steps and formations. Such dances express the lives of the people from which they arise and folk dances form an important part of a country's history and tradition. Living in a multicultural society, children are presented with a real richness in the diversity of dance forms available to them, which, in turn, fosters the development of their movement vocabulary and understanding of dance.

Young children often respond spontaneously to the rhythms of traditional dances and are eager to explore the new phrases and steps in a way that is quite distinct from creative dance. There is a particular satisfaction to be gained by learning and repeating traditional steps, patterns or dances (if you are not persuaded, go to a barn dance and see for yourself!). The adaptation and recombination of these traditional movements can open the way to countless new and creative dances.

Expressing and communicating ideas and feelings. Since dance need not rely on words, it can communicate on many different levels at once (Cohan, 1986), and this communication will be even stronger if it comes from strong emotional or imaginative experiences. From a very early age, children show their feelings through movement, and this can act as a foundation for a rich and personal movement vocabulary.

Games

Playing games has always featured strongly in the everyday experiences of children. Actions such as throwing, kicking and striking balls and other objects reflect spontaneity, total involvement and sheer enjoyment and it is in these early experiences that the foundation for future games play is laid. Aside from being part of our national heritage (DES, 1991), games have always occupied a central place in programmes of physical education where the aim is to 'provide a

Learning Story 6.2 The importance of games

One teacher and support assistant have planned a series of outdoor games activities for a nursery class. The children have been enjoying playing games such as 'Simon Says', 'Grandmother's Footsteps' and 'Follow-my-Leader' in the playground next to the nursery building. They have become more aware of belonging to a group and are beginning to understand how the concepts of rules are important in playing games. They have been very active during the sessions and later the teacher will use this opportunity to talk to the children about the changes to their bodies they have experienced through this exercise.

sequential programme of games activities within a well-balanced PE curriculum that will meet the needs of the child's total development' (Wetton, 1988: 102).

What does a games education have to offer children? Wuest and Bucher (1995) believe that games, as an integral part of a balanced curriculum, contribute to children's cognitive, affective and psychomotor development. Playing games provides many opportunities to engage children intellectually by solving problems and making decisions. In the simple game of 'Piggy in the Middle', where two players co-operate to keep possession of the ball from a third player, children are immediately involved in decisions about speed and direction of particular movements and about positioning and the characteristics of the other players in the game. There is much benefit too in children designing their own games, individually and with others, as this not only fosters creative thinking skills but also leads towards a greater understanding of structure and rule-making.

Much has been written about the relationship between games playing and the development of values (e.g. Bailey, 2000). For example, co-operating with others, establishing teamwork, trust and leadership skills are all developed through playing games. The former sports minister Iain Sproat extolled the virtues of games and highlighted the value of teamwork and team spirit as traits which many children would be unable to learn so vividly in other ways (Spencer, 1994). A year later, in *Sport: Raising the Game*, former Prime Minister John Major talked about instilling 'traditional values' in children by placing traditional team games back at the centre of school life (DNH, 1995). Although such games occupy only a small place in the games curricula of young children, and should be offered only in modified versions, fairness, adherence to rules and an ability to cope with winning and losing are valued traits in the personal development of children that involvement in games can offer. Of course, it is not only competitive games that offer such benefits. Research with pre-school children by Grineski (1992) found an increase in prosocial behaviours as a result of being taught co-operative games.

In teaching games to children, teachers should be aware of the importance of co-operation before (and alongside) competitive activities. If competition is introduced too early, some children may be denied the opportunity to succeed with the result that they become frustrated or bored and become disaffected. Games in the early years should be participation and enjoyment for everybody.

A range of motor skills are employed and developed through a games education. Knapp's textbook definition, referring to a skill as 'an act or whole collection of actions in which there is a clearly defined goal or set of goals' (1964: 3), embraces the plethora of physical skills in evidence when children play games. According to Gallahue (1982) there are three main categories of games skill: *locomotor* skills, such as running, leaping, skipping and galloping; *stability* skills, such as balancing and dodging; and *manipulative* skills, such as throwing, kicking and striking with a bat. These remain fundamental motor skills, being of a more generic nature and developed in early and middle childhood, and differentiated from sports-specific skills, which are used in the context of a specific sport, like football, netball or cricket (Thomas et al., 1988). It is these fundamental motor skills that form basis of games teaching in the early years, as a foundation for later participation and success.

The nature of a games education

The prime concern for games education is not in the development of future champions but in allowing children to explore the full range of opportunities that exist within games. For this to be achieved it is necessary to offer all pupils a balance of games experiences. Figure 6.3 illustrates the factors that are common to games relevant to children in the early years.

Teaching games

The Programme of Study for games at Key Stage 1 states:

Pupils should be taught to:

- travel with, send and receive a ball and other equipment in different ways
- develop these skills for simple net, striking/fielding and invasion-type games
- play simple, competitive net, striking/fielding and invasion-type games that they and others have made, using simple tactics for attacking and defending.

Traveling with, sending and receiving a ball and other equipment in different ways. Initially children in the Foundation Stage should experience free play and explore a range of games equipment. This vital familiarization stage includes holding, picking up, rolling and throwing balls and other objects of different shapes, sizes, weights and colours, using each hand, both hands and with a range of actions. Progressively, they should experience travelling, sending away

Formation	Time
individual	pupil-paced
partner/group	group-paced
class circle	teacher-paced
random	game
Playing area	**Score**
playground	object in goal
field	object into field of play
school hall	object over net/barrier
sports hall	points
Equipment	**Rules**
beanbags	attempts
balls	position of object on the ground
hoops	position of object in the air
bats	position of object in/out of play
quoits	fouls
ropes	penalties

Figure 6.3 *Factors common to games that are relevant to children*

and receiving skills as well as footwork skills to add challenge to the skills they are developing. The latter may well be the focus of the lesson in the early stages to ensure safe and efficient use of space and then become part of the warm-up (during the introductory phase of the lesson) in subsequent sessions. It is usual to begin with sending skills such as throwing to a target or into space before progressing on to receiving skills such as catching a ball from a partner.

Examples of these basic games skills are as follows:

- *Travelling*: use space, run, stop, dodge, carry, dribble.
- *Sending*: roll, throw, kick, bounce, push, strike.
- *Receiving*: stop, catch, gather, trap, field, intercept.

Developing these skills for simple net, striking/fielding and invasion-type games. The emphasis in Key Stage 1 is on teaching the foundation skills and concepts essential to games playing to this age group. As pupils improve their performance of skills and understanding, they can be lead into simple, inclusive games formats, which have the joint benefits of placing their skills into context and being great fun. As competency develops, children need to be challenged to improve levels of skill by increasing the level of difficulty in learning activities. Travelling, sending and receiving skills continue to be relevant, but they are increasingly used within specific activities. Conventionally, there are three main types of games, with each type adhering to certain basic principles of play (see Table 6.3).

Table 6.3 *The three main types of games*

Net games	Striking/fielding games	Invasion games
Tennis	Cricket	Football
Squash	Rounders	Hockey
Volleyball	Baseball	Rugby
Badminton	Softball	Basketball

This classification is based on adult forms of games, and these are rarely suitable for young children. The challenge for the educator is to adjust and adapt the relevant challenges of these games in such a way that children can take part at an appropriate level and achieve success. One strategy for consideration in the development of motor skills is target-setting, such as the following:

- Beat you own record.
- Weekly records: 'How many catches in a week?'
- Individual skills diary.
- Skills circuits.
- Pressure drills: 'How many bounces of the ball in 30 seconds?'

Playing simple, competitive net, striking/fielding and invasion-type games that they and others have made, using simple tactics for attacking and defending. The complexity of many traditional games has meant that some pupils rarely get the opportunity to use their skills, make decisions or understand basic principles of play. Pupils should learn simple tactics and strategies so they can match their skills against others. They should have knowledge of the common principles of each category of games and how these inter-relate. Once these principles are identified for each of the three games categories, it is then possible to teach these principles in a structured and progressive way. For example, all striking/fielding games are based upon principles such as hitting into space and trying to guess where your opponent is going to aim, and these are as valid within reception class rounders as in Major League Baseball.

Learning through play is a central feature in the effective teaching of games to children. Too much emphasis can be placed on isolated skills and traditional forms of play, which are likely to have detrimental effects on children's knowledge and understanding of games. Bunker and Thorpe's (1982) 'Teaching games for understanding' approach, characterized by early development of tactical understanding and use of modified games, and Graham's (1992) 'Play–teach–play' model, where skill practices are 'sandwiched' between games play, seek to make skill learning both meaningful and enjoyable.

Gymnastics

The movements intrinsically linked to gymnastic-type activities are easily observed in the natural movements of childhood. Building upon a solid base of basic movement experiences, such as running, jumping, rocking, rolling, twisting and turning, the teacher can support learning by encouraging children to combine, refine and elaborate, with control and poise.

What, then, is the specific contribution of gymnastics to the individual child and to the physical education programme? A common misconception is to confuse school or 'educational' gymnastics with the 'Olympic' version with which we are all familiar from the television. It is understandable, in light of this confusion, that some teachers question their capability to contribute to this aspect of the physical education curriculum. It needs to be stressed that educational gymnastics is centrally concerned with body management. It capitalizes upon children's understanding of their own bodies and leads them to use their bodies in increasingly diverse ways, with confidence and skill. So, gymnastics should be central to any physical education programme: it is concerned with the individual 'realising their own movement potential, striving for quality in movement, and coming to understand the potential of human movement in the most direct way' (Benn and Benn, 1992: viii).

The particular contribution of gymnastic activities to children's physical development and health is also worth emphasizing. They are excellent activities for building muscular strength, endurance and flexibility due to

---

Learning Story 6.3 Balance

A class of 5-year-olds have been learning about balance. In their gymnastics lessons they have balanced on various body parts and learnt the difference between balancing on large parts called 'patches', and smaller body parts called 'points'. They have shown a wide movement vocabulary in the variety of shapes they have held and increased control in the quality of stillness in these positions. In several weeks they will extend their learning by transferring their work on the floor on to apparatus.

---

the opportunities for bearing of weight and the involvement of both upper and lower body. In performing gymnastic activities, children learn to feel how their bodies move as a whole, how individual body parts move and movements can be combined. It is through learning of this sort that they begin to acquire body awareness, so vital in the control and efficiency of all movement. By exploring actions such as pulling, sliding, balancing and travelling on different surfaces and equipment, children learn about the versatility of human movement and their personal orientation in space. There is surely no better means to understand how to judge aspects of movement such as force, distance, direction and effort as they explore the environment and their relationships with it.

Opportunities exist for children to develop social responsibilities, such as co-operation, self-discipline and an awareness of safety. John Wright (1992) believes that the specific contribution of gymnastics extends beyond the physical realm, since confidence, curiosity, a capacity to exercise independent judgement, to think fluently and originally, and to play creatively with movement patterns are inherent characteristics of educational gymnastics. Similarly, Tony Reynolds (2000: 157) stresses the variety of aspects of the education process that come together through gymnastics, citing 'problem-solving, individuality and creativity in select-ing one's own actions, in refining those actions and applying them in different contexts and relationships'.

Distinguishing features of a programme of gymnastics

It is important that teachers develop some knowledge of the principles that underpin gymnastics. One simple framework for categorizing gymnastics content and that provides a useful basis for lesson planning is as follows:

- *Locomotion*: travelling actions that involve moving from one place to another and the use of different body parts.
- *Rotation*: movements that allow the body to roll, spin and turn.
- *Balance*: stillness and ideas involving achieving (reaching), maintaining (holding) and disturbing (overbalancing).

All gymnastics actions may be classified in terms of one or more of these headings. A scheme of work (and an individual lesson), therefore, may draw upon each of the themes or focus on only one. For example, during one lesson, children might consider and practise different ways of rolling across their mat (balance), and in the next they might progress to rolling into a held shape (rotation and balance), or travelling up to their mat, holding a tucked shape and finishing with a roll (travelling, balance and rotation).

None of these activities requires expert knowledge, just a little imagination and a basic gymnastics vocabulary of the sort described here.

Teaching gymnastics

The Programme of Study for gymnastics at Key Stage 1 states:

Pupils should be taught to:

- perform basic skills in travelling, being still, finding space and using it safely, both on the floor and using apparatus
- develop the range of their skills and actions
- choose and link skills and actions in short movement phrases
- create and perform short, linked sequences that show a clear beginning, middle and end and have contrasts in direction, level and speed.

Performing basic skills in travelling, being still, finding space and using it safely, both on the floor and using apparatus. Movement activities in gymnastics for children in the early years of education might comprise those things shown in Figure 6.4.

- Travelling activities, such as walking, running, hopping, skipping and crawling. Variations on these gross motor actions include walking on heels, hopping on alternate feet, skipping alongside a partner and crawling at different speeds and directions.
- Balancing and stillness activities, including balancing on large body parts (sometimes called 'patches' – back, side and front) and on smaller body parts ('points' – elbows, knees, feet and hands).
- Jumping and landing activities, incorporating the five basic jumping patterns – one foot to two feet, two feet to one foot, two feet to two feet, one to same foot and one to the other foot.
- Rolling activities, including rolls from different starting positions, rolls to different finishing positions, at different speeds and in different directions.
- Turning activities, such as through the head-to-foot axis (bottom spinning, standing and spinning), side-to-side axis (forward, backwards and rolls around a pole), front-to-back axis (cartwheels).
- Hanging, swinging and climbing activities, utilizing single and double ropes, ladders, beams and climbing frames.

Figure 6.4 *Movement activities in gymnastics*

Developing the range of their skills and actions. A programme of gymnastics should be developmental. One way to think about this is in terms of progressions of skills and practices. So, for example, children's skills can progress in difficulty by trying increasingly challenging tasks (balance on feet with a wide stance – balance with a narrow stance – balance on one leg). They can also be developed by increasing the complexity of movements (one roll – two rolls – a travelling action and two rolls), or the quality of movement (by encouraging children to carry out movements with greater control, grace or explosiveness). Finally, children's skills can be progressed in terms of variety (through adopting a number of themes to facilitate the development of a wider movement vocabulary).

Choosing and linking skills and actions in short movement phrases. Using the movement categories from above, a further way to progress learning is by linking actions together. The categories of movement provide many opportunities for this, through work on the floor and mats and extending on to small apparatus. Examples of these are shown in Table 6.4.

Creating and performing short, linked sequences that show a clear beginning, middle and end and have contrasts in direction, level and speed. Linking actions together to create short movement motifs is an inherent element in gymnastics. Although sequence work can be included from the early stages, it should be remembered that children must have sufficient body management skills to allow them to perform the actions safely and correctly. Most children derive a great deal of satisfaction from composing their own short sequences, practising and performing them. Valuable learning also takes place through talking about their own sequences and those of others. In developing sequence work with young children, opportunities exist for teachers to include dynamic qualities, such as level,

Table 6.4 *Linking actions together*

Floor	Apparatus
Travel around on hands and feet, then roll sideways	Run along a bench and jump off the end
Jump up and add a turn in the air	Get on to the climbing apparatus, then jump off in different ways
Balance, step and repeat the same balance	Choose two balances you can do on the floor. Try them on the bench
Roll, spin and jump up high	Roll to arrive at the apparatus, travel on it using hands and feet, then get off it safely
Move around on hands and feet, going forward then going backwards	Climb in/out of the apparatus twisting and turning as you travel

speed and direction, to movements, to work with partners and to incorporate apparatus work, and adding music can add an interesting dimension to compositions. Some examples of movement challenges in sequence work are shown in Figure 6.5.

Swimming

Swimming is an essential survival skill and considered so important that an early government publication, *Movement*, stated that 'the ability of every individual to swim should be regarded as a civic responsibility' (DES, 1972: 83). Common sense suggests that the earlier children become 'water happy' (Wetton, 1988: 173) the better. Early experiences at home of moving in the bath, gurgling water and getting the face wet, and later in pre-school settings of water trough play, filling and emptying containers, all help to build this confidence with water and understanding of its particular properties.

Children do seem to have a fascination with water and it provides a stimulating and fun movement experience. They delight in the immediate tactile experience that follows from being buoyant and free from their normal body weight, discovering new orientations and the thrill of immersion and of moving through water.

Hardy (2000) divides swimming content into the three sections:

1 confidence
2 propulsion
3 water safety.

Confidence requires a knowledge of different water environments and control of the body position in water, whilst propulsion involves elementary motion and the basis for efficiency in basic strokes, and water safety is empowering children to make reasoned judgements to keep safe in different water environments.

- Can you show me a sequence which has one balance, one roll and one jump?
- Make a sequence of three balances using different body parts.
- On the climbing frame, select two hanging shapes you know and combine in a sequence.
- Use your three favourite gymnastic movements and join them together in sequence.

Figure 6.5 *Movement challenges in sequence work*

Although swimming and water safety activities are at the school's discretion during the early years, many schools still choose to teach this area. Non-statutory guidelines (DfEE/QCA, 2000) propose that pupils should be taught to:

- move in water;
- float and move with and without swimming aids;
- feel the buoyancy and support of water and swimming aids; and
- propel themselves in water using different swimming aids, arm and leg actions and basic strokes.

Of course, more fundamental than any of these aims, and more important in terms of children's long-term development and physical activity, is that they are allowed to develop confidence and satisfaction in water-based environments.

Outdoor play

Play is what young children do when they are not eating, sleeping, or complying with the wishes of adults. Play occupies most of their waking hours, and it may literally be viewed as the child's equivalent of work. Children's play is the primary mode by which they learn about their bodies and movement capabilities. It also serves as an important facilitator of cognitive and affective growth in the young child. (Gallahue and Ozmun, 1998: 193)

Outdoor play holds a special place in the education of young children, offering countless experiences that contribute to their healthy development. Features in their natural surroundings are explored excitedly and can act as added stimuli for their activities. As children react to the sights, sounds and movements of the outdoors, there is often a new intensity to their physical play. Lasenby (1990: 5) neatly summarizes the role of the outdoor environment as 'an integral part of early years provision and ideally should be available to children all the time'.

Sutcliffe (1993) acknowledges that outdoor activity is integral to the whole learning environment but suggests that, in addition, it offers particular opportunities to promote physical skills and to satisfy children's sense of adventure. Outdoor physical activities have the potential to satisfy our human need for excitement and challenge in a positive way. Equipment such as climbing frames, stepping stones, playground markings, wheeled toys, trikes and bikes can facilitate children's physical development and encourage them to make decisions about the equipment they use in their play. Additionally, in these contexts, children can learn to trust their bodies, assess risks, co-operate with others, and use and develop their growing repertoire of physical skills.

Research findings point to wide variation in children's outdoor play experiences. Henniger (1985), for example, reports that some children are socially inhibited in indoor environments and that dramatic play in boys and older children is strongly influenced by the outdoor environment. Hutt and her colleagues (1989) found boys more decisive in their choice of activities outdoors than girls, whilst Cullen (1993) found that the way boys and girls used the outdoor areas reflected gender stereotypes in play found in other studies.

Bilton (1999: 38) gives useful advice when organizing learning in the outdoors. She suggests that consideration be given to the following:
In addition, attention needs to be given to the types of activities that are encouraged and resourced.

- The layout.
- The amount of space available.
- The way the environment is arranged.
- The use of fixed equipment.
- The effects of the weather.
- The need for storage.

Transition from the Foundation Stage to Key Stage 1

Physical education in the early years of education from 3 years to 7 should seek to provide a firm foundation of basic movement skills upon which later stages of children's education can successfully build. The Early Learning Goals provide a solid base for planning in the six areas of learning in the Foundation Stage and set out expectations for the majority of children to reach by the end of their year in the reception class. Planning for physical development, as in other areas, should help children make progress towards and, where it is appropriate, to go beyond the goals (DfEE/QCA, 2000).

Recommendations for planning from the *Curriculum Guidance for the Foundation Stage* (DfEE/QCA, 2000: 100) suggest that practitioners should give attention to:

- planning activities that offer appropriate physical challenges;
- providing sufficient space, indoors and outdoors, to set up relevant activities;
- giving sufficient time for children to use a range of equipment;
- providing resources that can be used in a variety of ways or to support specific skills;
- introducing the language of movement to children, alongside their actions;
- providing time and opportunities for children with physical disabilities or movement impairments to develop their physical skills, working as necessary with physiotherapists and occupational therapists;
- using additional adult help, if necessary, to support individuals and to encourage increased independence in physical activities.

By the time they are 5, most children will have had a minimum of two terms full-time education in a reception class and experiences in nursery or other pre-school settings. Some will be working towards the physical development Early Learning Goal, whilst others in the Foundation Stage will have moved beyond this. For this second group of children achievement may be described using the level descriptions of the National Curriculum. In applying judgements which 'best fit' children's learning and performance in physical education, it needs to be emphasized that these judgements should be made across the four aspects of the Programmes of Study, namely:

● Acquiring and developing skills.
● Selecting and applying skills, tactics and compositional ideas.
● Evaluating and improving performance.
● Knowledge and understanding of fitness and health.

As Patricia Maude (2001) points out, these descriptions strive to produce not only performers but also children with a broad and balanced view of physical education, who can talk about what they know, are able to select and apply skills, evaluate and analyse and demonstrate understanding. The attainment target at Level 1 of the National Curriculum requires that children 'talk about how to exercise safely, and how their bodies feel during an activity', which extends the statement within the Early Learning Goal for physical development which states that most children will be able to 'recognise the changes that happen to their bodies when they are active'. Levels 2 and 3 extend this further and progress pupil attainment through the Key stage.

Tables 6.5 and 6.6 illustrate how the content of physical education is progressed from the Early Learning Goals through the Programmes of Study at Key Stage 1 of the National Curriculum.

Conclusion

This chapter has emphasized the significance of movement in the lives of children. The appeal of movement rests in its directness and immediacy and can be observed in the everyday experiences of young people and in the skilled performances of elite athletes. Echoing the words of Jensen (2000: xii) that 'movement is about living and living is about learning', we have suggested that movement is a feature of our whole existence and a powerful, natural vehicle for learning.

Table 6.5 *Activities to support the physical development Early Learning Goals*

Statements	Activities
Move with confidence, imagination and in safety	• Exploring different ways of moving (e.g. running, skipping galloping, crawling, climbing) • Adjusting speed and direction to move safely around • Performing stories and action rhymes through movement • Moving to music showing pleasure and expression
Move with control and co-ordination	• Playing board games with dice and counters • Performing basic actions on the spot and then moving • Being able to hold a shape or remain in a fixed position • Move around on wheeled vehicles safely
Show awareness of space, themselves and of others	• Moving using fingers, hands, feet, tummies, elbows • Performing action songs with an emphasis on parts of the body • Exploring personal space: 'Pretend you are in a bubble. . .' • Playing 'Follow my leader' type games around the space
Recognize the importance of keeping healthy	• Understanding why hand washing and keeping clean are important • Knowing that exercise is important to keep the body healthy • Distinguishing between 'healthy' and 'unhealthy' foods • Recognizing the need for rest after being active
Recognize the changes to their body when active	• Not overexerting themselves physically • Recognizing that the heart beats faster after exercising • Appreciating that they may be out of breath after being active • Beginning to verbalize changes: 'My legs feel heavy!' 'I feel hot!'
Use a range of small and large equipment	• Enjoying playing on bikes, trikes and other wheeled toys • Experiencing activities with balls, bats and simple games equipment • Exploring large indoor and outdoor climbing apparatus • Participating in parachute games with the whole class
Travel around, under, over, through equipment	• Using indoor apparatus to scramble, slide, rock and jump on/off • Using outdoor apparatus to scramble, slide, rock and jump on/off • Showing different skills on the above apparatus • Moving on and off equipment set at different heights and levels
Handle objects safely and with increasing control	• Practising (un)dressing skills • Using knives, forks, chopsticks, paint brushes and crayons • Playing with jigsaws, construction sets and small toys • Practising skills of cutting, pasting, moulding, threading, posting

Table 6.6 *Activities to support National Curriculum physical education (Key Stage 1)*

Statements	Activities
Dance Use movement imaginatively, responding to stimuli and performing basic skills	• Exploring different actions in response to stimuli (e.g. stories, poems, photographs) • Copying and repeating simple stepping patterns • Utilizing leaps, twists, turns, jumps into their dances showing imagination
Change the rhythm, speed, level and direction of movements	• Varying directions – up/down/left/right/forwards/backwards • Varying speed – fast and slow • Varying level – high, medium, low
Create and perform dances, including those of different times and cultures	• Making up dances individually or with a partner • Performing hand gestures in an Indian dance with a four-beat rhythm • Stepping patterns from traditional British folk dances (e.g. a maypole dance)
Express and communicate ideas, feelings	• Using vocabulary to describe movement, such as 'melting', 'exploding' • Talking through ways to make their dances more expressive • Responding to different styles of music: 'The music makes me happy/sad . . .'
Games Travel with, send and receive a ball and other equipment	• Travelling through the teaching space with balls, hoops, skipping ropes, beanbags • Practising sending skills with such equipment to a space, a target or to a partner • Practising retrieving skills with such equipment with hands, feet, other body parts
Develop these skills for simple net, striking/fielding and invasion type games	• Improving skills of hitting a ball over a barrier to a partner (net games) • Getting better at striking a ball away from opponents (striking/fielding games) • Developing skills of sending a ball to a partner accurately (invasion games)
Play simple, competitive games that they and others have made, using simple attacking and defending tactics	• Participating in running and chasing games • Playing games such as Dodge Ball, Keep the Basket Full, French Cricket • Devising their own games which involve awareness of attack and defence strategies
Gymnastics Performing basic skills in travelling, being still, finding space using floor and apparatus	• Practising travelling skills on the floor to include stopping and starting • Making full use of floor space available • Performing basic skills on small apparatus

Develop their range of skills and actions	• Performing core actions such as balancing, jumping, rolling, turning • Improving skill in such core actions • Transferring basic skills on to small apparatus (e.g. benches, mats, small trestles)
Choose and link skills and actions in short movement phrases	• Selecting appropriate actions from one's own movement vocabulary • Combining specific actions together from the same movement category (e.g. rolling backwards and rolling forwards) • Combining specific actions together across movement categories (e.g. jumping forwards and turning)
Create and perform short, linked sequences that have contrasts in direction, level and speed	• Individually making up a short movement phrase of specific actions (e.g. a roll, a jump, then a balance at a low level) • Individually making up a short movement phrase of specific actions (e.g. a jump, a roll to the side, then a balance) • Individually making up a short movement phrase of specific actions (e.g. two fast forward rolls, a balance and a jump)

Suggested further reading

Bailey, R.P. (2001) *Teaching Physical Education*. London: Kogan Page.
Doherty, J. and Bailey, R.P. (2002) *Supporting Physical Development and Physical Education in the Early Years*. Buckingham: Open University Press.
Maude, P. (2001) *Physical Children, Active Teaching – Investigating Physical Literacy*. Buckingham: Open University Press.

References

Alexander-Hall, J. (1986) 'A case for the retention of team games in the secondary education curriculum', *British Journal of Physical Education*, 17(5): 163–4.
Arnold, P.J. (1979) *Meaning in Movement: Sport and Physical Education*. London: Heinemann.
Arts Council (1993) *Education: Dance in Schools*. London: Arts Council of Great Britain.
Bailey, R.P. (1999a) 'Play, health and physical development', in T. David (ed.) *Young Children Learning*. London: Paul Chapman Publishing.
Bailey, R.P. (1999b) 'Physical education: action, play and movement', in J. Riley and R. Prentice (eds) *The Curriculum for 7–11 Year Olds*. London: Paul Chapman Publishing.
Bailey, R.P. (2000) 'The value and values of physical education and sport', in R. Bailey (ed.) *Teaching Values and Citizenship across the Curriculum*. London: Kogan Page.
Benn, T. and Benn, B. (1992) *Primary Gymnastics: A Multi-Activities Approach*. Cambridge: Cambridge University Press.
Bilton, H. (1999) *Outdoor Play in the Early Years: Management and Innovation*. London: David Fulton.
Bjorkvold, J.-R. (1989) *The Muse Within – Creativity and Communication, Song and Play from Childhood through to Maturity*. New York, NY: HarperCollins.
Brinson, P. (1993) *Dance as Education*. Lewes: Falmer Press.

Brinson, P. (1993) 'Everybody Dances', in Arts Council, *Education: Dance in Schools*. London: Arts Council of Great Britain.

Bruner, J. (1983) *Child's Talk – Learning to Use Language*. Oxford: Oxford University Press.

Bunker, D. and Thorpe, R. (1982) 'A model for the teaching of games in the secondary school', *Bulletin of Physical Education*, 18(1): 56–8.

Clay, G. (1997) 'Standards in primary physical education: OFSTED 1995–6', *Primary PE Focus*, Autumn: 4–6.

Cohan, R. (1986) *The Dance Workshop*. London: Unwin.

Cullen, J. (1993) 'Preschool children's use and perceptions of outdoor play areas', *Early Child Development and Care*, 89: 43–53.

Department of National Heritage (1995) *Sport: Raising the Game*. London: HMSO.

DES (1972) *Movement: Physical Education in the Primary Years*. London: HMSO.

DES (1991) *Physical Education for Ages 5–16*. London: HMSO.

DfEE (1999) *The National Curriculum for England and Wales*. London: DfEE/QCA.

DfEE/QCA (2000) *Curriculum Guidance for the Foundation Stage*. London: QCA.

Gallahue, D.L. (1982) *Developmental Movement Experiences for Children*. Chichester: Wiley.

Gallahue, D.L. and Ozmun, J.C. (1998) *Understanding Motor Development: Infants, Children, Adolescents, Adults*. Boston, MA: WCB/McGraw-Hill.

Graham, G. (1992) *Teaching Children Physical Education: Becoming a Master Teacher*. Champaign, IL: Human Kinetics.

Grineski, S. (1992) 'What is a truly developmentally appropriate physical education program for children?' *Journal for Physical Education, Recreation and Dance*, 63(6): 33–5.

Hardy, C. (2000) 'Teaching swimming', in R. Bailey and T. Macfadyen (eds) *Teaching Physical Education, 5–11*. London: Continuum.

Henniger, M.L. (1985) 'Preschool children's play behaviours in an indoor and outdoor environment', in J.L. Frost and S. Sunderlin (eds) *When Children Play: Proceedings of the International Conference on Play and Play Environments*. Wheaton, MD: Association for Childhood Education International.

Hopper, B., Grey, J. and Maude, T. (2000) *Teaching Physical Education in Physical School*. London: RoutledgeFalmer.

Hutt, S., Tyler, S., Hutt, C. and Christorpherson, H. (1989) *Play, Exploration and Learning: A Natural History of the Pre-school*. London: Routledge.

Jensen, E. (2000) *Learning with the Body in Mind*. San Diego, CA: The Brain Store.

Knapp, R. (1964) *Skill in Sport*. London: Routledge.

Laban, R. (1975) *Modern Educational Dance*. Plymouth: MacDonald & Evans.

Lasenby, M. (1990) *Outdoor Play*. London: Harcourt Brace Jovanovich.

Maude, P. (2001) *Physical Children, Active Teaching. Investigating Physical Literacy*. Buckingham: Open University Press.

Mosston, M. and Ashworth, S. (1986) *Teaching Physical Education*. Columbus, OH: Merrill.

Reynolds, A. (2000) 'Teaching gymnastics', in R. Bailey and T. Macfadyen (eds) *Teaching Physical Education 5–11*. London: Continuum.

Russell, J. (1975) *Creative Dance in the Primary School*. London: MacDonald & Evans.

Schmidt, R.A (1988) *Motor Control and Learning: A Behavioural Emphasis*. Champaign, IL: Human Kinetics.

Shreeves, R. (1990) *Children Dancing*. East Grinstead: Ward Lock Educational.

Sleap, M. (1984) *Mini Sport*. London: Heinemann.

Smith, R. and Cale, L. (1991) *Primary Gymnastics Key Stages 1 and 2: A Resource Book for Teachers*. Loughborough: Ludoe Publications.

Smith-Autard, J. (1995) *Dance Composition*. London: A. & C. Black.

Spencer, D. (1994) 'No winners in PE order', *The Times Educational Supplement*, 18 November: 9.

Sutcliffe, M. (1993) *Physical Education Activities: Bright Ideas for Early Years*. Leamington Spa: Scholastic Publications.

Talbot, M. (2001) 'The case for physical education', in G. Doll-Tepper and D. Scoretz (eds) *World Summit on Physical Education*. Berlin: International Council of Sport Science and Physical Education.

Thomas, J.R., Lee, A.M. and Thomas, K.T. (1988) *Physical Education for Children. Concepts into Practice*. Champaign, IL: Human Kinetics.

Werner, P. (1979) *A Movement Approach to Games for Children*. London: C.V. Mosby.

Wetton, P. (1988) *Physical Education in the Nursery and Infant School*. London: Croom Helm.

Wetton, P. (1992) *Practical Guides: Physical Education*. Leamington Spa: Scholastic.

Williams, A. (1989) 'The place of physical education in primary education', in A. Williams (ed.) *Issues in Physical Education for the Primary Years*. London: Falmer Press.

Wright, J. (1992) 'Gymnastics: ideals for the 1990s', *British Journal of Physical Education*, 22(3): 8–14.

Wuest, D. and Bucher, C. (1995) *Foundations of Physical Education in Sport*. St Louis, MI: Mosby.

Creative development: learning and the arts

Roy Prentice, John Matthews and Helen Taylor

> *. . . to have a good life, it is not enough to remove what is wrong from it. We also need a positive goal, otherwise why keep going? Creativity is one answer to that question: It provides one of the most exciting models for living . . . if the next generation is to face the future with zest and self-confidence, we must educate them to be original as well as competent.*
>
> (Csikszentmihalyi, 1997: 11)

Introduction

Through the application of creative capacity it is possible for each of us to demonstrate a vital dimension of human intelligence. It is the purpose of this chapter to reaffirm the importance of this dimension of human intelligence and to support its growth. The claim that 'creativity is fundamental to successful learning' (DfEE/QCA, 2000: 116) provides a useful starting point for discussion. However, the term *creativity* means different things to different people in different situations and at different times. Understandably, this is both confusing and inhibiting for many adults with a responsibility for fostering and supporting the creative development of young children. Misunderstandings about creativity – what it is, how it is 'acquired', the forms it takes – continue to distort the ways in which we view the relationship between education and creativity. Likewise, confusion often clouds discussions about alternative modes of learning and the appropriateness of criteria applied to determine outcomes of learning deemed to be 'successful'. Furthermore, in our society, the strong association of creativity with the arts adds yet another layer of complexity. Whilst creativity is central to the arts, and through their rich diversity unlimited possibilities for its development are available, the arts are not the exclusive province of creativity; far from it. Sometimes the arts and creativity are discussed in terms that suggest they are synonymous. When this happens it contributes to a reinforcement of a false dichotomy between one field of human endeavour, the arts, in which creativity is regarded as being essential, and other fields in which, by implication, it is not. From such a position it is easy to see how adults' expectations of children's creative potential are often applied to particular ways of knowing, and to some curriculum subjects and not to others.

For early years educators in particular, this state of affairs proved difficult to cope with as tensions had to be grappled with as a result of shifts in emphasis in successive government policies. In recent years many deeply held views and cherished beliefs that historically have underpinned early childhood education (for example, the importance of play) have been challenged. Centrally imposed directives designed to promote a more prescriptive 3Rs-dominated curriculum also demanded a more didactic pedagogical approach at Key Stage 1 which, in turn, impacted on the reception year. Following the introduction of National Strategies for Literacy (1998) and Numeracy (1999) a narrow curriculum and a mechanistic approach to learning, experienced by many 5–7-year-olds, confirms that creativity has not always been regarded as 'fundamental to successful learning' by policy-makers.

Changes related to educational policy and provision for children between 3 and 7 years of age have created new opportunities to establish more conceptually coherent and robust practice informed by recent research evidence across a range of early years settings. In order to clarify what this means for the development of creative thought and action it is necessary to draw attention to:

- the nature of creativity;
- the conditions that foster creativity;
- creative development and learning dispositions;
- drawing and thinking;
- creativity and the arts;
- art and design education; and
- music education.

The nature of creativity: towards a definition

Creativity is a slippery and complex concept. It is difficult to pin down because it has multiple meanings. Being multifaceted it is capable of being developed through different modes of communication and expression and of being applied in a variety of contexts as the work of Gardner (1993) on multiple intelligences makes clear. It can be argued, also, that creativity is relevant to everyone and to everyday life, and embraces both individual and collective efforts. As Csikszentmihalyi (1997: 23) points out, 'creativity does not happen inside people's heads but in the interaction between a person's thoughts and a sociocultural context'.

From a wide range of literature and other forms of evidence through which it is possible to gain insight into the nature of the creative process, it is apparent that 'relevant criteria but no definitive criteria' exist for creativity (Fryer, 1996: 26). Relevant criteria include a sense of curiosity and wonder, inventiveness, flexibility, exploratory behaviour, imagination and originality. A capacity to take risks, to tolerate ambiguity and break established boundaries, along with an openness to experience and a freshness of perception, are also widely regarded as fundamental features of creativity. A useful working definition of creativity was devised by the National Advisory Committee on Creative and Cultural Education (NACCCE), which was set up by the present government. In an attempt to prioritise inclusion (rather than perpetuate exclusion and elitism) creativity is characterized as 'Imaginative activity fashioned so as to produce outcomes that are both original and of value' (NACCCE, 1999: 29).

By focusing on each of the fundamental features of this working definition it is possible to overcome criticisms that creativity is associated with vagueness, incoherence and formlessness.

Imaginative activity

There is broad acceptance that creativity involves in some way imaginative and inventive ways of thinking and doing, as a result of which something new comes into being. Whatever form imaginative activity takes, in whatever field of endeavour, it is always generative and it always leads to some kind of outcome that can be called original. For this to be achieved it is essential for the individual to be engaged in ways of thinking or doing that allow unusual connections to be made between ideas, objects, materials and processes. This requires a freshness of vision, a capacity to see familiar things from different perspectives, to envisage alter-natives, to break conventional boundaries that separate things and to transcend routines. Very often creative insights occur when existing ideas, objects, images or materials are combined to reveal new and unexpected relationships. Too often, from an early age, our ways of thinking, perceiving and responding become predictable because they are context bound. Ideas become dulled if they are bound to literal interpretations and denied opportunities for exploration at a deeper level, through a rich use of analogy and metaphor. The evidence of sense impressions and intuitive responses is a central dimension of these processes and they reaffirm how important insights into experience can be gained through ways of human functioning other than linear, logical, rational patterns of behaviour (Claxton, 1997). Contrary to popular belief it is precisely this non-linear mode of functioning – including imaginative leaps – that allows creative connections to be made in such fields as science, mathematics and technology as well as in the arts.

The production of outcomes

Creative activity involves making. Whilst the exact nature of creative outcomes cannot be known at the outset, the activity – mental and physical – through which they evolve is purposeful, deliberate and driven by strong self-motivation and energy. This is borne out time and time again through accounts of the behaviours of highly creative adults (Csikszentmihalyi, 1997). However, in the process of shaping and reshaping ideas and media it is necessary to remain open to unexpected possibilities, new opportunities, alternative directions and solutions that could not have been envisaged before work commenced. This requires a sensitivity towards emergent ideas and forms as the work develops and on the basis of which they are accepted, rejected or modified. The quality of the interplay that evolves during the creative process is analogous to a conversational exchange. It is through this kind of reciprocal relationship that ideas flow and change. Central to creative behaviour of this kind is an ability to evaluate from within the activity that which has come into being through the activity. In the arts the dual role of creator and critic is well documented. This dynamic inter-relationship between generative and evaluative modes of working is also acknowledged across all fields of creative activity (NACCCE, 1999: 3). Above all, outcomes that are regarded as being 'creative' are not the result of linear progress made at a regular pace in order to achieve some predetermined resolution or reach a prespecified target.

Originality

In order to avoid confusion about the relationship between creativity and originality it is helpful to differentiate between three categories of originality (Boden, 1992). First, an individual's work may be original in relation to previous personal efforts. Secondly, it may be original in the immediate context of a peer group; and, thirdly, it may be uniquely original in terms of its contribution to knowledge in a particular field of human endeavour. Too often, achievements at the level of the third category dominate discussions about creativity at the expense of developing understanding about the nature of achievements in the other two categories. It is through an acknowledgement of what it means to be original in relation to the first and second categories that a more informed basis for creativity as a feature of early childhood education is likely to become more securely established.

Value

The value that is placed on the outcome of a given creative activity requires us to make judgements about it – to adopt a critical stance in relation to it: for example, a painter is 'both creative and responsive' (Shahn, 1967: 49) as the painting takes shape. Criteria, on the basis of which judgements are made, will vary from one field to another in order to address, for example, the usefulness of an outcome in science or technology or the aesthetic qualities of a work of art. Central to this process is an ability to make critical evaluations. The skills required for an evaluative mode of functioning during the creative process are as important as the skills required for production using equipment and materials. Creative responses in any field are not the feverish outpourings of uncritical activity; a critical stance, in relation to ongoing work and resolved outcomes, is essential, and this requires a reflective approach; a capacity to 'stand back' from the process of making. Different evaluations can be shared and as a result of being shared judgements are open to modification over a period of time. At the heart of this reflective dimension of creative development lies a fluent use of critical language.

The conditions that foster creativity

Having considered the nature of creativity, the conditions that are likely to maximize its development in early years settings can now be highlighted.

Active engagement

For creative behaviour to flourish in any educational context it is vital that learners are actively involved in their own learning. Accounts of creative ways of thinking and doing in diverse situations all draw attention to a fundamental feature: *engagement*. Sustained engagement with experience leads to a very different relationship with the world from that based upon a succession of brief encounters. In her description of experiential learning, Salmon (1995: 24) refers to a way of learning in which 'knowledge is not divorced from knowers, where personal feeling, spontaneity and intuitive responses are encouraged'. This view of learning (that enables children's creative development to flourish) requires of adults a particular combination of qualities, skills, knowledge and understanding in order to support it. Such adults are aware that we each construct and reconstruct our personal view of the world through the nature and quality of the relationships we develop with ideas, people, events and the material world. They are also aware of the need to present young children with rich opportunities to engage with the world, and make sense of experience, in different ways, through a range of representational modes; enabling them to make imaginative connections between past and present experience.

Getting acquainted

For young children the stimulus for creative activity is very often the direct manipulation of materials and objects, sounds and movements. At the commencement of an activity children need to be guided and supported by sensitive adults as they begin to explore the potential of ideas and media. A particularly flexible form of scaffolding is required to support the development of investigative, productive and critical facets of creative activity. Encouragement is needed to increase children's confidence, on which inventive behaviour depends. Sufficient time to play with ideas and toy with materials is central to this process of 'getting in touch' (Eisner, 1998: 14). By allowing time for this exploratory, getting acquainted stage of an activity children develop confidence in their own abilities to direct the course of their activities and further refine and share their ideas with adults and their peers.

However, from an early age it is essential that children acquire appropriate technical skills and secure a sound knowledge base in order to underpin sustained activity. This requires a subtle shift in the kind of support provided as the freedom that is necessary for exploration leads to a need to gain greater control over ideas, materials, tools and processes. Throughout activities of this kind children need the support of empathetic adults who understand the unpredictable pace, the messy nature of, and risks and uncertainties involved with, making creative responses. By supporting the development of a range of different responses to a given starting point the value of individual interpretation is reinforced as being central to learning.

Creative development and learning dispositions

Skills and abilities

The relationship between our dispositions towards learning and our success as learners is widely acknowledged. A positive disposition towards learning is a prerequisite for the kind of learning outcomes that have personal meaning for the learner and can be used to advantage through their flexible application in different situations. The term *learning dispositions* is prominent in the current debates about the changing nature of early childhood education and the kind of curriculum, environment and ethos that are most likely to develop the skills and abilities (habits) required of autonomous learners.

Whilst alternative ways of conceptualizing such dispositions exist they have in common key characteristics that include self-motivation, involvement, perseverance, determination, concentration, flexibility and risk-taking. The importance of sensitive adult interventions to help children from the earliest possible age to learn how to learn is indisputable. How a young child learns is recognized as being equally important as what is learnt, in determining that individual's ability to function as a proactive, lifelong learner. However, it is clear that different perspectives on the nature of the curriculum for 3–7-year-olds place different degrees of emphasis on ways of learning and subject content. Indeed, it is a declared aim of this book to articulate an approach to the curriculum and pedagogy in all early years settings that is informed by an awareness of the interdependence of learning how to learn and subject knowledge. This awareness is vital for the support of creative development in general and learning in the arts in particular.

Too often the case for learning dispositions appears to exist in a vacuum. It is sometimes implied that the acquisition of a repertoire of desirable generic skills and abilities can be achieved in isolation, detached from any subject-specific content. Unconnected from intellectually challenging content it is difficult to see how curiosity can be fuelled and skills acquired and extended through sustained engagement in activities. Without support from adults, who themselves are curious about the world and able to draw upon, and share, a strong knowledge base, opportunities for children to be initiated into different ways of knowing and alternative modes of responding to experience will, inevitably, remain limited. Such adults display a kind of cultural curiosity and deeper understandings rooted in a firm grasp of concepts, principles and issues. As a result, they are able confidently to adopt a more flexible and creative approach to their interactions with young learners that enables them to remain 'open to children's ideas, contributions, questions and comments' (Aubrey, 1994: 5). Imaginative connections are more likely to be explored between ideas and media, and interactions between adults and children are more likely to reflect sustained shared thinking when they are qualitatively different from approaches that perpetuate stereotyped ways of thinking and behaving. In short, creative adults demonstrate their capacity to generate alternatives through which the conditions are created in early years settings for learners to function creatively.

Drawing and thinking: children observed

The account given in Learning Story 7.1 of children closely observed reveals insight into the relationship between thinking and drawing. Some of these children are moving from one activity to another – for example, from actions made in three-dimensions of space, to the drawing surface, where actions are encoded into two dimensions. It is as if these children are forming a metaphorical space on the drawing surface which analogues the space of the real world (Wolf and Fucigna, 1983). Echoing their play with the flying toys, the children, in their drawing, associate vocalizations which vary in stress and cadence according to the changing characteristics of their actions. The children seem to match the character of their vocalization with the character of their drawing actions. For example, one child first underscores decisive impacts of the brush with explosive sounds and then accompanies a softly stirring brush with quiet shushing sounds.

Learning Story 7.1 Drawing and thinking

A group of 3 and 4-year-olds are playing, drawing and painting in a nursery class. Some are working at a table; others at easels and others on the floor. A 3-year-old and his 2-year-old sister play with a mouse-operated computer paintbox programme. Still other children are investigating a videocamera. Moving freely in between these groups, some 3 and 4-year-olds play with hand-held toys, gracefully sweeping them through arcs in space, talking softly to themselves as they do so, or synchronizing vocalized sound effects to the object's movements; onomatopoeic cryings and croonings which rise and fall with the ascent and descent of the flying craft. They whirl these toys through graceful orbits whilst simultaneously rotating the objects on their own axes, like spacecraft in free-fall.

In making these actions, the children carefully co-ordinate and calibrate their entire musculature, ranging from large-scale motor actions of the trunk, waist, hips and legs, down to the small-scale manipulations of their fingers and the finest adjustments of their eye focus, as they manipulate the toys and visually track them as targets in space. Even though the children move the toys through a variety of spiralling and oscillating movements they manage to stay 'locked-on-target'; maintaining a single view of the object. One girl even clamps a hand over one of her eyes in order to obtain a monocular view – a single image – of the flying object.

Drawing and ICT

Use of the computer

Children using a computer will also investigate the causal relations between their actions and the resultant effects. With pencil and paper, this relationship is direct. With electronic paint, the relationship is different. Here, the drawing surface and the visual display – the monitor screen – are at right-angles to each other and are adjacent but separate. Yet, by investigating this new medium with strategies with which they explore other media, the children will start to see that, with the computer too, they can still be the agents of change. With actions essentially the same as those used with traditional drawing media (pushing, pulling, fanning and stabbing gestures), the children will test this new, electronic device. The results of these strategies have both similarities with, and differences from, the results obtained when the same actions are applied to crayons or pencils (see Learning Story 7.2).

Learning Story 7.2 Using the computer

Robert, aged 3 years 10 months, who can make pencilled ellipses, now applies the same rotational action to the mouse-driven paintbox programme. This also results in elliptical shapes, but this time not in physical pigments but in textureless tracings of light on a glass screen. Also, because of the scale in which Robert describes his rotation, only a segment of it is displayed upon the monitor. This means that, in this electronic medium, relative rather than absolute, spatial correspondences may be made between drawing action and shape (Matthews and Jessel, 1993).

This learning story gives us an important clue about the interaction between the same, self-generated expressive strategies and their impact across a range of media. It means that generalized categories of movement (in themselves emergent conceptual categories) interact with the different media in different ways, resulting in what one might think of as theme and variation. Sometimes, the same strategy has very different effects when the medium is changed. A good example is when, after making horizontal arcs with a pencil, a child then transfers this movement to a musical domain when she repeatedly trails a beater from side to side across a xylophone (Young, 2000).

In this case, the horizontal arc strategy requires little modification. But sometimes the same type of action, when adapted for a new medium, leads to whole new avenues of possibilities. For example, a stabbing action (vertical arc) – very effective for producing dots or spots when used with pencils or paintbrush – requires radical revision when applied to a mouse-driven paintbox – that is, when the mouse is banged against the table!

By careful experimentation, Robert in Learning Story 7.2 checked the causal relationship between the different actions he performed with the moving mouse and their effects upon the screen. His younger sister used even more basic techniques to check out this relationship. At just 2 years of age, she had to get up and look behind the monitor!

Use of a videocamera

In 'front of and behind' relationships, lines of sight and points of view are also utilized by children using a videocamera. With a minimum of instruction from the adults ('don't drop the camera – keep the strap around your neck – don't touch the lens because that's like poking the camera in the eye'), children learn about this medium by basing their investigation of it upon their emergent concepts of lines of sight, points of view and the concept of going through a bound volume or tube. Whereas in their drawings they make elements go through passages or corridors created by pencil lines or in play, with toy figures going through tubes, or in the playground by inserting their entire bodies through tubes, here they learn that light can travel in a straight line through this electronic, virtual tube. Within a few minutes they are able to make their own videomovies (Matthews and Chan, 2002; Ma Ying and Leong, 2002)(see Learning Story 7.3).

Learning Story 7.3 Using videocameras

Two adults stand by. Mostly they appear to do very little. Sometimes they offer a few words of advice to the children. Sometimes this is about the safety and maintenance of equipment, the children's own safety; sometimes brief comments are made about a child's work. There is one aspect of the adults' contribution, however, which is very striking. This is the seriousness with which they take the children's actions. Most of the actions employed by the children are commonplace and even trivial looking. Indeed, many adults not only disregard the actions, assuming them to be of no educational importance, they do their best to prohibit them! Yet these adults watch carefully even the most trivial-seeming actions and sometimes discuss these with the children. This is because these adults have knowledge of the development of representational and expressive thought, and how best to identify and support its growth. They know that, within chaotic-seeming actions, the children are running profound experiments in expression and representation, which will form the substrate for the child's later understanding and use of symbol systems of all kinds, including linguistic and logicomathematical signs.

These children moved through a self-initiated, self-driven sequence of representational and expressive structures which are carried from one media domain to another. They developed these modes in order to form understandings of reality, their relationship to it and how it might be represented in signs and symbols. Without this background, their use and understanding of semiotic systems they will encounter in school and in the outside world will be, if not impossible, then restricted at a very primitive level. We will now focus particular attention on the example of drawing, but bearing in mind that this forms part of an entire assembly of interacting modes based upon a small range of emergent structural principles.

Drawing, mark-making and kinaesthetic movement

Learning Story 7.4 Drawing

Children are drawing with great enthusiasm. They have not been told what to draw. Some of the children simply investigate the marks the pencil and paints will make. They seem to find these marking actions sufficiently rewarding in themselves to warrant repetition. They test the drawing materials in a variety of ways, using movements which initially issue from the natural swayings and oscillations of their musculature and their skeletal frame (Smith, 1983). However, these rhythmic, instinctive-looking actions are quickly refined and adapted – sometimes within seconds. The children are clearly alert to the suggestions of structure which emerge on the drawing surface.

The children in Learning Story 7.4 are using this drawing surface as both a playing area and work surface upon which to test hypotheses about structure and representation. The children have started to discover certain shapes which result from certain actions. Guided by the visible feedback of their actions, they learn to navigate the pencil, using controlled accelerations and decelerations; switchback direction changes, and precise stoppings and startings. Achieving this level of skill, they realize that they may combine actions to form new families of shapes. From swayings, pushings and pullings of the pencil, they form cruciforms, grids and other right-angular structures. Some of the children find that if they open up fanning or push-pulling actions of their wrist they can form continuous rotations of the pencil. They become engrossed in swirling layers of ellipses, one over another. They quickly find that if this circular action is curtailed to a single orbit, then single-line, roughly circular, closed shapes may be made. Some of the children stab their pencils inside and outside these closed shapes. Other children also realize that passages might be formed between lines, through which the pencil or brush might be traced. Those who have started to make right-angular joins between lines realize they can also attach lines to the perimeter line of closed shapes, so forming a shape called a 'core and radial' (Athey, 1990; Matthews, 1999). Other children find that if, after attaching a line at approximate right-angles to a baseline, instead of stopping the line they curve it around to rejoin the baseline, they can form a cell-like unit. I call this a 'U shape on a baseline' (Matthews, 1994; 1999; 2002). Some of the children found that such U shapes may form the baseline of further U shapes and that, in a reiterative process, cell-like aggregates might be constructed.

These discoveries are not made once and for all but require repeated practice and opportunities for replication, variation and transformation. This can happen only if certain optimal conditions prevail, including the companionship of adults who can identify these systems of representation as they emerge.

In addition to this fervent structural investigation, some of the children not only formed lines and shapes but also associated their drawing actions with other vocalizations and sound effects. Some were onomatopoeic; the sounds of imagined projectiles flying and exploding. Other children made gentle cooing, singing and shushing sounds in synchrony with their drawing actions. One-to-one correspondences were made between singing and the softly moving brush, the skidding pencil. Perhaps one may even speak of analogues or metaphors being formed. It may be said that these very young children are forming visual structures which have various levels of meaning, ranging from the formal, to the representational, to the symbolic or metaphoric. Still other children narrated stories in accompaniment to the drawing actions. Some of these children talked of 'an aeroplane flying', 'crashing' or 'bursting into flame'. These representations seemed to be of simple flight-paths from A to B, plotting the trajectory from its starting point to its point of arrival or moment of impact. Others of the children described more complex events – for example, a 3-year-old girl, whilst running a line through a complex course across the paper, said: 'it is a man running away, he falls down, he falls into a dustbin.'

The centrality of learning in the arts to creative development will now be considered.

Creativity and the arts

The arts, unlike any other group of subjects in the curriculum, are repeatedly required to justify their existence. It is commonplace for the arts in education to be justified in terms of how they might support learning in academic subjects rather than for their intrinsic value. The notion of learning through the arts is well established, and the centrality of the arts to the promotion of creative development and positive, transferable learning habits is widely recognized. Less clearly articulated very often is the case for the arts in the curriculum for their own sake. The main point here is that, unless the arts are valued for the *distinctive* contributions they make to children's learning – as alternative ways of knowing – it is unlikely that connections between the arts and other subjects will be achieved, other than at a superficial level. It is to help early years educators develop and support a coherent and relevant arts curriculum for 3–7-year-olds that the discussion now focuses, in turn, on art and design and music education.

■ Art and design education

Another way of organizing experience

An education in art and design is primarily about understanding how art and design can be used as a mode of organizing experience. However, art and design is not merely a non-verbal means of communicating ideas that already exist. Through our involvements in an increasingly wide range of art and design experiences we are able to explore new possibilities, to generate new ideas, give them form and, in the process, make personally significant meaning. Thus, engagement in art and design is a powerful learning activity, offering endless opportunities for meaning to be constructed and recon-structed. It is, of course, the way in which this meaning-making comes about that makes learning in art and design distinctive. As Gentle points out:

> Art is profoundly important for the full growth of the individual because it deals with ideas, feelings and experiences visually and develops a language of visual, tactile and spatial responses which create and sustain images. To develop an intelligence about visual matters is not a haphazard affair any more than it is with other languages. (1985: 96)

Some fundamental features of art and design education are revealed by Gentle's remarks. First, it is reaffirmed that art and design has the power to change people. Through their active engagement in art and design experiences of quality that offer cognitive challenge, children have opportunities to demonstrate and develop their intelligence in a way that otherwise would be denied. Secondly, it is recognized that experiential learning of this kind involves the whole person; it embraces in a holistic way thinking and feeling, perceiving and doing. Thirdly, attention is drawn to the fact that children need to be initiated into a framework within which the language of art and design operates as a means of communication and expression. Fourthly, it makes it clear that for children to function as effective learners in the field of art and design the positive, sustained interventions of knowledgeable adults are vital.

Investigating, making and responding

Ways of approaching these interdependent aspects of an art and design cur-riculum in early years settings are now considered. Through our *investigations* of the world we begin to make some sense of it. Investigations can take many different forms and lead to different outcomes. We observe how babies find out about the nature of an immediate world they inhabit through their direct con-tact with it, and sensory exploration of it. Early learning through tactile experiences provides potentially rich starting points from which increasingly complex skills, knowledge and understanding can be developed. Young children develop what might be called an 'intelligence of feeling' through bodily contact with diverse surfaces and through the manipulation of a range of materials and artefacts. Play is central to this learning process and a prerequisite for the development of investigative behaviour in art and design.

Playing with sand, water, wooden blocks and clay, for example, helps to develop a sense of weight, balance, softness, warmth, coolness and moistness, as well as angular and curved, large and small, forms and movements. The essential characteristics of learning of this kind are captured by Barrett (1977: 41) in his description of a child's exploration of and increasing control over a piece of clay:

> The hand holding the clay has a sensate experience of its wetness and coolness; by moving the hand the clay is found to be plastic and malleable, ie. it retains and records the movement of the hand over the clay. The fingers and eyes are conscious of this change of shape and the manipulator becomes aware of the forms created, the potential for change and the creation of new forms. These forms engender ideas, impulses and feelings which, in turn, create needs and possibilities for further manipulation and consideration of alternative forms to develop the concept.

A similar observation of a child's exploration of a resistant material, for example cardboard, wire or wood, would reveal a growing awareness of very different qualities and properties. Through an acquisition and application of further investigative skills such as bending, joining, interweaving, squeezing, pinching and rolling, children gain increasing control over their handling of both resistant and plastic materials.

Young children also make marks on surfaces with whatever media are to hand: jam, toothpaste, crayons or a stick trailed through wet sand. Enjoyment of such activity, for the very young child, is rooted in kinaesthetic sensation. With increasing age children's levels of enjoyment and confidence, when communicating ideas graphically, are influenced by the quality and range of mark-making media to which they have access and over which they have been assisted to gain some control.

Learning through explorations

The *Curriculum Guidance for the Foundation Stage* (DfEE/QCA, 2000) with reference to art (rather than art and design) and the National Curriculum for art and design at Key Stage 1 (DfEE, 1999) both draw attention to the relationship between exploratory behaviour and learning in art and design. Through their explorations of the visual, tactile and spatial qualities of materials, children begin at Key Stage 1 to understand how the elements of a visual vocabulary (colour, shape, pattern, texture, form, line) can be organized to convey ideas and feelings.

Through the process of *making* children give form to experience, and the motivation to make something in the early years frequently comes from a desire physically to handle materials and tools to find out how they might be used or combined for different purposes. In order to communicate intentions effectively through art and design activities it is necessary to use a visual language. As with any other language children need to be initiated into it and understand how its components work in combination. They need to be taught how to use it in increasingly complex ways and for different purposes that might include ways of investigating and recording things observed and expressing feelings about things imagined and remembered. By becoming familiar with different modes of visual communication, codes and conventions, children's awareness of visual possibilities is extended.

A repertoire of possibilities

By making available to young children a broad-based two-dimensional and three-dimensional art and design curriculum, a rich repertoire of possibilities for future use is established at the Foundation Stage. At Key Stage 1, it is important to build upon earlier forms of experiential learning (in particular, exploratory play and experimentation) in order to become familiar with media and processes not previously encountered. However, it is important at Key Stage 1 to provide opportunities for children to sustain their engagement in a given activity for a sufficiently long period of time for them to explore alternatives, solve problems, acquire and practise skills and gain satisfaction from work that is resolved. Children become demotivated and art and design is trivialized when effort evaporates and unfinished work proliferates. Between the work in progress and the maker a conversation-like exchange evolves. At one moment the maker is energetically engaged in the manipulation of visual images, tools and media, whilst at the next it is necessary to stand back and reflect upon the situation in order to 'find out' how the work should continue. Uncertainties have to be lived with if decision-making is to remain open for sufficiently long periods of time to encourage explorations of alternative approaches and interpretations, and different ways of solving visual or technical problems. Risks need to be taken in order to move beyond safe, stereotyped ways of seeing and doing things.

Sometimes the ways in which children are introduced to media determines the parameters within which such media are used. Indeed, the National Curriculum for art and resign (DfEE, 1999) is in danger of perpetuating rather narrow and traditional approaches to drawing, painting, printmaking, sculpture and textiles by the way such terms are used. Whilst it is necessary for children in early years settings to begin to develop skills through which media associated with these areas can be used with confidence and purpose it is also important to encourage children to challenge concepts of appropriateness, as far as choice of media for creative work is concerned.

Breaking boundaries

Many contemporary artists and designers work in ways that do not fit into neatly defined categories of painting, sculpture and so on. Increasingly, ideas and issues are explored through inventive combinations of media, processes and imagery using old and new technologies. Collections of objects – often humble, discarded or ephemeral things – videos, photographs, projected light, sound and performance – are used by installation artists to create environments. Such work requires the active participation of the 'viewer', without which it would remain incomplete, devoid of meaning. Young children, too, can break boundaries, challenge predictable ways of seeing and thinking about visual things and bring a freshness of vision to the ways they use materials for making in art and design. It is an important part of an adult's role in early years settings to introduce children to the work of contemporary artists and designers. Not to do so will merely perpetuate what is commonly referred to as a 'school art orthodoxy' at later stages of education.

Responding to art

The development of children's *responses* to their own creative work and to the work of a wide range of artists, crafts people and designers has been a somewhat neglected aspect of the early years art and design curriculum. Given the traditional emphasis placed on art making this is hardly surprising. However, at both the Foundation Stage and at Key Stage 1, curriculum guidance makes it clear that knowledge, skills and understanding should be developed to support two modes of engagement with art and design experience: making and responding.

Critical skills

The capacity to respond to work in progress is an integral part of creative behaviour. Provision should be made for children in early years settings to acquire and apply reflective skills at different stages of the making process. The deeper insights gained by 'standing back' and viewing work afresh, and by thinking about it, in turn, inform and shape ideas and future actions. Individually and in groups children can be helped to understand how ideas grow and change. Gradually they come to recognize that art and design activity encourages alternative ways of perceiving and responding – that there are no single 'right answers' to be found. It is also necessary to ensure children develop a critical vocabulary through which they are able to respond to an increasingly rich and varied visual and material culture. An important purpose of art and design education is to develop children's critical skills and in so doing their confidence to adopt a particular critical stance in relation to works of art and design and to visual things in general. Language, particularly talking, is central to this process. At the ages of 3 and 4 children should be encouraged to talk about visual things and express their likes and dislikes about their own and other artists' work.

Building on such foundations, 6 and 7-year-olds should feel confident enough to enter into discussion about works of art and design and their immediate visual environment and, most importantly, to justify their views.

At the Foundation Stage it is recognized that to support learning of this kind it is vital to have access to 'resources from a variety of cultures to stimulate different ways of thinking' (DfEE/QCA, 2000: 116). The need to make available resources that engage children with different kinds of art, craft and design is seen as being essential to enrich children's involvement in art and design at Key Stage 1 and beyond. It is suggested that good use can be made of the local built environment, visits to museums and galleries, reproductions, videos and Internet sites. Clearly such enrichment can by extended when early years settings create for children 'opportunities to work alongside artists and other creative adults' (DfEE/QCA, 2000: 116). It is to this key factor – the nature of creative adults' interventions to support children's learning in, and through, art and design activities – that attention is now turned.

Supporting children's learning in art and design

The quality of learning outcomes in art and design is determined by the conditions created by adults to support children's engagements in art and design experience. In order to provide a continuum of effective support for art and design education across the Foundation Stage and Key Stage 1, early years educators are invited to consider the following factors in relation to their current practice.

A stimulating environment

The working space should be arranged and managed with care in order that it operates as a coherent resource to support children's learning. The layout (visual, tactile and spatial richness of a room or area, inside or out of doors) supports certain ways of thinking and behaving whilst discouraging and being unsupportive of others. A flexible design allows space to be changed to meet the particular requirements of diverse activities and individual and group work. The nature and amount of space available for an activity, the arrangements for gaining access to materials and tools, the ease with which it is possible to share ideas with peers and adults, all operate as controls over what children can do in a given space. A clear set of guiding principles needs to be established on the basis of which materials are selected, introduced and used. Familiar things placed in unfamiliar contexts and unfamiliar things placed in familiar settings are likely to stimulate fresh ways of looking at and thinking about images, artefacts and events. Opportunities should also be grasped to take advantage of different locations for learning in art and design through visits to exhibitions, museums and galleries, studios and workshops of local artists, crafts people and designers, site-specific work and websites.

Breadth of experience

At the Foundation Stage adults should provide children with a broad-based art and design curriculum. Through structured play, opportunities to explore and enjoy handling an increasingly wide range of materials and processes can be exploited in order to initiate children into a wide range of sensory experience. With the sensitive support of adults, attention is focused and engagement is sustained for progressively longer periods of time. At this stage children should be encouraged to collect, look at, arrange and talk about different kinds of objects that have different functions and come from different cultures at different historical times. As children develop their work in art and design within the National Curriculum framework, adults need to be mindful of an extended concept of breadth of study to embrace alternative starting points for practical work, working on different scales and collaborative projects. It is essential that, between the ages of 3 and 7, children gain direct experience of the wide range of possibilities art and design offers as a mode of communication and expression. It is particularly important for children at Key Stage 2 to be able to draw upon a rich repertoire of art and design experiences acquired at Key stage 1 given the disturbingly narrow range of art and design activities currently available for 7–11-year-olds in many schools.

The role of language

Central to teaching and learning in art and design is an adult's ability to focus children's looking through a rich use of language. The boundaries between investigating, making and responding are blurred. Through the process of making, ideas and media continue to be investigated, and responses to ongoing work and to the work of other artists and designers inform future decision-making. It is through spoken language that adults are able to empathize with young learners and support their creative development in art and design by using appropriate technical terms and well-chosen similes, metaphors and analogies.

Various frameworks have been proposed to help adults structure ways in which personal responses to a wide range of art and design experiences can be invited and extended. For example, Gentle (1985: 172) suggests four categories in which mark-making media can be placed in order to accentuate their particular qualities:

1 soft and smudgy;
2 waxy and greasy;
3 wet and runny; and
4 hard and linear.

In addition to providing a simple organizational structure for graphic media, this also encourages a focused way of thinking and talking about the range and characteristics of the marks and images they are capable of producing. A useful approach to the framing of open questions can be developed based on an understanding of the need to support children's verbal responses at an informational and descriptive level before interpretations of images are attempted. Another useful strategy to focus attention and sharpen perceptions addresses the similarities and differences in relation to images, artefacts, environments, materials and processes. Throughout, sensitive adults use language to guide children's observations – teaching them how, rather than what, to see and encouraging critical judgements.

Subject knowledge

Given that a large number of adults have never experienced art and design as a meaningful dimension of their own lives it is hardly surprising that they lack the confidence and understanding required to initiate young children into art and design experiences of quality. Inevitably, this state of affairs impacts on the quality of support primary teachers are able to provide when attempting to implement the requirements of the National Curriculum for art and design. Even more worrying than the marginalization of the arts in the primary school curriculum in recent years is what Galton and MacBeath (2002: 5) refer to as 'a decline in teachers' own sense of creativity'. It is only when children's creative endeavours are supported by the informed interventions of creative adults that their full potential for development in the arts is realized. For this reason it is heartening that curriculum guidance for the Foundation Stage draws attention to the need for children in early years settings to 'work alongside artists and other creative adults' (DfEE/QCA, 2000: 116).

To support children's learning in art and design adults need to have engaged at their own level in art and design activity in order to know what learning in art and design 'feels like' from the 'inside'. Only then is it possible to empathize with the struggles and creative efforts of others and to offer considered and focused support in response to constantly changing needs.

From such a position it is possible for adults to support children's ideas and intentions, to encourage them to explore alternative approaches, to persevere to overcome setbacks, to take risks, to try out new ways of doing things. Above all, adults with a secure subject knowledge are able to transform their experience of learning in art and design into appropriate ways of 'scaffolding' children to achieve highly personal outcomes. It is the quality of such transformations of subject knowledge (into subject-specific pedagogical knowledge) that provides the basis on which creative, reciprocal relationships between children and early years educators evolve. Thus, by its very nature, the sustained shared thinking that promotes learning in art and design is energized and enriched by adults' cultural curiosity and commitment to a concept of continuous creative development.

■ Music education

> Children are both sophisticated listeners and music-makers from early infancy onwards and the ways that they understand music are constantly evolving.
> (Hallam, 2001: 11)

This section considers the nature and purpose of music education. In order to meet the challenges of providing support for young children's musical learning it is important to establish what constitutes effective music education. Through the stories of several young children and their engagement with music making we consider some key questions that explore how to create appropriate environments for this learning to occur. These questions are:

- Why do music with children in the early years?
- What might be the end-product of music education in the early years?
- What do we need to know to support young children's musical development and progress?
- How do we provide an effective music education in the early years?

From the answers to these questions we can formulate approaches to initiating and sustaining musical opportunities that ensure young children can develop at their own pace and to their full potential (see Learning Story 7.5).

Learning Story 7.5 A puzzling question!

James, who is 4, is working hard playing on the coloured chime bars using two beaters. James and his friends are getting ready to lead a music workshop for their parents and carers. A 'very important visitor' asks him what he is doing. James looks puzzled and continues playing. The visitor asks again and this time James says: 'Playing music man!!' with a look that says 'I would have thought that was obvious!'

Why do music with children in the early years?

James would find this question equally puzzling. Why do adults need an answer to this? James's mother and teacher would be quick to respond and give reasons why it is important that he should have access to music education. They see the advantages this experience offers. James is confident and independent in his musical exploration and experimentation. His concentration is focused and sustained for extended periods. He is happy and proud when he is playing, sharing and showing his music. He is creating musical ideas of his own. James *might perhaps* become a famous rock star and bring fame and fortune to the family!

It is clear from Hallam's (2001) investigation into the nature of learning in and through music that young children are already 'sophisticated listeners and music-makers'. Responding to music, and an enthusiasm to join in with musical activities, comes naturally to very young children. In the early years children remain responsive to a wide range of musical styles and genre. From her review of Hargreaves and North (1999), Hallam found that the research suggests young children have 'a willingness to accept different musical styles . . . with phases of "open-earedness" in early childhood up to age eight years . . .' (2001: 10).

Perhaps, therefore, the first question should be 'why not "do" music?' rather than 'why "do" music?' The justification for music in the curriculum has been extensively debated since the development and review of the National Curriculum. The place of music within the Foundation Stage curriculum is clearly embedded and acknowledged as important in the development of young children. Singing, moving to music, exploring sounds and sound makers are essential aspects of young children's musical experience. Whilst music has a specific place in the creative development area of learning, the *Curriculum Guidance for the Foundation Stage* document (DfEE/QCA, 2000) suggestions for teaching in the other five areas highlight music, with the particular use of songs, as a means to learning. The power of music as a learning tool is therefore recognized throughout the Foundation Stage document. At Key Stage 1 music is also considered for use across the curriculum and within the National Literacy and Numeracy Strategies. However, music has a place in its own right in the development of young children, and the exploration of the above questions will help us to consider what that place is.

What might be seen as the 'end-product' of music education in the early years?

To have made something which is yours, and yours alone, is real achievement.
(Paynter, 1992: 22)

Learning Story 7.6 Harry, Nasreen and Jo

Harry, Nasreen and Jo, all 7 years old, are about to make a recording of their latest composition. They are positioning the microphone near to the computer and the tables with their variety of sound makers and instruments. Nasreen explains that they have put sounds on the computer because when they started they didn't have enough people to play all the instruments: 'but it's really good that that happened 'cause the computer bit makes it sound cool!' They are recording the whole piece they have been working on for several weeks. Harry explains: 'We had got all the bits and how it went but we kept getting it wrong when we did it so we've had to do it over and over and over and well . . .' He shrugs with a 'hope we can get it right this time'. The piece is a fixed composition using carefully selected un-tuned percussion and voice sounds, both spoken and percussive. It lasts about a minute and has a defi- ▶

nite start, middle and end. They listen very carefully to one another as they fit their own part in. They watch Jo who nods at them when they have to come in. The concentration is so intense you can almost feel it. The recording is a success and their joy and relief are expressed with shouts, laughter and jumps. Harry says: 'that was hard!'

Engaging young children in music needs to have a clear purpose. With a clear purpose, it is possible to articulate the nature and aims of music education, and to do this requires an exploration of this second question. For each child to reach his or her full musical potential would be the first and obvious answer. Is the aim to produce people who can all make a living as musicians? This would be absurd. In many countries around the world there is no word for 'musician' and therefore by definition there can be no concept of 'non-musician'. Perhaps this holds the key?

The aims for a music education

We should aim to support children's musical learning to enable them to delight in music through listening to and, practically, making music. This in turn will give them the opportunities to develop, express and communicate their musical ideas and feelings. These aims might translate into the following types of children. Those who:

- are confident to experiment with sound media, elements and conventions;
- can use these music frameworks to express themselves in music and convey their music ideas to others;
- delight in sharing musical experiences and opportunities with others; and
- have had the opportunity to develop and discover their music potential in order to enrich their emotional, social, cultural, intellectual, physical and spiritual lives.

The children are then free to choose how, and to what extent, they become involved in music in adult life. They will have the skills, knowledge and understanding in music to be able to make these choices.

The role of adults' to support music education in the early years

Learning Story 7.7 Michelle

Michelle's dad is sitting on the carpet with her and they have several simple percussion instruments around them. They are trying out different ways of making sounds and are involved in a 'mini competition' to see who can find unusual methods to get sounds. Michelle, who is 5, is holding the shaker handle between her hands and rolling it slowly. She is making her dad listen to it and he is trying to copy. He looks up and says: 'This is great this, didn't think I'd do it . . . see she's better at it!'

Music education involves not only the children themselves but also the adults who facilitate and encourage the children in their musical endeavours. There is a clear role for these adults. Whether the adults are within the educational settings or in the home and community, their primary purpose for engaging in music education should be for the sake of the child's musical development. Not all adults who work with, or care for, young children are confident about music. However, the music potential, understanding, skills and enjoyment of the adults can be developed as they work with the children. Adults who enjoy music model enthusiasm and motivate the children with whom they are working. They are also more likely to provide opportunities to make music.

Imitating the model that the children themselves offer, for some adults, might lead to a reconnection with practical music making and to the building of confidence and skills in expressing musical ideas. Support in how to learn with, and from, the children through skills in observation of emergent, musical behaviours may be needed. Developing an understanding of what counts as musical behaviour will support this informed observation. It is not enough just to recognize the musical behaviour. It is important to develop an understanding of how and when to interact with the children to consolidate and to extend their musical behaviour. Educationalists and parents need to engage with the children in these activities.

Musical development and progress

> Every piece of music is a new adventure of thinking and making in which – almost without realising it we become aware of things that matter to us; of our commitment to ideas and our determination to see the task through to the end and to stand by the decisions we take . . . the first people who must be satisfied with the finished pieces of music are those who compose them. (Paynter, 1992: 21)

How do we enable progress to occur? There are two aspects to this question:

1 The adults' level of understanding of music.
2 The level of understanding of what constitutes sound practice in early childhood education.

Understanding of music

An interest in, and understanding of, music, music skills, approaches and processes needs to be developed. It is possible to acquire this subject knowledge whilst working with children and these understandings and skills do need to be developed. There is no easy way for this, but learning with and from the children can provide the adult with many aspects of the understanding of music education necessary to facilitate sound learning experiences for pupils.

Learning to sing in tune comes through daily singing opportunities. This does not require the ability to produce beautiful tones or to sing to an audience but to be able to sing naturally and spontaneously with the children. Motor co-ordination to experiment with a range of sound makers is well within the capabilities of adults and does not necessarily involve pianistic skills or standard instrumental skills such as playing the guitar. However, strumming and plucking the strings of a guitar is not a difficult task. Walking your fingers over the keys of a piano or pressing two keys simultaneously are easily achieved. These are skills that can show children the way to experiment with the many different sounds they can make with a given sound maker.

Practitioners in the early years possess skills and understandings that are required in order to create opportunities for learning. Music is the intentional manipulation of sounds and silences over a specific time period. The process of making music and putting sounds together requires the following:

- Time to explore and experiment with the sound media, music elements and ideas at each stage.
- Making choices about:
  - types of sounds to use;
  - changing sounds; and
  - how many sounds to use and when.
- Time to show and share at each stage.
- Opportunity for the children to reflect upon and evaluate their own and others' music through:
  - developing music-specific vocabulary;
  - talking about their choices and ideas;
  - supporting them to make judgements about their own and others' music; and
  - talking about their present work in relation to previous efforts.

To be able to make music, sounds have to be:

- produced using sound makers (sound media);
- put together using the music elements (e.g. pitch, duration);
- approached drawing upon the music conventions (e.g. composing, improvising); and
- chosen for musical purposes (expressing musical ideas).

This provides a simple template to consider the provision of opportunities and experiences that are needed by children in order to support their learning in music. The children should be helped to make informed choices about the sound media and elements within the music conventions.

So what are these media, elements and conventions?

Sound media

The sound media are the variety of sound makers that can produce sounds to be used for musical purposes. The term 'sound maker' is being used in preference to 'instrument'. The possibilities for making musical sounds include traditional musical instruments but also extend beyond these. Sound makers include the voice, which can be used for:

- singing;
- humming;
- rhythmic speaking;
- chanting; and
- voice percussion.

The tongue, teeth, lips, throat and breathing can be used to produce unusual sounds which young children both enjoy and make naturally when they play. Voice percussion is used to accompany singing as an alternative to instruments, particularly in a cappella (unaccompanied by an instrument) singing.

Other sound media include the following:

- Found objects (e.g. plastic bottles, pan scrapers, old combs).
- Un-tuned percussion instruments (e.g. claves, tambours, shakers making different pitches depending upon size and thickness).
- Tuned percussion instruments (e.g. glockenspiel, xylophone, chime bars).
- Body percussion (e.g. hand sounds: rubbing, clicking, clapping).
- Electronic manipulation of environmental sounds.
- Standard instruments from various music traditions and countries.
- Use of electronic and computerized hardware and software which can produce a whole raft of sounds previously unobtainable.

These sound makers provide the rich sound pallet for children to use when making their music.

Music elements

Music elements are used to change the sounds made by the sound media. The changes can be gradual from one state to another (such as becoming louder or higher) or they can be sudden by leaping from a high note to a low note. These elements are identified in the National Curriculum for music (DfEE, 1999):

- pitch
- duration
- timbre
- tempo

- dynamics
- texture.

It is important to note that they are all comparative. A sound is only loud in comparison to another sound if the second sound is quieter. Therefore any questions and interactions, for example, are best phrased:

> Can you make that sound last longer? Was that sound louder this time? Can you sing higher than this? The shaker was faster than the tambourine.

and not:

> Can you play a long sound? That sound was loud? Can you sing a high note? Play the shaker fast.

Duration

No sound can be made without it having a length in time (duration). The combination of different lengths of sounds produces rhythms. If the sounds are all the same length this produces a regular beat. This is the heartbeat of the music. If sounds are different lengths a rhythm pattern occurs. Clapping every syllable of the words to a song is an example of this. This is the rhythm pattern made up of longer and shorter sounds.

Pitch

All sounds have a pitch, which produces low to high sounds. However, only certain sound makers and instruments have the notes tuned to specific pitches. A thick piece of wood will sound lower than a thin piece of the same length, but they have not been intentionally tuned to produce a specific pitch. Bottles filled with different levels of water can be intentionally tuned to the notes of a scale.

Timbre

The quality of the sound is determined by the choice of the sound maker. A tune played on a xylophone sounds very different from singing the same tune. The timbre of an individual sound maker can be changed by using a different method to make the sound. A tambourine skin could be scratched or rubbed giving two very different timbral qualities.

Tempo and dynamics

Tempo and dynamics are used to change the speed and the loudness of the sounds being made. Sounds can be changed using just one of these or combinations. The combination of loud and fast or quiet and slow is technically easier to produce than loud and slow or quiet and fast sounds. Singing 'Happy Birthday' slowly and loudly will sound very different from singing it faster and more quietly. Try it to see what effect it has!

Texture

Texture is used to make the music interesting. All the sounds happening all the time throughout the music can become boring. Deciding where the sounds and silences occur creates the texture. Choices have to be made about how many sounds occur at the same time and when the sound should start and stop in relation to other sounds. Listen to your favourite song and listen for instruments coming in and out.

Music conventions

The music conventions are the ways we 'do music'. We can 'do music' by:

● listening
● improvising
● composing
● performing
● recreating other people's music.

Listening

Listening underpins all musical activity and it is an active participation in the music. Different types and ways of listening are required for the different conventions and they have different qualities.

● Working alone trying out sounds to see what we like or dislike requires open and critical listening.
● Performing and fitting in with others to sing a song requires speed listening and concentration.
● Listening as an audience enables the music to be perceived as a whole.
● Listening and watching as an audience will be different from listening to a tape or CD with no visual element.

Improvising

Improvising and composing both require music to be invented. However, improvisation is not fixed and will be different each time it is played. Young children naturally invent extended improvisations (see Learning Story 7.8).

Learning Story 7.8 Caroline

Three-year-old Caroline sang a song on and off during a morning about her daddy's new red car. The song at various times included voice percussion of the brakes and acceleration. It was never quite the same and had a rambling style.

Composing

Composing is 'putting sounds together'. As the choices are made they have to be fixed and remembered:

- What sound makers did we use and how many of each?
- What order did we do, who started, who came in next and who finished?
- What rhythms and pitches were used?

Once the choices have been fixed the music can be repeated on subsequent occasions (see Learning Story 7.9).

Learning Story 7.9 James

James is 4 and his tune on the chime bars was remembered by the colours in a certain order. He was able to fix the order, and therefore the pitches, but was having trouble fixing the rhythm. The adult with him clapped one of the patterns that James seemed to use more than others. He clapped it and then tried it on the chime bars. He now knew the rhythm but got angry with himself because he made mistakes as he tried to play it. His technical skills were lagging behind his rhythmic understanding but the composition was on its way to completion.

Performing

Performing is the demonstration and sharing of music. Music only occurs when it is actually being played. When children show a friend or adult what they are doing, by playing to them, they are performing their music. Performing can range from informal to formal (see Learning Story 7.10).

Learning Story 7.10 Michelle

Michelle and her dad were performing informally while Harry, Nasreen and Jo went on to perform their piece to the whole school (see also Learning Stories 7.6 and 7.7).

How do we provide an effective music education in the early years?

To develop young children's ability to express and communicate their musical ideas they need the following:

- A repertoire of the sound possibilities that come from experience of a wide range of sound makers.
- Experience and time to explore the many possibilities that the manipulation of the music elements do to change those sounds.

- The opportunity to try doing music by improvising, composing, performing, recreating and listening in different ways.
- Opportunities for reflection and time to talk about their own and other's music.

To provide these opportunities adults need to use knowledge and understanding of both:

- music, the media, elements and conventions; and
- careful observation of musical behaviour.

This is underpinned by an understanding of *intervention* and *interaction* throughout both Key Stages 3–7 years.

Two further issues need to be taken into consideration as we use the above to develop the children's music learning. First, that music is greater than its parts and should be treated holistically rather than separating the ingredients falsely. Children sing songs using all the music elements together to make the whole song work.

Second, it is children's own ideas and musical expression that are being developed. This necessitates strategies that enable the children to have ownership of the music. They will invest a lot of time in the music they make and where they have made the choices. The music may sound like a 'musical scribble' to adult ears but the child will perform proudly. This 'musical scribble' is providing the adult with the information about the child's stage of musical thinking and her level of skills and understanding at that moment. Any intervention has to be carefully considered in order to support and extend learning opportunities rather than impose directed tasks that give no space for the child's own ideas and experimentation.

Musical observation

The musical development of young children will relate both to innate predisposition to music and, more importantly to the life experiences and opportunities to explore music that they have been given within and beyond the educational setting. Stages of development are often difficult to judge by relating them to specific ages. Children at 4, with a rich musical experience, can outperform children of 7 who have not had this access to music. It is, therefore, more important to look at what each child is capable of through careful observation of musical behaviour and interaction to make judgements about levels of understanding. From this decisions can be made about:

- the type of music environments and opportunities to offer; and
- the possible ways that the adult can interact and intervene to support consolidation and progression.

Music observation with children in early years is integrated into observing the child as a whole. As all experienced early years educators will know a child will display various categories of behaviour at certain times. Within the space of a minute a child might focus on:

- social interaction;
- emotional engagement;
- subject-specific activity;
- physical activity; and
- intellectual activity.

This makes observing the subject-specific activity in music a challenge and means that it is important for the observer to be able to draw upon the areas in musical behaviour that make observation more focused and informed. Using the framework developed here of the sound media, music elements, music conventions and the expression of musical ideas, it becomes easier to observe specific behaviours and to create appropriate environments, strategies and interactions.

The *Curriculum Guidance for the Foundation Stage* (DfEE/QCA, 2000) is not explicit about the content of a curriculum for music education. However, the Framework for Music (see Figure 7.1) provides a useful summary to support the planning of rich musical opportunities for early years children.

Through the learning stories we have highlighted a range of musical behaviours that occur from 3 to 7. To finish, Learning Stories 7.11–7.13 present a few more narratives. We ask you to look at the framework to see how you think these stories came into being.

Learning Story 7.11 The trouble with lullabies

A group of nursery children fell about laughing when I picked up the teddy bear and roughly, quickly and loudly shouted out 'Rock a bye baby'. I stopped and asked what was wrong. Some shouted 'no', others shook their heads and one said 'not like that!' This child took the teddy and started to sing in a quiet and gentle voice rocking the teddy very carefully and slowly. The other children joined in.

These children demonstrated a deep understanding of the lullaby genre and could make informed judgements about the appropriateness of the use of timbre, tempo and dynamics for a lullaby. They had analysed my faults and had the answers to the problem.

CONVENTIONS	SOUND MEDIA	MUSIC ELEMENTS	EXPRESSION
Doing music through . . .	Choice/range of instruments	Music building blocks	Musicianship
IMPROVISE Made up at the time Cannot be repeated e.g. JAZZ	VOICE ● Singing ● Humming ● Speaking (chants) ● Percussion	DURATION Rhythm = Beat = Pattern PITCH Horizontal = Tunes, Vertical = Harmony	
COMPOSE To put sounds together Fix ideas Can be repeated	BODY ● Percussion	TIMBRE Choice of instruments Sound quality	CREATING ● Moods ● Music ● Associations
PERFORM Showing of work Informal/formal Appropriate to occasion	OBJECTS ● Metal ● Wood ● Plastic ● Etc.	DYNAMICS Volume TEMPO Speed	MOODS CONVEYING IDEAS
RECREATE Interpret: ● Someone else's work ● Revisit own work (includes decoding notations)	PERCUSSION ● Tuned ● Untuned ETHNIC/FOLK CLASSICAL ELECTRONIC	TEXTURE How many sounds STRUCTURE Beginnings – Middles – Ends AB / ABA / ABACAD Binary / Ternary / Rondo	EXPRESSING EMOTIONS

LISTENING

Appraising, Knowledge and Understanding

Figure 7.1 *The framework for music*

Learning Story 7.12 James and his mum

'It's alright mum, you can choose.' James is 4 and is leading a music workshop with a group of other 4-year-olds. His mother is one of several parents/carers sitting with chime bars trying to play music. The children have been working with a musician each week for a year and are very confident in exploring a range of instruments. The coloured chime bars have been a particular favourite. James is comfortable with the chime bars as a sound medium. He has explored the musical element of pitch and can use his understanding of putting pitches together to make up tunes. Through his explorations he has understood that he has a 'right' to choose and that he can put his own ideas together to make his piece of music. There is a clear sense of musical pur-pose in his choices of the chime bars and which should go next. He is able to repeat his few chosen notes and has practised his tune so that he can show it to the musician, his teacher and his mum. The concentration and listening that James exhibits are noted by all who watch and listen.

James's mother is very tentative when playing the chime bars and needs to be told which notes to play. As an adult she has the motor co-ordination that James at times lacks but he has the ideas and the confidence to experiment and use his musical ears and mind whilst his mother is inhibited by a need to 'get it right' and to play a recog-nized tune. She is trying to play 'Twinkle, Twinkle' but James is trying to encourage her to make up her own tune and is helping her, when she feels she played the 'wrong' note, by saying it is alright to choose your own notes.

Learning Story 7.13 Raj

Raj, who is 5, hit the drum twice, banged his hand on the tambour and shook the jingle stick continuously whilst singing his own song without words. The song was improvised and accompanied by a sequence on the drum, tambour and jingle stick. The singing was quiet but the accompaniment was loud and enthusiastic. He played quite slowly and deliberately. The song and accompaniment speeded up once he was shaking the jingle stick.

Conclusion: a fundamental human activity

An effective music education in the early years relies on an appreciation of music as a fundamental human activity. Paynter (1992) discusses the signifi-cance of music to human beings. He makes clear that many writers and composers have tried over the years to identify the relevance and importance of music and to answer the question: 'What is music?' Music making has been a part of human existence from the beginning of time and is an essential aspect of each day for most people: 'Music does matter, world-wide, and clearly has done so for as far back as we can see across the centuries. Could its hidden significance be that it acts to mitigate a deep-rooted concern, even though that relationship may not be immediately apparent?' (Paynter, 1992: 15).

We have a responsibility to foster in young children this significant aspect of human life. It is crucial to ensure that within the learning environments we create for children they have opportunities to develop and progress in musical understanding and skills throughout these formative years. Music education should aim to avoid young children developing into adults who become disconnected from music and who feel obliged to offer apologies for being 'tone deaf' or 'unmusical'. Once pupils in the Foundation Stage and Key Stage 1 have developed confidence, skills and understanding in music making, they will continue to learn and grow in, and through music for their entire lives.

Suggested further reading

Craft, A. (2000) *Creativity across the Primary Curriculum*. London: Routledge.

Matthews, J. (1999) *The Art of Childhood and Adolescence: The Construction of Meaning*. London: Falmer Press.

Matthews, J. (2002) 'The art of infancy', in A. Kindler et al. (eds) *Learning in the Visual Arts: Handbook of Research and Policy in Art Education*. Vancouver, BC: University of British Columbia Press.

Matthews, J. and Jessel, J. (1993) 'Very young children and electronic paint: the beginnings of drawing with traditional media and computer paintbox (shortened version)', *Early Years*, 13(2): 15–22.

Morgan, M. and Robinson, G. (1997) *Developing Art Experience 4–13*. Oxford: Nash Pollock Publishing.

Schiller, W. (1998) *Issues in Expressive Arts: Curriculum for Early Childhood*. London: Gordon & Breach.

Young, S., and Glover, J. (1998) *Music in the Early Years*. London: Falmer Press.

References

Athey, C. (1990) *Extending Thought in Young Children: A Parent–Teacher Partnership*. London: Paul Chapman Publishing.

Aubrey, C. (ed.) (1994) *The Role of Subject Knowledge in the Early Years of Schooling*. London: Falmer Press.

Barrett, M. (1977) *Art Education*. London: Heinemann.

Boden, M. (1992) *The Creative Mind*. London: Abacus.

Claxton, G. (1997) *Hare Brain, Tortoise Mind*. London: Fourth Estate.

Csikszentmihalyi, M. (1997) *Creativity*. New York, NY: Harper Perennial.

David, T. (2001) 'Curriculum in the early years' in G. Pugh (ed.) *Contemporary Issues in the Early Years*. London: Paul Chapman Publishing.

DfEE (1999) *National Curriculum for England and Wales*. London: DfEE.

DfEE/QCA (2000) *Curriculum Guidance for the Foundation Stage*. London: QCA

Eisner, E. (1998) 'Does experience in the arts boost academic achievement?' *Art Education*, 51(1): 7–15.

Fryer, M. (1996) *Creative Teaching and Learning*. London: Paul Chapman Publishing.

Galton, M. and MacBeath, J. (2002) *A Life in Teaching: A report commissioned by the National Union of Teachers*. London: National Union of Teachers.

Gardner, H. (1993) *Multiple Intelligences*. New York, NY: Basic Books.

Gentle, K. (1985) *Children and Art Teaching*. Beckenham: Croom Helm.

Hallam, S. (2001) 'Learners: their characteristics and development' in *Mapping Music Education Research in the UK*. London: BERA

Hargreaves, D.J. and North, A.C. (1999) 'Developing concepts of musical style', *Musicae Scientiae*, 3: 193–216.

Matthews, J. (1994) *Children and Visual Representation: Helping Children to Draw and Paint in Early Childhood*. London: Hodder & Stoughton,

Matthews, J. (1999) *The Art of Childhood and Adolescence: The Construction of Meaning*. London: Falmer Press.

Matthews, J. (2002) *Children and Visual Representation: Helping Children to Draw and Paint in Early Childhood* (2nd edn). London: Paul Chapman Publishing.

Matthews, J. and Chan, R. (2002) 'Very young children use videocameras.' Unpublished research paper.

Matthews, J. and Jessel, J. (1993) 'Very young children use electronic paint: a study of the beginnings of drawing with traditional media and computer paintbox (original version)', *Visual Arts Research*, 19(1).

Ma Ying, J. and Leong, A.L.J. (2002) *The Art of Childhood and Adolescence: An Exhibition*. Catalogue for the art exhibition: 'The Art of Childhood and Adolescence', 26 January 2002–28 February, The Art Gallery, National Institute of Education, Nanyang Technological University, Singapore.

National Advisory Committee on Creative and Cultural Education (NACCCE) (1999) *Report: All our Futures: Creativity, Culture and Education*. Sudbury: DfEE.

Paynter, J. (1992) *Sound and Structure*. Cambridge: Cambridge University Press.

Salmon, P. (1995) 'Experiential learning', in R. Prentice (ed.) *Teaching Art and Design*. London: Cassell.

Shahn, B. (1967) *The Shape of Content*. Cambridge, MA: Harvard University Press.

Smith, N.R. (1983) *Experience and Art: Teaching Children to Paint*. New York, NY: Teachers College Press.

Wolf, D. and Fucigna, C. (1983) 'Representation before picturing.' Paper presented at the symposium on Drawing Development, British Psychological Society International Conference on Psychology and the Arts, University of Cardiff.

Young, S. (2000) 'Young children's spontaneous instrumental music-making in nursery settings.' PhD thesis, University of Surrey.

Index